Great Places to Learn

How Asset-Building Schools Help Students Succeed

NEAL STARKMAN, *Ph.D.*

PETER C. SCALES, *Ph.D.*

CLAY ROBERTS, *M.S.*

Forewords by Sara Pierce and Mary Beth Blegen

Search
INSTITUTE

Practical research benefiting children and youth

This resource has been made possible in part by the generous support of the Kansas Health Foundation, Wichita, Kansas. It is also part of Search Institute's Healthy Communities • Healthy Youth initiative, which seeks to unite individuals, organizations, and communities for children and adolescents. Lutheran Brotherhood, now Thrivent Financial for Lutherans, was the founding national sponsor for Healthy Communities • Healthy Youth. Thrivent Financial for Lutherans Foundation has provided Search Institute with generous support.

Library of Congress Cataloging-in Publication Data

Starkman, Neal.
    Great places to learn : how asset-building schools help students succeed / Neal Starkman, Peter C. Scales, Clay Roberts ; forewords by Sara Pierce and Mary Beth Blegen.
        p.   cm.
    Includes bibliographical references.
    ISBN 1-57482-722-7
    1. School improvement programs—United States. 2. School environment—United States. 3. Child development—United States. 4. Academic achievement—United States. I. Scales, Peter, 1949–   . II. Roberts, Clay, 1949–   . III. Title.
LB2822.82.S84   1999
371.2—dc21   99-38749

10   9   8   7

    Search Institute
    615 First Avenue NE, Suite 125
    Minneapolis, MN 55413
    612-376-8955
    800-888-7828
    www.search-institute.org

Editor: Kathryn (Kay) L. Hong
Design: Diane Gleba Hall
Production: Rebecca Manfredini, Jeannie Dressel
Typesetting: Stanton Publication Services, Inc.
Cover photographs courtesy of Culp Productions, Seattle.

Contents

Handouts

Chapter 1

Chapter 2

Chapter 3

Chapter 4

Chapter 5

Chapter 6

Chapter 7

Chapter 8

Chapter 9

Chapter 10

Foreword: Belonging to a School Community

I was asked by my high school counselor to write this foreword and to try to tell you, the reader, how we can make our schools better and safer for our young people. I would like to think that I have made some useful effort in this direction, and the best way that I have personally seen to improve our schools has come to my attention in the form of the developmental assets framework.

While the list of assets includes many things, from support and empowerment to boundaries and expectations, one of the most important things this tool promotes is positive identity in youth. No matter how much a young person is told that he or she is worth it, it does no good unless they believe it. I think that this is the single most important factor in determining anyone's future. Someone with a positive sense of self is more likely to make positive decisions in everything from choosing friends to doing that day's math homework.

I don't want anyone to think that this sort of change in a school can happen overnight. It is not enough simply to send the list of assets home with every student and then expect things to change. Remember, high school students are quite possibly the most stubborn group of people on the planet! There needs to be a gradual integration of the asset framework into the school. And even before looking to the asset framework, the phrase "school community" needs to become a reality.

Many of the students I know, including people who are my friends and people who are not, do not have this sense of a school community backing them up. Too many of my peers don't think that they matter. This is one of the first things that need to change, in high schools, middle schools, and elementary schools. This is what they need most, just to be bombarded with the idea that people do care. A number of the assets are about caring relationships, but other assets are about young people being respected and seen as resources. In fact, sometimes the best way to get the idea of caring across is to make sure that each young person feels valued and needed, and schools can help encourage that through service-learning projects. If young people are invited into the community to help make it better, by being a candy striper at the hospital or working at a neighborhood daycare center or building houses for disadvantaged people, an interesting side effect arises. Not only is the community improved, but the person responsible for that is also improved, and close new relationships often grow out of the experience.

The school, then, is part of the wider community, not an institution standing separate, filled with separate, unconnected individuals. Every interaction students experience within the wider community and within the school community can build connections and assets, or it can increase the distance between people. And it is the adults in a student's life who can be the greatest positive influence, be they parents, educators, or other community members. For these reasons, educators and other school adults should take advantage of every chance to "live the assets" and share an experience with a student, whether it is a conversation about something that was discussed in class that day or just a smile and a greeting as they pass in the hall.

Every little effort can make a difference in the life of a student. And as each young person becomes more connected to the people in the school, and the asset chain that connects the student to the school is strengthened, he or she will want to make the school better. This often manifests itself in better grades and motivation to become even more involved in the school. That could mean joining a club, playing a sport, becoming a student representative on a committee, or perhaps even starting a new club. Very rarely will students turn away from the opportunity to form connections or become involved, if they are invited and made to feel welcome.

School communities should adopt the developmental assets framework because it promotes the belief in students that they are important. Today's students are tomorrow's leaders, and anything that can be done to improve their lives and their experiences in schools and the communities in which they live should be used as fully as possible. Everyone deserves a chance to succeed, and the asset framework increases that chance for everyone who is touched by it and by those people in their lives who try to build assets for and with them.

In short, what students need in school to make it better is the opportunity to have a hand in that improvement. Every time they help, the spirit of the school builds in that student and a little part of the student is left behind in the school's spirit. It is this spirit of school and community that builds the assets for and with children and youth. School must be more than just a place to learn—even a great place to learn—it should be a place to belong.

Sara Pierce
Senior, Overland High School, Aurora, Colorado

Foreword: No More Strangers in Our Schools

I teach a class that comes over from a charter school to the Department of Education in Washington, D.C. The kids are in that school because they have been in trouble with the law. It is a small school with caring teachers where the kids just might make it. On Monday I asked my class to tell me what people see when they look at them. I would like you to "hear" the words of one young man. He wrote, "What do they see? They see a black young man, a survivor, a crazy guy, they see heartless, niceness, a soldier, a boy who wants to make it. They see pain, they see someone who doesn't give a damn. They see me." He's full of contradictions. I watch him as he swaggers down the street talking too loud. I watch him as he sits in class writing about his dead brother.

This is about kids, real live kids. A second grader grabs the hand of a teacher when he needs reassurance. A young teacher squeezes that hand if only for a second and in squeezing sends a message to that second grader. A high school junior can't grab the hand of his teacher. Too many are there to point fingers, but a junior needs a squeeze back even more than a second grader. A junior needs to know that his thoughts and ideas are worth being heard. He needs to know that his inner turmoil is expected. He needs to know that his dreams are valid. This is about kids, real kids, kids who cry and laugh, ache and bubble, stretch and scream. Kids who need to learn more in order to enter this incredibly complex society we adults are giving to them. Kids who say they want to learn, kids who push away just when we believe we have reached them, kids who are messy and challenging, frustrating and exhilarating. What is the most important thing we do for kids?

What is the most important thing we do for the hundreds of bright young people who enter our schools needing to discover their place in this world, needing to discover the joy of learning, and needing to find skills that will allow them to thrive in this chaotic world we adults have created? Those kids need us in schools and communities to have conversations about real stuff, about real kids and about real learning. They need us to talk about helping them make sense of this raucous and chaotic and wonderful world. They need us to talk and work together to find the balance in our classrooms, the balance between the passion of knowing and listening to kids and helping them know themselves through learning and the structure of knowledge and its requirements. They need us to dream together as adults and kids. They need us to change.

In 1999, our kids need honesty in listening and knowing and being known in a learning community in a school which is created as a place where they can take risks. In safe classrooms where new and challenging ideas collide passionately with the comfortable and the familiar and with a structure that sets the stage for thinking and questioning and doubting and deciding for all kids. Our kids need relationships within those schools, which mean that when they are gone from school they are missed, when they are grumpy and depressed, somebody notices, and when they need to rejoice, someone is there to rejoice with them because we know them. Because we know what is going on, because we won't allow strangers in our schools anymore. We won't allow teachers to be strangers; we won't allow kids to be strangers. We won't allow kids to come to school and to go from school without someone noticing.

Our kids need classrooms where they are challenged to discover their ability to think and to reason and to create and to process, classrooms in schools where teachers are engaged in ongoing and scheduled conversations about what we do in our schools and why we do it. Together in our schools and in our communities we must ask important questions, but more importantly, we must listen for the answers. We must look to real kids, kids like those who put a sign on my wall that read, "With kids like us, who wouldn't be teacher of the year?" (Believe me, I saved that sign!)

Asking the right questions and pursuing the answers to those questions means we put aside that which has stopped us from change in the past. Can we afford to put aside the past, and our agendas, and our fear in order to ask those questions? Can we ask hard questions and listen for the answers in places where we'll hear the answers that will truly tell us what our kids need in 1999 and 2000 and 2010? Before testing, before accountability, before curriculum, and before standards must come questions that will truly tell us if kids are learning. If they are learning, if we know they are learning, if we want them to learn.

Are all kids in our schools known well by an adult? Study after study tells us that kids are looking for relationships. They are looking to be known in a society that asks them to do it now and to do it faster. They are looking for places where someone will listen to their thinking, their frustration, and their person. But our kids are spending more and more time alone. Their relationships with adults come in the form of brief encounters with parents, bosses, and teachers.

In Patricia Hersch's book *A Tribe Apart,* she says the most stunning change for adolescents today is their aloneness. And Peter Benson, who is the president of Search Institute, has come to the conclusion that America needs to discover anew how to raise healthy kids. So I ask, what is the role of schools working together with communities to rediscover ways to raise healthy kids? In saying to them, that not only do we want them not to be alone but that we are willing to listen to them. To hear what they have to say, to help them hear themselves as they figure out what it means to grow up. Kids are looking to be known in a school setting that encourages passion and discovery, but offers enough structure so the passion can be discovered.

We must also ask, where are the silences in our schools and communities? What are the unstated issues that are so powerful or harmful or dangerous and that play such a role with our kids that they cause our kids to retreat from discovery, from learning, but more importantly, from themselves? Are we allowing silences to take the place of open, meaningful discussions about difficult but important topics like what it means to grow up, the mixed blessings of new technology, sexual identity, and race and class in American culture? Our students need chances to reflect on and teach us about who they are and the times they are living in, opportunities to make real decisions, and the support to make sense of it all.

In 1999, the schools they come to are in turmoil. While searching for the best methods of teaching and administering, schools face an increasingly diverse and challenging student population. We understand that we are in the last years of the twentieth century and schools writhe in their attempts to meet the needs of all of these kids growing up in this competitive technological society. The messages pouring in from everywhere for our kids challenge childhood, threaten adulthood, and promise quick and frequently false answers to human dilemmas, but that same society asks that those kids be better prepared, be more flexible, and be ready to solve problems we haven't even yet imagined with technology that changes before our very eyes.

⚘

I knew I wasn't going to be in a classroom for a while and I needed to know what was going on with my kids. I needed to make connections between teaching and learning, between school and reality, so I asked them a question. I wanted them to respond honestly and anonymously. I wanted to hear what they had to say. I asked this: "If you could tell your parents something that would surprise them, what would you tell them?" Their answers were startling and profound, shocking and thrilling. Their answers were honest.

One wrote, "Our intelligence. They would be surprised to find out that we can think for ourselves. We're not a group of mindless zombies; most of us do not take pleasure in rebelling against our parents. Most of us have either hit, seen, or taken a jump into the drug world. We've gained experience, found some new friends, and lost some also. Yes, I believe my parents would be shocked by our intelligence, how wise we have become and how much we already know."

Another wrote, "I'm smart, but I'm no scholar. I'm friendly, but I'm not ideal. I've been confirmed, but I'm no Christian. Whatever I've been told not to do, I've done. When I'm given responsibility I slack off. My parents wonder why I'm always gone. It's to be away. They wonder why I never leave. It's because there's no point. I've seen the world as much as I care to. I've seen people. Not many stand up anymore. I see people falling down all around me and I'm helpless to avoid the vacuum. What's the point?"

As people who say we care about kids, we have the wonderful, frightening, and awesome responsibility of helping all kids find the point, of knowing them, of bringing them to learning, of helping them find the structure and discover the passion in learning, but most importantly, of helping them to a level of self-discovery which will help them find their way through the almost chaotic times they will encounter in their lives. We have the responsibility of helping them know their dreams and beginning to see their way through to those dreams.

⚘

The developmental assets provide a framework for all the things I've written about here. It is a framework from which educators can build the kind of relationships that will lead students to the process of self-discovery and open door after door to learning, knowing, and being known.

Mary Beth Blegen
National Teacher of the Year, 1996

Acknowledgments

Three names appear on the cover of this book as authors, but many more people need to be acknowledged as contributors.

First, thank you to all the principals, teachers, students, support staff, community workers, coordinators, and other people in school communities who selflessly gave of their time, energy, and thoughts, and who supplied us with a variety of materials for use in the book. Your contributions to this book are a reflection of your contributions to your school communities.

Second, thank you to all the people at Search Institute who provided us with guidance and suggestions in an effort to make this book useful and readable, and especially to Kay Hong, whose incisive editing, insightful comments, and overall stewardship of the project helped bring this book to life.

Finally, thank you to all the asset builders in *our* lives—especially our families. They've given us the caring, respectful relationships, the asset-rich environment, and even the "programs and practices" that contribute to whatever success we may have achieved.

Neal Starkman
Peter C. Scales
Clay Roberts
June 1999

1

⚜

Why We Should Build Assets

in School Communities

Outside, it's cold. The Colorado winter has been unusually harsh, and Denver has felt its force. Motorists clench their steering wheels, trying to navigate across sheets of ice and through drifts of newly fallen snow. Pedestrians wear not only overcoats, boots, and scarves, but also ski masks and every manner of hat so as not to expose skin to the biting, numbing air. Everyone moves slowly, tentatively, as if not to antagonize the environment and make it even more hostile. Giovanny DeLeon turns onto East 33rd Avenue, the last of 11 blocks she walks every weekday morning and every weekday afternoon. She passes the brightly colored mural painted on the front wall of Mitchell Elementary School. The mural is a representation of people who achieved in school and succeeded in life—people like her. Giovanny enters the doors of the school.

Inside, it's warm. Giovanny's teachers, Ms. Doyle and Mr. Fox, stand by the front office laughing about something they saw on TV the previous night. They both say hi to Giovanny, and Ms. Doyle reminds her that later in the afternoon Giovanny will be leading the three of them—plus Giovanny's mother—through a quarterly conference. Giovanny asks Mr. Fox if during lunch he can help her with some of the questions she's going to ask her mother, and he says he'll be glad to.

Giovanny walks down a hall and into the library. Off the library is a little room with a computer and a machine that looks something like a printer and something like a lathe. Giovanny boots the computer and checks out the words that later in the morning she'll print on vinyl, cut out, and affix to the wall outside the auditorium. The words are musical terms, and Giovanny makes a note to herself to look up the word "coda." She smiles when she thinks that she almost turned down an invitation to work on the vinyl-words business team. She'd thought, cutting out words and slapping them on walls? That's work! But the work somehow became—fun: There was the selling of the vinyl words to other schools, for example. There was the choosing of the themes—Spanish words, computer words, cooking words. There was the pride of seeing her work appear throughout the school. Now doing the "work" is one of the highlights of Giovanny's day.

She hurries back to her room, stopping once to give a hug to a teacher and another time to get a pat on the shoulder from a secretary. She realizes that she's actually looking forward to the conference with her mother and her teachers. Everyone says she's doing well; she knows she's doing well. Anyway, doing less is really not acceptable. Just before taking her seat and visiting with her friends, she thinks, "I really like it here."

Giovanny DeLeon goes to a school that's rich in what we call "developmental assets"—a school characterized by strong adult-student relationships, an environment that provides opportunities for every student to excel, and programs and practices that help young people grow up healthy, caring, and responsible. When Giovanny goes to school, she feels *cared for*. She believes that she *matters*. She is given chances to *contribute* and make a difference in the life of the school. She is *involved*, emotionally and intellectually. She *enjoys* going to school. Moreover, this "asset-richness" delivers two bonuses: Children who have high levels of developmental assets achieve more and are involved in fewer high-risk behaviors. Simply put, children who feel better about school *do* better in school.[1] Let us repeat that, not only because it's important but also because more than a few people believe otherwise: *Children who feel better about school do better in school.*

What specifically are developmental assets? They're the positive "building blocks"—relationships, experiences, values, attitudes, and attributes—that all children and youth need for success. "Developmental" refers to how the building blocks both emerge from and help shape how children and youth grow and develop. "Assets" points to the fact that these building blocks are positive, that they give strength to young people. *Developmental assets help children thrive.*

We wrote this book to help you build assets in *your* school community, to help *your* students thrive.

About This Book

What can you expect as a result of having read this book? You can expect to:

- ◆ Understand the concept of developmental assets and the reasons why building assets is important;
- ◆ Learn how to intentionally incorporate developmental assets into the goals, missions, and standards already existing in your school;

- ◆ Be able to recognize how assets are being built in your school community and to make those efforts more productive;
- ◆ Be able to identify a variety of strategies that will build and sustain developmental assets in your school community—as a matter of routine; and
- ◆ Be able to put those strategies into effect.

In the first part of this book, we'll show you how building developmental assets is consistent with and indeed contributes toward schools' fulfilling their missions: to foster academic achievement and to provide a safe and healthy environment in which that achievement can best occur. We'll explain how "developmental assets" came about and why it's important to augment the good things you're already doing by intentionally building developmental assets. We'll describe how developmental assets relate to students from kindergarten through high school so you can begin to focus in on how to best use the information in the rest of the book. We'll give you the data supporting the relationships between developmental assets and academic success, and we'll show you how developmental assets can help you address some of the important educational issues you grapple with every day.

Next, we'll outline a process to help you build developmental assets in your own school and district. Not only will we lay out the process step by step, but we'll also provide stories from school communities throughout the country that illustrate the points we're making. Finally, we'll give you some suggestions on what you can do *now*—what you can do on your own and what you can do as part of a school community.

You should know some other things about this book, too. First, although we wrote it primarily for teachers, administrators, and other adults who work with students in schools, we recognize that within the broad category of "members of school communities," there's a great amount of diversity. Individuals are distinct from one another. So are students. So are schools. Because of this diversity, we have tried not to be too prescriptive in writing this book. While the overall framework of the developmental assets and the processes of building those assets can be applied in any school community, some of the specific strategies we discuss may work for you, and others may be less appropriate. You know your school community far better than we do; you know the who's, the what's, the why's, and even the why not's. So take from this book what makes sense for you. We'll tell you what the research indicates about the connections between school success and the developmental assets. We'll tell you what's working or being tried in some school communities around the country. And we'll give you ways to make some of this information "your own."

A second thing to know is that although our comments—like those in the preceding paragraph—are directed at "you," that "you" is really many people. Later in the book, we'll discuss just who the people in the school community are and what roles they can play. Understand, however, that although the principles underlying developmental assets are basic and—to some people—intuitive, building and sustaining developmental assets at a peak level in school communities happens when many individuals and groups are committed to building assets. "You" alone can't build assets in a school community; it's everyone's job to build assets. So as you read the book, think about the colleagues who can benefit from this information.

Finally, we wrote this book to be relevant for a range of readers and accessible on many different levels. We're giving you a mix of research findings, conceptual philosophies, and practical ideas. We're discussing change in individuals and in systems. We want to give you the necessary background information so that you explicitly choose to build assets in your school community, and we want to give you concrete examples so that you're able to build those assets.

One hint: If your time is limited and you're not sure what you could get out of reading this book, turn to Chapter 7, 8, or 9 first. There you'll find real-life stories from people around the country who are using the framework of developmental assets to organize and guide their actions to improve their school and their students' success. We hope you'll be moved and inspired, first to read the rest of the book and then to start building developmental assets yourself.

The Unique Role of Schools

Healthy Communities • Healthy Youth is an initiative of Search Institute that seeks to motivate and equip individuals, organizations, communities, and their leaders to join together in nurturing competent, caring, and responsible children and adolescents. As part of more than 400 Healthy Communities • Healthy Youth initiatives throughout the country, people are working together in new and creative partnerships, using the framework of developmental assets, to contribute to young people's well-being. Schools have a specific, unique, and important role in this effort. Consider:

- ◆ Young people spend more of their waking hours in school than in any other place outside the home.
- ◆ It's not just that young people are *in* school; it's that they're there— ostensibly—to *learn*.
- ◆ Schools are the social and civic center of many communities, particularly small communities. Activities—basketball games, fund drives, political campaigns, many of the other events that define a community—center either physically or conceptually around the school.
- ◆ Schools have been a major participant in community efforts to build developmental assets. Fully 30 percent of all Healthy Communities • Healthy Youth initiatives have been initiated and led by schools— more than town councils, more than youth-serving organizations,

more than municipalities, more than congregations. And over 90 percent of community efforts have included schools.

Beyond all those reasons for focusing on schools, though, think about this one: One mission of schools is to educate young people—to maximize their abilities, to provide them with knowledge and skills and the ability to acquire more knowledge and skills, that is, to develop intellectually. To do that, schools also need to provide young people with a safe, secure, healthy environment while they're being educated. That's part of a second mission of schools—to help young people develop physically and emotionally, and to maintain healthy growth and development. A third mission is to help young people develop socially—as citizens and meaningful contributors to society.[2] Building developmental assets helps schools accomplish all three missions.

Antecedents to Achievement

Helping all students achieve means doing more than just working toward higher standards, grades, or test scores. In a comprehensive review of the research on adolescent development, Search Institute researchers recently concluded that "schools that nurture positive relationships among students and among students and teachers are more likely to realize the payoff of more engaged students achieving at higher levels."[3]

It's not really surprising, is it? If students experience school as positive, and if they have good relationships with the people who guide them and teach them, aren't they more likely to learn and achieve to their potential? Building students' developmental assets contributes to their academic achievement. At a time when demands for higher scores on standardized achievement tests pressure schools to focus narrowly on "the basics," it's affirming to have a research-based conceptual framework that clarifies how the pieces—strong relationships, challenge and expectation, music and the arts, social skills, character and values, and academic achievement—all fit together.

A New Approach

For the past few decades, the most common strategy for working with young people has been to try to reduce the number and extent of risk factors in their lives, to help them avoid problems like school failure, drug use, and teen pregnancy. Programs targeted to one or another of these problems have flourished, with mixed success. The research shows that many of the effects of these programs have, in the absence of "booster" sessions, disappeared over time, and some of the programs were quite costly to implement in the first place.[4] In addition, many of them—e.g., curricula that, essentially by themselves, are supposed to build self-esteem, prevent adolescent pregnancy, or eliminate drug abuse—put the burden of solving these problems right on the shoulders of teachers and other school staff.

In contrast, the developmental assets approach recognizes what researchers increasingly are finding: The seemingly separate problems among youth—for example, the aforementioned school failure, drug use, and teen pregnancy—tend to cluster. Young people who are failing at school are more likely than other children also to be users of alcohol and other drugs, and to have their first sexual intercourse at younger ages and with less chance of being protected against pregnancy or disease. The good things young people do tend to cluster as well. Young people who are succeeding at school are also more likely to be physically healthy and to be able to overcome adversity.[5] It makes sense, then, to "cluster" the positive things we all provide to young people, as the asset framework does.

After all, family, school, friends, and community simultaneously shape young people, so it's difficult to ascribe to any one source the predominant influence on how a child thinks and behaves at a given time. The pieces of young people's lives interlock to make pictures as varied as their experiences, and in any given 24-hour period, a young person might be influenced by any of these sources. What are the implications of this? Something simple yet profound: The job of raising healthy, caring, productive, happy children and youth doesn't belong to families, or schools, or community resources alone—it belongs to all of us.

Social science has confirmed something else that educators have known for a long time: Teachers in the early grades can often pick out the children who, if they don't get extra support and attention, are likely to have problems—academic and otherwise—later on. Teachers have vast amounts of data: children's behavior with adults and peers, the social skills they acquire, the expectations that surround them, and the way their behaviors seem to indicate how they feel about themselves. Young people don't suddenly emerge at adolescence with successes and failures that were wholly unpredictable. Success during adolescence is made more possible by childhood success, and in turn makes a successful adulthood more possible.

Recognizing that these earlier stages of life influence later stages, researchers and others began in the 1970s to look at young people's lives, and at points earlier in their development, for critical moments when young people's development could be influenced. The search for better understanding ranged over a vast landscape of research on child and adolescent development; it proved particularly fruitful in mining the field of studies on resilient children, children who "made it" despite enormous odds against them, for example, living in a poor or violent neighborhood, or living with drug-abusing parents. For example, one study followed Hawaiian children for more than 30 years, discovering that young children who could attract a large circle of caring adults had a stronger sense of their scholastic abilities at age 10 than did children with fewer caring adults in their lives.[6]

Such studies have shown that upper elementary-school children, young adolescents, and older youth, while obviously having some different developmental needs, nonetheless need many of the same experiences and conditions. Different words are used to describe these experiences and conditions, but they all boil down to the same things: All children and youth need a stable, positive sense of self and an ability to increasingly regulate themselves, a belief in their overall competence and skills at social problem-solving, and a connection to caring adults.[7] Children and youth who experience those conditions are able to create more coherent and sensible lives, and can more easily find positive pathways as they grow up. Positive conditions and experiences like these are what make up the framework of developmental assets.

Over the last 10 years, Search Institute has exhaustively reviewed the research from numerous fields related to child and adolescent development. It has also conducted its own research—using successive versions of the institute's *Profiles of Student Life: Attitudes and Behaviors* survey—with more than one million 6th- to 12th-grade students. In addition, in the last few years, Search Institute researchers have extensively examined the early childhood literature and interviewed practitioners in early childhood programs to gain a better understanding of developmental assets among children below grade 6.

Through this work, the institute has identified 40 specific developmental assets—20 "external" assets and 20 "internal" assets. External assets are the relationships and opportunities that are provided to young people. They comprise four categories: Support, Empowerment, Boundaries and Expectations, and Constructive Use of Time. Internal assets are the values and skills that young people develop to guide themselves. They also comprise four categories: Commitment to Learning, Positive Values, Social Competencies, and Positive Identity.

The most recent aggregate sample of Search Institute data, and the source for most of the statistics on levels of developmental assets we cite, includes nearly 100,000 6th- to 12th-grade students from 213 U.S. communities. What we've found about the presence or absence of assets in young people's lives generally holds true for both males and females and across racial/ethnic groups and socioeconomic status.

Handout 1.1 shows the 40 assets and their definitions. These definitions, developed for adolescents, express best what we mean in talking about each of the 40 assets.

Many of these assets may seem commonsensical; they are. And their power to positively influence young people is backed up by hundreds of scientific studies. Young people who have more of these assets engage in more positive behaviors and fewer high-risk behaviors. For every increase in the level of assets, there's a corresponding increase in positive behaviors and a decrease in high-risk behaviors, as you can see in Handouts 1.2 and 1.3. These examples illustrate specifically the effects of higher levels of developmental assets on school success (1.2) and problem alcohol use (1.3), but we have found the same relations for all the thriving indicators and high-risk behaviors we've studied.

Given the clear value and importance of the developmental assets, we obviously wish that most young people experience most of the assets. Ideally, we believe, all youth should have 31-40 assets, that is, they would be "asset rich." After all, many

40 Developmental Assets

Category	Asset Name and Definition
	External Assets
Support	**1. Family support**—Family life provides high levels of love and support.
	2. Positive family communication—Young person and her or his parent(s) communicate positively, and young person is willing to seek advice and counsel from parent(s).
	3. Other adult relationships—Young person receives support from three or more nonparent adults.
	4. Caring neighborhood—Young person experiences caring neighbors.
	5. Caring school climate—School provides a caring, encouraging environment.
	6. Parent involvement in schooling—Parent(s) are actively involved in helping young person succeed in school.
Empowerment	**7. Community values youth**—Young person perceives that adults in the community value youth.
	8. Youth as resources—Young people are given useful roles in the community.
	9. Service to others—Young person serves in the community one hour or more per week.
	10. Safety—Young person feels safe at home, at school, and in the neighborhood.
Boundaries and Expectations	**11. Family boundaries**—Family has clear rules and consequences, and monitors the young person's whereabouts.
	12. School boundaries—School provides clear rules and consequences.
	13. Neighborhood boundaries—Neighbors take responsibility for monitoring young people's behavior.
	14. Adult role models—Parent(s) and other adults model positive, responsible behavior.
	15. Positive peer influence—Young person's best friends model responsible behavior.
	16. High expectations—Both parent(s) and teachers encourage the young person to do well.
Constructive Use of Time	**17. Creative activities**—Young person spends three or more hours per week in lessons or practice in music, theater, or other arts.
	18. Youth programs—Young person spends three or more hours per week in sports, clubs, or organizations at school and/or in the community.
	19. Religious community—Young person spends one or more hours per week in activities in a religious institution.
	20. Time at home—Young person is out with friends "with nothing special to do" two or fewer nights per week.

40 Developmental Assets (cont.)

Category	Asset Name and Definition
	Internal Assets
Commitment to Learning	21. **Achievement motivation**—Young person is motivated to do well in school. 22. **School engagement**—Young person is actively engaged in learning. 23. **Homework**—Young person reports doing at least one hour of homework every school day. 24. **Bonding to school**—Young person cares about her or his school. 25. **Reading for pleasure**—Young person reads for pleasure three or more hours per week.
Positive Values	26. **Caring**—Young person places high value on helping other people. 27. **Equality and social justice**—Young person places high value on promoting equality and reducing hunger and poverty. 28. **Integrity**—Young person acts on convictions and stands up for her or his beliefs. 29. **Honesty**—Young person "tells the truth even when it is not easy." 30. **Responsibility**—Young person accepts and takes personal responsibility. 31. **Restraint**—Young person believes it is important not to be sexually active or to use alcohol or other drugs.
Social Competencies	32. **Planning and decision making**—Young person knows how to plan ahead and make choices. 33. **Interpersonal competence**—Young person has empathy, sensitivity, and friendship skills. 34. **Cultural competence**—Young person has knowledge of and comfort with people of different cultural/racial/ethnic backgrounds. 35. **Resistance skills**—Young person can resist negative peer pressure and dangerous situations. 36. **Peaceful conflict resolution**—Young person seeks to resolve conflict nonviolently.
Positive Identity	37. **Personal power**—Young person feels he or she has control over "things that happen to me." 38. **Self-esteem**—Young person reports having a high self-esteem. 39. **Sense of purpose**—Young person reports that "my life has a purpose." 40. **Positive view of personal future**—Young person is optimistic about her or his personal future.

40 elementos fundamentales del desarrollo

El Instituto Search ha identificado los siguientes elementos fundamentales del desarrollo como instrumentos para ayudar a los jóvenes a crecer sanos, interesados en el bienestar común y a ser responsables.

Elementos fundamentales del desarrollo externos

Apoyo

1. **Apoyo familiar**—La vida familiar brinda altos niveles de amor y apoyo.
2. **Comunicación familiar positiva**—El (La) joven y sus padres se comunican positivamente. Los jóvenes están dispuestos a buscar consejo y consuelo en sus padres.
3. **Otras relaciones con adultos**—Además de sus padres, los jóvenes reciben apoyo de tres o más personas adultas que no son sus parientes.
4. **Una comunidad comprometida**—El (La) joven experimenta el interés de sus vecinos por su bienestar.
5. **Un plantel educativo que se interesa por el (la) joven**—La escuela proporciona un ambiente que anima y se preocupa por la juventud.
6. **La participación de los padres en las actividades escolares**—Los padres participan activamente ayudando a los jóvenes a tener éxito en la escuela.

Fortalecimiento

7. **La comunidad valora a la juventud**—El (La) joven percibe que los adultos en la comunidad valoran a la juventud.
8. **La juventud como un recurso**—Se le brinda a los jóvenes la oportunidad de tomar un papel útil en la comunidad.
9. **Servicio a los demás**—La gente joven participa brindando servicios a su comunidad una hora o más a la semana.
10. **Seguridad**—Los jóvenes se sienten seguros en casa, en la escuela y en el vecindario.

Límites y expectativas

11. **Límites familiares**—La familia tiene reglas y consecuencias bien claras, además vigila las actividades de los jóvenes.
12. **Límites escolares**—En la escuela proporciona reglas y consecuencias bien claras.
13. **Límites vecinales**—Los vecinos asumen la responsabilidad de vigilar el comportamiento de los jóvenes.
14. **El comportamiento de los adultos como ejemplo**—Los padres y otros adultos tienen un comportamiento positivo y responsable.
15. **Compañeros como influencia positiva**—Los mejores amigos del (la) joven son un buen ejemplo de comportamiento responsable.
16. **Altas expectativas**—Ambos padres y maestros motivan a los jóvenes para que tengan éxito.

Uso constructivo del tiempo

17. **Actividades creativas**—Los jóvenes pasan tres horas o más a la semana en lecciones de música, teatro u otras artes.
18. **Programas juveniles**—Los jóvenes pasan tres horas o más a la semana practicando algún deporte, o en organizaciones en la escuela o de la comunidad.
19. **Comunidad religiosa**—Los jóvenes pasan una hora o más a la semana en actividades organizadas por alguna institución religiosa.
20. **Tiempo en casa**—Los jóvenes conviven con sus amigos "sin un propósito en particular" dos noches o menos por semana.

	40 elementos fundamentales del desarrollo (cont.)
	Elementos fundamentales del desarrollo internos
Compromiso con el aprendizaje	**21. Motivación por sus logros**—El (La) joven es motivado(a) para que salga bien en la escuela.
	22. Compromiso con la escuela—El (La) joven participa activamente en el aprendizaje.
	23. Tarea—El (La) joven debe hacer su tarea escolar por lo menos durante una hora cada día de clases.
	24. Preocuparse por la escuela—Al (A la) joven debe importarle su escuela.
	25. Leer por placer—El (la) joven lee por placer tres horas o más por semana.
Valores positivos	**26. Preocuparse por los demás**—El (La) joven valora ayudar a los demás.
	27. Igualdad y justicia social—Para el (la) joven tiene mucho valor el promover la igualdad y el reducir el hambre y la pobreza.
	28. Integridad—El (La) joven actúa con convicción y defiende sus creencias.
	29. Honestidad—El (La) joven "dice la verdad aún cuando esto no sea fácil".
	30. Responsabilidad—El (La) joven acepta y toma responsabilidad por su persona.
	31. Abstinencia—El (La) joven cree que es importante no estar activo(a) sexualmente, ni usar alcohol u otras drogas.
Capacidad social	**32. Planeación y toma de decisiones**—El (La) joven sabe cómo planear y hacer elecciones.
	33. Capacidad interpersonal—El (La) joven es simpático(a), sensible y hábil para hacer amistades.
	34. Capacidad cultural—El (La) joven tiene conocimiento de y sabe convivir con gente de diferente marco cultural, racial o étnico.
	35. Habilidad de resistencia—El (La) joven puede resistir la presión negativa de los compañeros así como las situaciones peligrosas.
	36. Solución pacífica de conflictos—El (La) joven busca resolver los conflictos sin violencia.
Identidad positiva	**37. Poder personal**—El (La) joven siente que él o ella tiene el control de "las cosas que le suceden".
	38. Auto-estima—El (La) joven afirma tener una alta auto-estima.
	39. Sentido de propósito—El (La) joven afirma que "mi vida tiene un propósito".
	40. Visión positiva del futuro personal—El (La) joven es optimista sobre su futuro mismo.

of the assets seem to be common-sense things. But the research indicates that "common sense" doesn't necessarily lead to "common" attention to young people's needs. Unfortunately, the reality is that fewer than 10 percent of young people we've surveyed report experiencing that many assets. In fact, the typical 6th- to 12th-grade

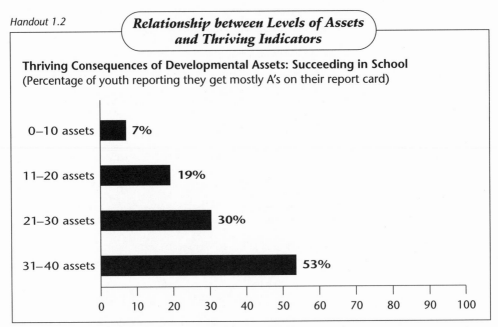

Relationship between Levels of Assets and Thriving Indicators

Thriving Consequences of Developmental Assets: Succeeding in School
(Percentage of youth reporting they get mostly A's on their report card)

0–10 assets 7%

11–20 assets 19%

21–30 assets 30%

31–40 assets 53%

0   10   20   30   40   50   60   70   80   90   100

From P.L. Benson, P.C. Scales, N. Leffert, and E.C. Roehlkepartain, A Fragile Foundation: The State of Developmental Assets among American Youth *(Minneapolis, MN: Search Institute, 1999).*

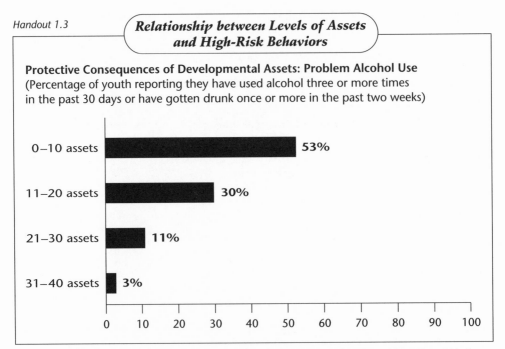

Relationship between Levels of Assets and High-Risk Behaviors

Protective Consequences of Developmental Assets: Problem Alcohol Use
(Percentage of youth reporting they have used alcohol three or more times
in the past 30 days or have gotten drunk once or more in the past two weeks)

0–10 assets 53%

11–20 assets 30%

21–30 assets 11%

31–40 assets 3%

0   10   20   30   40   50   60   70   80   90   100

From P.L. Benson, P.C. Scales, N. Leffert, and E.C. Roehlkepartain, A Fragile Foundation: The State of Developmental Assets among American Youth *(Minneapolis, MN: Search Institute, 1999).*

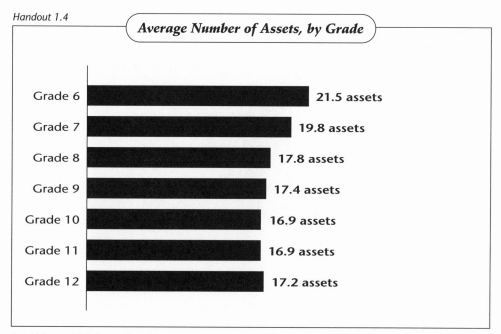

Handout 1.4

Average Number of Assets, by Grade

Grade 6	21.5 assets
Grade 7	19.8 assets
Grade 8	17.8 assets
Grade 9	17.4 assets
Grade 10	16.9 assets
Grade 11	16.9 assets
Grade 12	17.2 assets

From P.L. Benson, P.C. Scales, N. Leffert, and E.C. Roehlkepartain, A Fragile Foundation: The State of Developmental Assets among American Youth (Minneapolis, MN: Search Institute, 1999).

student surveyed reports experiencing less than half—18—of the 40 assets (see Handout 1.4).

What makes this low level of developmental assets among American youth so troubling is not just that young people with many assets make healthier choices about alcohol and other drugs and that they are more likely to do well in school. It's also that young people who already are vulnerable and at high risk of making poor health choices and being unsuccessful in school and other areas of life—because of abuse, violence, or other developmental deficits—experience an even greater positive impact from having developmental assets in their lives.[8] When vulnerable children's experience of developmental assets is limited, they miss a tremendous opportunity to become resilient.

Handout 1.5 gives us the data: Among highly vulnerable youth who experience all five developmental deficits Search Institute has studied (liabilities such as physical abuse, violence, or being home alone too much, which may be dangerous by themselves or may increase the odds that a young person will engage in high-risk behavior), those rich in assets (31–40 assets) engage in only two of ten high-risk behavior patterns (such as alcohol abuse or juvenile delinquency). In contrast, vulnerable youth who experience few assets (0–10 assets) engage in an average of six of the ten high-risk behaviors.[9] For the most vulnerable youth, the relation is powerful: more assets appears to translate into *many* fewer risks.

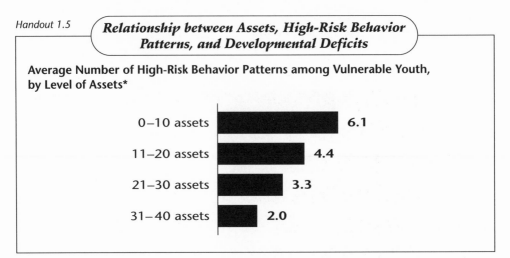

Handout 1.5

Relationship between Assets, High-Risk Behavior Patterns, and Developmental Deficits

Average Number of High-Risk Behavior Patterns among Vulnerable Youth, by Level of Assets*

0–10 assets	6.1
11–20 assets	4.4
21–30 assets	3.3
31–40 assets	2.0

*N = 4,063 6th- to 12th-grade students who report simultaneously the five developmental deficits: alone at home, TV overexposure, physical abuse, victim of violence, and drinking parties; a sub-sample from the aggregate sample of 99,462 who took the Search Institute Profiles of Student Life: Attitudes and Behaviors survey during the 1996–97 school year.

From P.L. Benson, P.C. Scales, N. Leffert, and E.C. Roehlkepartain, A Fragile Foundation: The State of Developmental Assets among American Youth (Minneapolis, MN: Search Institute, 1999).

Misconceptions about the Asset Approach

When people first hear about the framework of developmental assets, they sometimes develop misconceptions about the connections between the framework and their school's missions. Why? Perhaps some people make assumptions or jump to conclusions because they've heard about lots of other models and ideas. Sometimes people are frustrated by the numerous policy and practice changes that have come to them from legislatures or districts, and they feel resistant to initiating more change. Sometimes people don't have enough accurate information, or they feel too rushed and busy to familiarize themselves with the information they do have. Whatever the reason, in talking with educators from across the country, we've heard several misconceptions that apply specifically to building developmental assets in school communities. Here are four of them, followed by our observation of why they're incorrect.

Misconception 1

"Our school is already doing enough of this kind of thing. All our teachers are familiar with the developmental assets, and we try to be caring to all our students."

Actually, a lot of schools *are* already doing some of this kind of thing. It's a testament to the logic and relevance of developmental assets that the concept resonates so powerfully with school communities. There's something reassuring about focusing on the positive, on strengths, on things that people *can do*. And educators recognize actions they're already taking that look like asset building. But awareness is only a small first step, and being systematic is different from doing asset building in a hit-or-miss manner. If the awareness isn't translated into behaviors, and if the caring and high expectations aren't consistent throughout the school, and if students aren't affected by those behaviors, what has been accomplished? People may think they're doing something without really doing it sufficiently. For example, most educators would probably say that their schools are caring places, but a sobering reflection on schools' efforts in this category is our finding that *only 25%* of students in grades 6–12 report experiencing a "caring school climate."[10] Equally sobering are the following: Only 24% of students surveyed report having the asset of reading for pleasure, and only 41% report that both parents and teachers expect them to do well. The difference between what schools try to do or think they're doing and what students are experiencing indicates a need for schools to *change* what they're doing. Here's the bottom line: Many schools may already be "doing some of this kind of thing," but the chances are you could do more.

Misconception 2

"This sounds pretty good. I'll order the program as soon as I can."

It's not quite as simple as that. In fact, there is no neat, tidy, packaged program to help you build developmental assets. Building developmental assets is a conceptual framework, not a program. It's a tool for examining and organizing yourself, your relationships, and the environment of your school community that can lead you toward more success in helping young people develop in positive ways and achieve their academic potential. To be sure, a wide variety of programs can contribute to building assets, and we'll describe some of the best of them in this book. But all these programs will go for naught if the people behind them—teachers, administrators, other school adults—don't understand what they themselves need to do to build assets, and then go ahead and do it. So don't be put off by the mistaken notion that this is yet another program to implement. On the contrary, because using the asset framework is a way of approaching what you are already doing, you can incorporate building assets into virtually everything you currently do. Building assets is a *process*, not a product, a "how" more than a "what."

Misconception 3

"Schools aren't responsible for kids' problems; we're doing a good job.
Parents are responsible, and the media are responsible, and . . . ."

No one ever wins the blame game. Ensuring that children and youth grow up to be safe, healthy, responsible, and caring people is a difficult and complex job; there's plenty of responsibility to go around. Everyone has a stake in this, and everyone has a role to play. For the reasons we listed earlier, schools have a particularly good opportunity to contribute, and that's what we're focusing on in this book. However, the more that schools can coordinate with parents, media, and other parts of the broader community, and the more that all sources of influence for young people give clear, consistent, positive messages, the better the chance that the job will be completed.

Misconception 4

"It's nice to have a caring environment, but my school has to focus on achieving high academic standards. There's no time to do anything else."

Think about your own current work environment as well as previous work environments, and you'll see why this statement is a myth. Haven't you accomplished more when you felt good about coming to work? Aren't you spurred on to do greater things when you know that your colleagues will respect and be receptive to your ideas? Don't you feel more capable when everything and everyone around you supports who you are and what you do?

Students are no different. They're more able to focus on their studies when they're not thinking about getting beaten up by bullies or being made fun of for their weaknesses and uniquenesses. They're more able to succeed when they trust that school adults will listen to them. Building developmental assets in school communities increases the likelihood of student achievement. We'll show you the evidence for that very soon, but for now, if you hear this misconception, consider your own experience: most of us are more successful in a caring, nurturing environment where we're expected to do our best.

Enhancing What Schools Are Already Doing

As we mentioned, schools and districts in more than 1,000 towns and cities nationwide, involving more than one million 6th- to 12th-grade students who have taken Search Institute's survey of developmental assets, risks, deficits, and thriving behaviors—*Profiles of Student Life: Attitudes and Behaviors*—have used the results to spark changes in how individuals and institutions live and work with young people. More than 400 of those communities have formally mobilized residents around the theme of Healthy Communities • Healthy Youth, and many of those have used the survey results to increase understanding of the needs and strengths of young people in the community and to embark on a variety of actions.

But many schools and many communities subscribe to Misconception 1, which begins, "Our school (community) is already doing enough of this kind of thing." If you or your colleagues are in that camp, here are four additional points to consider.

First, even if a majority of the students are succeeding at your school, no student stands still for long. Children develop rapidly, and with each change in the school they attend and in the way they experience their world comes the possibility of new successes or failures, new or intensified confidences or insecurities. Today's happy and successful child can become tomorrow's unhappy and struggling young adolescent if we don't attend enough to the fit between their changing developmental needs and their daily experiences.

Second, children are not a homogeneous group. They're not all average, above average, equally privileged or equally vulnerable. Again: The more vulnerable children are, the more they benefit from high levels of developmental assets. Search Institute's extensive review of the research on adolescent development suggests that building developmental assets can be a valuable way of helping to narrow the achievement gap between high- and under-achieving students.[11]

Third, regardless of superficial similarities to others of their sex, age, or ethnicity, all children experience school, family, friends, and community life in their own way. So, even if students are achieving high grades and test scores—traditional measures of academic success—that doesn't ensure either that they'll continue to achieve at high levels, or that they're succeeding in other ways, such as being healthy, making contributions to their community, or being able to overcome adversity and be resilient inside and outside of school. High levels of developmental assets can reinforce school success, encourage student success in other ways that are important in their own right, and support continued success as a learner. Having a lot of developmental assets doesn't guarantee that a specific young person will avoid all problems, but it does dramatically change the odds.

Finally, as we noted earlier, despite schools' seemingly best efforts, Search Institute's data show that only 25 percent of 6th- to 12th-grade students say that their school is a caring place, only 29 percent say that their parents are involved with their schooling, and only 41 percent say that their parents and teachers have high expectations of them. Maybe teachers and other students really do care about young people, and maybe teachers as well as parents really do have high expectations for young people. Maybe the data reflect that the caring and high expectations don't get communicated sufficiently for most young people to notice. Or maybe the caring and high expectations tend to be centered around certain types of students, rather than reaching all students. Using the asset framework can guide you in sorting it out and making improvements in your school, so that you can help all your students be successful.

Intentionality

Caring for students, expecting the best from them, and giving them opportunities to be involved and succeed *as a deliberate strategy to build developmental assets* is much different from doing these things only by chance. When people in school communities are deliberate about building assets, they're more likely to reach more students and they're more able to focus their efforts where they do the most good. *We believe that schools and students will benefit tremendously by intentionally using the developmental assets framework as a central principle in the five school areas of curriculum and instruction, organization, cocurricular activities, community partnerships, and support services.* If school adults ensure that asset building fundamentally informs their relationships with students, the environment of the school, and the school's programs and practices—as well as its community partnerships—then they are giving a wide range of students a better chance of growing up healthy, caring, and responsible, in addition to achieving academic success.

To genuinely and intentionally build assets means that school staff need to identify and challenge some of their beliefs about schooling and some of their practices. Handout 1.6 shows how some of these beliefs and practices look—before being intentional about asset building and after making a commitment to using the asset framework.

Take a second look at the last three beliefs, each of which is about including everyone in the work of building developmental assets for students. Although schools obviously play an important role in promoting student achievement, it's vital to see that role in the context of the bigger picture. For example, some research suggests that the majority of differences among the states on students' achievement scores on the National Assessment of Educational Progress can be explained by a state's poverty level, the number of parents children have at home, the level of parents' education, and the type of community they live in.[12] Obviously, the level of poverty in a school district or the type of community a school is in does affect what schools can do, but the point is that what affects children's learning is broader than just what happens "in" schools. Research has long shown that parents' involvement in their children's schooling is tremendously important and, more recently, that parent involvement can exert even more influence on students' school success than families' socioeconomic status.[13] But the power of each of the factors that help students do well in school can be multiplied when the people involved—parents, teachers, neighbors, volunteers, and other concerned adults—are united by a common language and common goals.

The asset framework can provide that language and those goals. It's not a universal panacea, it's not the only thing that people in school communities need to do. But the research—and common sense—indicate that students benefit in many ways from having high levels of developmental assets. So how can school communities be effective asset builders? Several key features need to be in place:

Handout 1.6

Beliefs and Practices that Limit and Promote Asset Building

Beliefs and Practices that Limit Asset Building	Beliefs and Practices that Promote Asset Building
There's a program for everything, and the sources of success in working with students mostly come from formal programs.	We emphasize "informal" asset building based in the daily individual relationships students have with each other and with school adults.
"Interventions" for helping students are something we do to or for students.	We promote asset building with and not only for students, i.e., we encourage students' significant participation and leadership in building their own assets.
Once students attend a special intervention event or participate in a program, we've adequately helped them.	We commit to ensure that each student has repeated, ongoing opportunities for asset building, more than reliance solely on short-term special events or programs.
We believe that asset building is the job of only certain staff, such as teachers and counselors.	We believe that everyone in a school community is a potential asset builder—including students, custodians, bus drivers, paraprofessionals, nurses, teachers, administrators, and cafeteria workers.
We believe that asset building is for only certain students, such as "at-risk" students.	We commit to intentionally build assets throughout the entire school community, so that all students and school adults receive the benefits.
We believe that schools carry the burden of students' academic success.	We believe that accountability for students' performance should be a collective responsibility of the entire community, not just schools.

- ◆ Acceptance of the concept and active participation in the asset-building effort by a core team of committed and influential school community members;
- ◆ A growing awareness of the concept of developmental assets by as many members of the school community as possible;
- ◆ An assessment of how many assets students are currently experiencing and of how the school community is currently building assets and for whom;
- ◆ A way for the school community to infuse the assets into its routine;
- ◆ An emphasis on "informal" asset building based in the daily relationships students have with each other and with school adults;

- ◆ A commitment to intentionally build assets throughout the entire school community, so that all students and school adults receive the benefits;
- ◆ A belief that *everyone* in a school community is a potential asset builder;
- ◆ Asset building *with* and not only for students, i.e., significant encouragement of student participation and leadership in building their own developmental assets;
- ◆ A commitment to ensuring that each student has multiple, repeated, ongoing opportunities for asset building, more than reliance on special events, activities, or programs; and
- ◆ A way to sustain and nurture asset building.

We'll explore these features throughout the book, but before we do that, we want to talk about how asset building relates to children of all ages.

Notes

1. Goodenow, C. (1993). Classroom belonging among early adolescent students: Relationships to motivation and achievement. *Journal of Early Adolescence*, 13, 21–43.
2. The three missions of schools are drawn from the following:
   Carnegie Council on Adolescent Development (1992). *Turning points: Preparing American youth for the 21st century.* Washington, DC: Author.
   Lawson, H., & Briar-Lawson, K. (199x). *Connecting the dots: Progress toward the integration of school reform, school-linked services, parent involvement, and community schools.* Oxford, OH: The Danforth Foundation and the Institute for Educational Renewal at Miami University.
   National Education Goals Panel (1998). *National education goals report: Building a nation of learning 1998.* Washington, DC: Author.
   Sizer, T.R. (1992). *Horace's school: Redesigning the American high school.* Boston: Houghton-Mifflin.
3. Scales, P.C., & Leffert, N. (1999). *Developmental assets: A synthesis of the scientific research on adolescent development.* Minneapolis: Search Institute.
4. Dryfoos, J.G. (1990). *Adolescents at risk: Prevalence and prevention.* New York: Oxford University Press.
5. Benson, P.L., Scales, P.C., Leffert, N., & Roehlkepartain, E.C. (1999). *A fragile foundation: The state of developmental assets among American youth.* Minneapolis: Search Institute.
6. Werner, Emmy E., & Smith, Ruth S. (1992). *Overcoming the odds: high-risk children from birth to adulthood.* Ithaca, NY: Cornell University Press.
7. Garmezy, N. (1993). Children in poverty: Resilience despite risk. *Psychiatry*, 56, 127–136.
8. Benson, et al., op. cit.
9. Ibid.
10. Ibid.
11. See, for example: Berends, M. (1995). Educational stratification and students' social bonding to school. *Journal of Sociology of Education*, 16, 327-352; Eccles, J.S., & Midgley, C. (1990). Changes in academic motivation and self-perception during early adolescence. In R. Montemayor, G.R. Adams, & T.P. Gullotta (Eds.), *Advances in adolescent development: Vol. 2. From childhood to adoles-*

cence: A transitional period? (pp. 134–155). Newbury Park, CA: Sage. Lee, V.E., & Smith, J.R. (1993). Effects of school restructuring on the achievement and engagement of middle-grade students. *Sociology of Education*, 66, 164–187.

12. Evans, R. (1999). The great accountability fallacy. *Education Week*, Feb. 3, 1999, 28(21), 52, 35.
13. Epstein, Joyce L. (1987). Parent involvement: What research says to administrators. *Education and Urban Society*, 19, 119–136.

Marjoribanks, K. (1996). Ethnicity, family achievement syndrome, and adolescents' aspirations: Rosen's framework revisited. *Journal of Genetic Psychology*, 157, 349–359.

Chavkin, N.E., & Gonzales, D.L. (1995). *Forging partnerships between Mexican-American parents and the schools.* Charleston, WV: ERIC Clearinghouse on Rural Education and Small Schools (ERIC Document Reproduction Service No. ED 388 489).

2

❧

Assets and Development across the School Experience

As we've mentioned, schools have a specific, unique, and important role in the effort to build developmental assets for young people. We believe that building assets is important throughout all the years a young person goes to school. However, the assets will come to bear in different ways at different times in a young person's development. For example, building the asset of Resistance Skills could be more important for a 6th-grade student than for a 2nd-grade student; even though 2nd-grade students today do encounter invitations to use drugs, those situations are more common among 6th-grade students. The asset of Honesty, while important for people of all ages, might take on a greater significance for a 2nd-grade student than for a 6th-grade student, simply because parents usually teach their children the value of honesty at a young age. It's likely that, as children grow, different assets ebb and flow in importance, become internalized in new, deeper ways, and that is what we want to address in this chapter.

Pre-Kindergarten through Grade 4

Because the developmental assets framework was initially developed for adolescents ages 12–18, parts of it do not readily apply to very young children, such as the concept of "external" and "internal" assets. Although some children do start with biologically based temperaments that do indeed garner for them more adult attention and care, e.g., infants who smile early and often—most assets in infancy are external, i.e., provided by others. Gradually, children learn to internalize the values, beliefs, and self-perceptions that the internal assets describe. But the conceptual basis of the framework is still sound when applied to infants and young children, because all children need their caregivers to surround them with support as well as boundaries, keep them safe, and provide constructive opportunities for exploring their growing worlds. As Handout 2.1 shows, each of the 40 assets among youth is paralleled by a developmentally analogous, although sometimes not identical, asset in infancy and early childhood.

Before children begin kindergarten, of course, the groundwork has been laid at home and in pre-school settings for their success at school. Parents and other caregivers who are warm and loving, neither too permissive nor too strict, encourage the development of basic security in children, a foundation from which those children can safely explore the world around them. Parents and other caregivers can further enhance their children's readiness for school by reading to them and by giving them opportunities to manipulate objects, learn by doing things, see their parents reading and writing, and interact with other children and adults.[1]

In their early years in school, young children need to experience school as a place where they are cared about, where they are known and have useful roles, where rules and consequences are clear, where they do and learn interesting things, where they have opportunities to develop basic planning and decision-making skills, and where they can learn how to interact positively with other children and adults.

To help achieve these things at school, teachers can:

- Set and explain high standards for expected behavior;
- Model expected behavior;
- Use small-group and cooperative learning strategies; and
- Provide opportunities for children to assume responsibilities and help others.

As children learn to associate school with being a safe and enjoyable place, the foundation is being set for their development of assets such as School Engagement and Bonding to School. Being given plenty of opportunities to succeed at simple and fun learning tasks helps build the foundations of assets such as Personal Power, Planning and Decision Making, and Achievement Motivation. Finally, being exposed to a variety of group activities and learning how to get along positively with others helps build assets such as Interpersonal Competence and a Caring School Climate. Experiences such as these help young children develop the kind of positive perceptions about school that are the foundation for continued success at school.

Assets from Infancy through Adolescence

Asset type	Infants (Birth to 12 months)	Toddlers (Ages 13 to 35 months)	Preschoolers (Ages 3 to 5 Years)	Elementary-Age Children (Ages 6 to 11 Years)	Adolescents (Ages 12 to 18)
EXTERNAL ASSETS					
SUPPORT					
Asset #1			Family support		
Asset #2			Positive family communication		
Asset #3	Other adult resources			Other adult relationships	
Asset #4			Caring neighborhood		
Asset #5	Caring out-of-home climate			Caring school climate	
Asset #6	Parent involvement in out-of-home situations			Parent involvement in schooling	
EMPOWERMENT					
Asset #7	Child has place in family life	Children valued		Community values children	Community values youth
Asset #8		Children have roles in family life	Children given useful roles		Youth as resources
Asset #9			Service to others		
Asset #10			Safety		
BOUNDARIES AND EXPECTATIONS					
Asset #11			Family boundaries		
Asset #12	Out-of-home boundaries			School boundaries	
Asset #13			Neighborhood boundaries		
Asset #14			Adult role models		
Asset #15	Positive peer observation	Positive peer observation and early interactions	Positive peer interactions		Positive peer influence
Asset #16			Expectations for growth		High expectations
CONSTRUCTIVE USE OF TIME					
Asset #17			Creative activities		
Asset #18	Out-of-home activities			Child programs	Youth programs
Asset #19			Religious community		
Asset #20	Positive, supervised time at home			Time at home	

Asset type	Infants (Birth to 12 months)	Toddlers (Ages 13 to 35 months)	Preschoolers (Ages 3 to 5 Years)	Elementary-Age Children (Ages 6 to 11 Years)	Adolescents (Ages 12 to 18)
INTERNAL ASSETS					
COMMITMENT TO LEARNING					
Asset #21	Achievement expectation			Achievement motivation	
Asset #22	Engagement expectation			School engagement	
Asset #23	Stimulating activity			Homework	
Asset #24	Enjoyment of learning			Bonding to school	
Asset #25			Reading for pleasure		
POSITIVE VALUES					
Asset #26	Family values caring			Caring	
Asset #27	Family values equality and social justice			Equality and social justice	
Asset #28	Family values integrity			Integrity	
Asset #29	Family values honesty			Honesty	
Asset #30	Family values responsibility			Responsibility	
Asset #31	Family values healthy lifestyle and sexual attitudes			Healthy lifestyle and sexual attitudes	Restraint
SOCIAL COMPETENCIES					
Asset #32	Planning and decision-making observation		Planning and decision-making practice	Planning and decision making	
Asset #33	Interpersonal observation		Interpersonal interactions	Interpersonal competence	
Asset #34	Cultural observation		Cultural interactions	Cultural competence	
Asset #35	Resistance observation		Resistance practice	Resistance skills	
Asset #36	Peaceful conflict resolution observation		Peaceful conflict resolution practice	Peaceful conflict resolution	
POSITIVE IDENTITY					
Asset #37	Family has personal power			Personal power	
Asset #38	Family models high self-esteem			High self-esteem	
Asset #39	Family has a sense of purpose			Sense of purpose	
Asset #40	Family has a positive view of the future			Positive view of personal future	

Adapted from N. Leffert, P.L. Benson, and J.L. Roehlkepartain, Starting Out Right: Developmental Assets for Children (Minneapolis: Search Institute, 1997).

Grades 4–6 and 6–9

We link these grade groupings for two reasons. First, children in the late elementary through middle school grades are undergoing tremendous physical, social, emotional, and cognitive changes, and the great variation among children means that those changes can begin any time across these grades. In addition, the transitions from elementary school to middle school and from middle school to high school are critical times during which students' commitment to learning can either grow or wither. Especially for girls, the transition from a more intimate elementary school to a larger middle school may bring with it declines in both academic performance and self-esteem, especially if the middle school they're moving into really is just a high school for younger people—a literal "junior" high—and not a genuine middle school that's organized specifically around the developmental needs of young adolescents.[2] Programs begun in the 6th grade to help those students and their families connect with caring students and adults from their new middle school—e.g., encouraging summer visits to the new school, or pairing the new 6th-grade students with 7th- or 8th-grade student mentors—are a crucial part of the steps needed to keep building students' assets during the transition and beyond. Search Institute's data show that 12th-grade students report experiencing less of 22 of the 40 developmental assets by 10 percentage points or more than 6th-grade students do—and most of the decline happens during the middle-school years.[3] Thus, the period from grade 4 through grade 9, encompassing early adolescence, deserves particular attention from educators.

A school community that intentionally builds young people's assets responds well to several of the key developmental changes that occur during this period. Especially important changes occur in several areas.

Pubertal development

The most fundamental change of all for children in the 4th–9th grades, or roughly ages 9–15, is the transition into puberty. Young people are changing more rapidly during early adolescence than at any time other than infancy, and at a variety of different rates.[4] One of the effects of their great variety in maturation is that confident, friendly, self-assured 3rd- and 4th-grade students can become self-critical, doubtful, and reticent 5th- and 6th-grade students as they begin to compare themselves with others, noticing both the features, interests, and abilities they have and, too often, what they don't have. Girls tend to begin puberty about two years earlier than boys, a fact that adds further variation to any group of similar-age middle-school students.[5]

One practical implication of these developmental realities is that, in fostering the asset of Achievement Motivation, schools that stress competition and comparisons in the late elementary and middle grades—in contrast to learning for its own sake, personal improvement, and cooperative learning strategies—can easily exacerbate what is already a difficult aspect of adjustment during puberty, making school success less likely.[6] Schools can positively respond to adolescents' concerns about their changing bodies with comprehensive health education programs that emphasize accurate information about human sexuality, identification of personal and social values, development of social skills, and respect for self and others—content that helps build assets such as Caring, Restraint, Interpersonal Competence, Cultural Competence, Resistance Skills, and, indirectly, Self-Esteem.

Cognitive development

Why are at least half of adolescents bored quite a lot of the time at school?[7] For some students, school may never be a place of excitement that they look forward to participating in every day. But for many other students, what is taught and how it is taught can be the key. Students in grades 4 through 9 are beginning to think abstractly and are increasingly able to hypothesize, imagine, and identify exceptions and inconsistencies.[8] They also are trying to make sense of the different parts of their world, trying to understand how the parts connect into a whole and what their place in that world is.

That's why most young adolescents respond with interest to integrative curriculum that connects subjects such as language arts, the sciences, health, social studies, and mathematics through broad themes. In addition, when schools have available a variety of exploratory, mini-course opportunities, especially those that enable young people to connect to others in the community through service-learning or internship programs, they're providing ways of enabling young people to identify strengths and interests, and to develop a sense of themselves as a valuable part of a community, not as "just a student." In these ways, schools can help build assets such as Community Values Youth, Youth as Resources, High Expectations, Achievement Motivation, School Engagement, and Bonding to School.

Relationships with parents

Young people and their parents must renegotiate their relationships during early adolescence. Although young adolescents want and need greater autonomy and self-regulation, they also want and need closeness with and support from their parents. As we mentioned earlier, parents who are neither too permissive nor too strict seem to strike the right balance. In relation to school, this kind of parenting seems to help children develop positive attitudes toward school and motivate them to do well in school.[9]

Educators know that "parent involvement" as reflected in attendance at school functions tends to decrease as children move into higher grades, but a different kind of parent involvement remains important throughout adolescence. What parents do at home to support learning—expressing positive attitudes about schooling, talking with their children about what they're learning, encouraging and modeling reading, providing an environment conducive to studying—may be even more important than attending school meetings and events, especially as children mature.[10] Schools that support, encourage, and facilitate all those kinds of parent involvement can help build the asset of Parent Involvement in Schooling, but they may also help build assets such as Positive Family Communication, High Expectations, Time at Home, Achievement Motivation, School Engagement, Bonding to School, Homework, Reading for Pleasure, Responsibility, Planning and Decision Making, Personal Power, and Positive View of Personal Future.

Socializing and peer relations

The peer group grows in importance over grades 4 through 9. Research has shown that children who are liked and included by their classmates tend also to report that their teachers are more caring and supportive.[11] A common denominator in those peer and adult relationships seems to be the ability of socially successful children to use restraint, to control their emotions in ways appropriate to the situations in which they find themselves.

Allowing plentiful opportunities for children in this age-group to socialize with their peers, particularly through project-oriented and cooperative learning strategies, helps young people feel that they "fit in" as part of a valued group and maximizes the influence of positive peer pressure on behavior. These strategies may help build assets such as Caring School Climate, Positive Peer Influence, School Engagement, Bonding to School, and Interpersonal Competence. In contrast, too soon an emphasis on quiet, order, and independent work may shut off the potential for this kind of constructive social learning to occur.[12]

The competing pulls of independence and dependence

Children and young adolescents increasingly exert more autonomy, express more personal preferences, and accept less readily what their parents or other adults say. Yet studies have found, for example, that 7th-grade students commonly say their teachers give them less freedom to have input to curriculum content and the rules that govern the classroom than 6th-grade students say their teachers give them, even though 7th-grade students tend to be developmentally more capable of assuming those roles.[13]

The conclusion? Young people need increasing opportunities to influence their environment and regulate themselves, even as their need for close relationships with adults and peers continues. Thus, strong advisor-advisee programs, "looping" (keeping the same teachers and students together over several years), and other ways of sustaining caring, supportive relationships continue to be important through middle school and even on into high school, as do service-learning and other activities that give students a chance to take action and contribute to the common good. These strategies may help build assets such as Other Adult Relationships, Caring School Climate, Community Values Youth, Youth as Resources, Service to Others, Positive Peer Influence, Bonding to School, Planning and Decision Making, and Personal Power.

Grades 9–12

For too many adolescents, the transition from middle school to high school can be as striking a change as the one from elementary school to middle school. In high school, students usually are just one of a much larger number of peers, less likely to be well-known by several caring adults and more likely to feel anonymous. Schoolwork tends to become an individual rather than a small-group pursuit, and higher- and lower-achieving students become even more differentiated from each other, ever more firmly stuck in whatever "tracks" they were placed into years earlier. The young people who didn't like school much before can drop out, and more than 11 percent do each year, with three times that amount among Hispanic and Native American students.[14] Although the declines in reports of developmental assets that were observed in middle school are generally less dramatic during high school, few of the assets seem to increase over the high school years, and reports of some, like parental involvement in schooling, are less common in each succeeding grade; for most students, their asset profile when they leave high school is, at best, stuck right where it was when they entered high school. In its survey research, Search Institute did not follow the same young people from 6th grade through 12th grade, so these impressions from the data are limited in terms of telling us what happens in an individual youth's passage through those years. However, both the institute's comprehensive review of the research on adolescent development[15] and the consistency of these 6th- to 12th-grade trends across a decade of Search Institute studies give us a portrait of many young people's experiences and lend confidence to the view that youth do experience different levels of assets as they grow up.

Most of these "downward" trends are preventable. Many of the kinds of asset-building practices that make sense for young adolescents also make sense for most high school students. Many high schools have adopted models of school improvement—including creating intimacy through small houses or teams, using teachers as advisors, and emphasizing block scheduling and thematically integrated curriculum—that originated in middle schools. Not all techniques work for all children, of course, but the evidence is promising that these strategies do make a difference for most students who experience them.[16]

However, there are some important differences between middle school and high school students' needs. Researchers have found that while overall competence in middle childhood and early adolescence is made up of three dimensions—academic achievement, conduct, and social success with peers—for some young adolescents, and for most high school-age youth, two additional dimensions enter the picture: job competence (developing the skills necessary for success in the work world) and romantic competence (being able to initiate and maintain satisfying dating and love relationships).[17] Therefore, although maintaining much of the middle school approach would make high school a more nurturing and challenging time for more students, some additional, developmentally specific approaches also are needed.

These older adolescents are more able to regulate themselves than their young adolescent counterparts, and so they need more opportunities for self-direction and supervised independent study. However, because developing job competence in today's world increasingly means knowing how to work effectively in teams, older students must also continue to work collaboratively with others on longer-term projects. While young adolescents need to explore their place in their families, schools, and communities, high school students need to begin making some decisions about their roles in society. Expanded opportunities for a variety of service-learning, peer counseling, peer mediating, and community internship experiences respond to those developmental needs. Of course, older youth also need a special kind of caring adult relationship, preferably with both a teacher and a guidance counselor—as well as other adult mentors—through which they can sharpen their focus on the intersection of their interests, talents, and values. That kind of supportive relationship is a necessary adjunct to broader "career awareness" activities.

In the increasingly diverse United States, there also are moral, democratic, and practical reasons for students (and school staff) to understand, become comfortable with, and be respectful of those from cultural, religious, or socioeconomic backgrounds different from their own, as well as understanding and appreciating their own cultural background. Because of the rapid diversification of our society, heightened emphasis on strengthening cultural competence is an important asset-building focus in the high school years. Finally, students at the high school level increasingly face decisions that affect their own and others' health and well-being, particularly around sexual behavior and use of alcohol and other drugs. Comprehensive health education continued from and building on the health education provided in the elementary and middle school years helps reinforce the positive values and social competencies that enable young people to make wise decisions. Together, these strategies can help students build assets such as Other Adult Relationships, Youth as Resources, Adult Role Models, High Expectations, Achievement Motivation, School Engagement, Responsibility, Restraint, Planning and Decision Making, Interpersonal Competence, Cultural Competence, Resistance Skills, Sense of Purpose, and Positive View of Personal Future.

Assets and Developmental Realities

The 40 assets that Search Institute has identified are based on these kinds of developmental realities, and they strongly contribute to positive child and youth development. As the foregoing indicates, schools already use a variety of school organization and curriculum strategies to build the developmental assets that all children and youth need. The approach we suggest in this book, however, is to become more systematically intentional about building assets throughout the entire school community. That means using the developmental assets framework as the primary lens through which to view and affect day-to-day relationships—among staff and students, among students, and among schools, families, and communities—as well as the climate of the school community and the programs and practices implemented there. As Handouts 2.2–2.9 show, there are many actions school staff can take that help build the eight categories of external and internal assets. Most of these are individual behaviors, not formal programs. In the next chapter, we'll focus more specifically on the assets that most directly relate to academic success, and on what schools can do to build those developmental assets.

Handout 2.2

Building the Support Assets

Grades	How to Build the Assets
4-6	◆ Encourage children's passions and interests. ◆ Answer children's questions. If you don't know the answer, admit it and work together to find it. ◆ When you and a child disagree, show you still care, and encourage other adults to do the same.
6-9	◆ Be available to listen. ◆ Answer students' questions. If you don't know the answer, admit it and work together to find it. ◆ Affirm independence and interdependence. People need each other.
9-12	◆ Find out what teenagers care about and advocate for their causes. ◆ Ask teenagers for their opinion or advice.

Adapted from Pass It On! Ready-to-Use Handouts for Asset Builders (Minneapolis, MN: Search Institute, 1999).

Building the Empowerment Assets

Grades	How to Build the Assets
4-6	◆ Encourage children to write letters to public officials about issues that are important to them. ◆ Ask children what they like and don't like about their school routines. Try to make changes to improve them.
6-9	◆ Encourage teenagers to volunteer at least one hour a week. Have them write about or talk in class about what they learn from these experiences. ◆ Talk with young people about their feelings and fears about safety. Work together to help young people feel more safe.
9-12	◆ Help teenagers spend time contributing to their communities. This could range from finding out about opportunities and how to get involved to simply figuring out ways to get them there. ◆ Encourage teenagers to take leadership roles in addressing issues that concern them.

Adapted from Pass It On! Ready-to-Use Handouts for Asset Builders *(Minneapolis, MN: Search Institute, 1999).*

Building the Boundaries-and-Expectations Assets

Grades	How to Build the Assets
4-6	◆ Encourage schools, neighbors, organizations, and communities to have consistent boundaries and consequences so children know how to act in different settings. ◆ Be firm about boundaries that keep kids safe at school. Don't negotiate these boundaries. ◆ Challenge children to do their best in school, and help them whenever you can.
6-9	◆ Be patient, calm, and consistent as young teenagers test the boundaries you set. ◆ Negotiate new boundaries as children grow older. Work together on what's acceptable and what's not.
9-12	◆ Help teenagers think about their goals for the future and what kind of boundaries they'll need to meet them. ◆ Continue to have boundaries for appropriate behaviors and consequences for violating those boundaries. ◆ Challenge teenagers to learn through school and other activities.

Adapted from Pass It On! Ready-to-Use Handouts for Asset Builders *(Minneapolis, MN: Search Institute, 1999).*

Building the Constructive-Use-of-Time Assets

Grades	How to Build the Assets
4-6	◆ Teach children to balance their time so they gradually learn how to avoid getting too busy or too bored.
	◆ Volunteer in activities for children, such as sports, clubs, and music.
6-9	◆ Help young people look for positive, stimulating activities that match their talents, interests, and abilities.
9-12	◆ Encourage teenagers to be involved in at least one activity that may continue into their adult years.
	◆ Help teenagers think about how the time they spend on different activities helps or hinders them in reaching their goals.
	◆ Volunteer in cocurricular programs and activities for older teenagers. Take time to get to know the young people involved.

Adapted from Pass It On! Ready-to-Use Handouts for Asset Builders *(Minneapolis, MN: Search Institute, 1999).*

Building the Commitment-to-Learning Assets

Grades	How to Build the Assets
4-6	◆ Assign appropriate homework for children, and teach them effective study skills.
	◆ Let children read to you every day as they learn to read. Show them that you are excited and proud about their reading.
	◆ Help children find ways to learn more about subjects that really interest them.
	◆ Encourage young people to collect things like stamps, postcards, leaves, dried flowers, or quotes they like.
6-9	◆ Find creative ways to help young people link their interests with school subjects, such as doing special projects.
	◆ Ask young people to teach you a new skill.
9-12	◆ Help teenagers think about their goals and the discipline required to reach them.
	◆ Encourage teenagers to take an interesting community education class.
	◆ Place emphasis on lifelong learning and not just on graduation.

Adapted from Pass It On! Ready-to-Use Handouts for Asset Builders *(Minneapolis, MN: Search Institute, 1999).*

Building the Positive-Values Assets

Grades	How to Build the Assets
4-6	◆ Have children write thank-you notes or show their appreciation in some other way when they're treated especially well by someone at school.
	◆ Encourage families to participate in service activities together.
	◆ Talk to children about specific examples of people acting on their values.
6-9	◆ Interact in caring, responsible ways with people of all ages. Encourage young people to do the same.
	◆ Discuss the values of characters from popular television shows.
	◆ Within the guidelines of your district policies and regulations, talk with young people about their values regarding honesty, sexual activity, drug use, and other topics.
9-12	◆ Encourage teenagers to volunteer with at least one organization.
	◆ Help teenagers write letters to newspaper editors or to politicians about their views on issues.
	◆ While being aware of the relevant policies and regulations of your school and district, talk with teenagers about how their values guide their choices and behaviors. Let them know how your values influence you.

Adapted from Pass It On! Ready-to-Use Handouts for Asset Builders *(Minneapolis, MN: Search Institute, 1999).*

Building the Social-Competencies Assets

Grades	How to Build the Assets
4-6	◆ Encourage children to use words—rather than just actions—to communicate.
	◆ Encourage children to develop more skills in areas that interest them.
	◆ Find ways for children to spend time with people who look, act, think, and talk in different ways.
6-9	◆ Help young people use healthy coping skills when difficult situations arise.
	◆ Be gentle and supportive in how you respond to young people's fluctuating emotions.
	◆ Help young teenagers find ways to resolve conflicts peacefully.
9-12	◆ Slowly begin to allow teenagers more freedom to make their own decisions, e.g., choosing projects or ways to complete assignments.
	◆ Ask teenagers about their dreams for the future and help them plan how to achieve them.
	◆ Encourage teenagers to practice healthy responses to situations in which they might feel pressured or uncomfortable, such as being offered drugs by a friend or being challenged to fight.

Adapted from Pass It On! Ready-to-Use Handouts for Asset Builders *(Minneapolis, MN: Search Institute, 1999).*

Building the Positive-Identity Assets

Grades	How to Build the Assets
4-6	◆ When children are facing problems or difficult times, help them think of all the possible ways they could address the situation. Then help them choose what they want to do.
	◆ Encourage children to find inspirational, positive role models.
	◆ Talk with children about what gives your life meaning and a sense of purpose.
6-9	◆ Expect young people to experience ups and downs of self-esteem during these years and for their self-esteem to increase as they get older.
	◆ Avoid comparing young people with each other.
9-12	◆ Let teenagers know that you are proud of and excited by their talents, capabilities, and discoveries.
	◆ Support teenagers as they struggle with issues and questions of identity.
	◆ Let teenagers know that you're willing to listen if they want to talk about their sense of purpose in life, including their ideas about how they'd like to contribute to the world.

Adapted from Pass It On! Ready-to-Use Handouts for Asset Builders *(Minneapolis, MN: Search Institute, 1999).*

Notes

1. Bredekamp, Sue (Ed.) (1986). *Developmentally appropriate practice.* Washington, DC: National Association for the Education of Young Children.

2. National Middle School Association (1997). *This we believe.* Columbus, OH: National Middle School Association. See also Simmons, R.G., & Blyth, D.A. (1987). *Moving into adolescence: The impact of pubertal change and school context.* New York: Aldine de Gruyter.
   Eccles, J.S., Midgley, C., et al. (1993). The impact of stage-environment fit on young adolescents' experiences in schools and in families. *American Psychologist*, 48, 90–101.

3. Benson, P.L., Scales, P.C., Leffert, N., and Roehlkepartain, E.C. (1999). *A fragile foundation: The state of developmental assets among American youth.* Minneapolis, MN: Search Institute.

4. Feldman, S.S., & Elliot, G.R. (Eds.) (1990). *At the threshold: the developing adolescent.* Cambridge, MA: Harvard University Press.

5. Ibid.

6. Reviewed in Scales, P.C., & Leffert, N. (1999). *Developmental assets: A synthesis of the scientific research on adolescent development.* Minneapolis: Search Institute.

7. Ibid.

8. Feldman & Elliot, op. cit.

9. Steinberg, L.; Mounts, N. S.; Lamborn, S. D.; & Dornbusch, S. M. (1992). Authoritative parenting and adolescent adjustment across varied ecological niches. *Journal of Research on Adolescence*, 1, 19–36.

10. Reviewed in Scales & Leffert, op. cit.

11. Wentzel, K.R. (1991). Relations between social competence and academic achievement in early adolescence. *Child Development*, 62, 1066–1078.

12. Eccles, J.S., & Midgely, C. (1990). Changes in academic motivation and self-perception during early adolescence. In R. Montemayor, G.R. Adams, & T.P. Gullotta (Eds.), *Advances in adolescent development: Vol. 2. From childhood to adolescence: A transitional period?* (pp. 134–155). Newbury Park, CA: Sage.

13. Ibid.

14. U.S. Department of Education (1998). *No more excuses: The final report of the Hispanic dropout project.* Washington, DC.

15. Scales & Leffert, op. cit.

16. Lee, V.E., Smith, J.B., & Croninger, R.D. (1995). Another look at high school restructuring. *Issues in Restructuring Schools* (Wisconsin Center for Education Research), Issue Report No. 9, 1–10.

17. Masten, A.S., Coatsworth, J.D., et al. (1995). The structure and coherence of competence from childhood through adolescence. *Child Development*, 66, 1635–1659.

3

⚜

Developmental Assets and

Academic Success

A schoolwide focus on building developmental assets can help a school attain a rare status: becoming a school that reinforces the reasons of the heart that drove most educators to take up their field in the first place; and becoming a school that helps its students achieve not only traditional measures of school success but also success in broader terms—becoming healthy, caring, responsible citizens who contribute to society in a productive way.

A school thus has multiple missions, even if its primary mission is to help students become academically successful: Part of a student's "school success" is "academic success," part may be "citizenship success," and part may be "health success." The 40 developmental assets as a whole can contribute to school success broadly defined, but some assets have a more direct relationship with academic success. In this chapter, we're going to focus more on academic success.

So: How do we know if a student is academically successful? Traditional definitions of academic success include student grades and achievement test scores, high school graduation, and post-secondary education, such as attendance at college or trade school, or entry into an adequately compensated career-track job after high school. There are problems with these definitions: One problem is that they tend to mask individual differences among students. A student who regularly gets D's and who then manages to get a B may be more "successful" than a student who regularly gets B's and then manages to get an A. Another problem is that they tend to underrate qualities like creativity, resilience, persistence, and independent thought. For these reasons alone, it would seem to be prudent for educators to seek out new, more relevant, more meaningful definitions of success. But regardless of how individual administrators, teachers, parents, or students feel about the usefulness of these traditional markers of academic competence, either in general or for particular students, schools today do use them and, in many cases, are required to use them. Any definition of academic success has to take indicators like grades and standardized test scores into account.

However, there are plenty of disagreements about how completely those indicators serve to give us a perspective on students' success: Grades can be given for reasons other than academic accomplishments, some tests may give unfair advantage to some students, and so on. In addition, while grades and test scores can be measured in the present and for the short-term future, it may take many years to see if students have attained other traditional outcomes of academic success related to employment, family, and civic life.

Elements of Academic Success

Because it can take years to observe some of those desired outcomes, we want to look at several short-term elements of academic success. Research indicates that the following beliefs and behaviors are strongly related to students' achieving high grades and test scores, as well as other traditional measures of school success[1]:

- ◆ Attendance;
- ◆ Conduct;
- ◆ Motivation to achieve;
- ◆ Pursuit of learning for its own sake more than for grades;
- ◆ Value attached to learning;
- ◆ Engagement in school;
- ◆ Bonding to school;
- ◆ Sense of group membership, belonging, teacher support;
- ◆ Hours spent on homework; and
- ◆ Reading for pleasure.

As we'll see later, some of the developmental assets appear to directly affect these beliefs and behaviors, but most of the assets at least indirectly support the optimal conditions for learning that these beliefs and behaviors describe. In addition, research consistently shows that academic success is strongly related to students' social competence and their ability to adapt to different environments.[2] Students with such skills and attitudes as stress management, self-control, self-direction, and personal responsibility have higher achievement levels. This leads some researchers to say that student progress on social competence, even more than intellectual measures, "might be the best primary measure" of academic success.[3]

Collectively, the elements of academic success, whether cognitive or social, involve students' motivations, perceptions, values, and skills. These are significantly influenced not only by school, but also by peers, families, and other influences in the community outside school. Therefore, the asset-building teacher, administrator, or other school adult recognizes the critical importance of partnerships with parents and community resources. As Barbara T. Bowman of the Erikson Institute at Loyola University in Chicago writes, "school competence results from the interaction between children, their various environments, and their families' and communities' previous experience, rather than from a single factor, such as the school, the home, or the child's natural environments."[4] All the short-term elements of academic success are affected by those multiple influences in the lives of children and youth.

The Commitment-to-Learning Assets

Search Institute includes several of the elements of academic success as the specific developmental assets that make up the category called Commitment to Learning. The Commitment-to-Learning assets describe students who care about their school and their schoolwork, try hard (including doing homework daily), are usually interested in school, and have started on the path of lifelong learning by reading regularly for their own enjoyment. These are the Commitment-to-Learning assets:

- Achievement Motivation: Youth is motivated to do well in school.
- School Engagement: Youth is actively engaged in learning.
- Homework: Youth reports doing one or more hours of homework every school day.
- Bonding to School: Youth cares about her or his school.
- Reading for Pleasure: Youth reads for pleasure three or more hours per week.

As Handout 3.1 shows, numerous studies have found that, among adolescents, each of the Commitment-to-Learning assets is associated with numerous direct markers of school performance, such as grades and achievement test scores, as well as with effects that support student learning, such as level of effort or decreased drug use. For example, Bonding to School is associated with more time spent on homework and with less drug use, and Achievement Motivation is associated with increased achievement in reading and math as well as greater personal expectation of success and better control of stress and anxiety.

These specific Commitment-to-Learning assets, then, are related in important ways to academic success, and the research shows that those relationships generally hold for girls and boys, students at different ages and grades, and students from various

Effects of Commitment-to-Learning Assets on Outcomes Related to Academic Success

Commitment to Learning Asset	Association with Outcomes Related to Academic Success
Achievement Motivation	◆ Increased high school completion ◆ Increased enrollment in college ◆ Increased reading and math achievement ◆ Better grades ◆ Increased positive perceptions of teachers ◆ Increased effort at school ◆ Greater expectancies for success ◆ Greater personal control ◆ Greater goal setting ◆ Better management of stress and anxiety ◆ More effective communication skills ◆ Less sexual intercourse and childbearing ◆ Less drug use
School Engagement	◆ Better attendance ◆ Higher academic self-concept ◆ More time on homework ◆ Increased college attendance ◆ Greater use of "deep" study techniques ◆ Greater feelings of support at school ◆ Greater feelings of support at home ◆ Less drug use ◆ Less adolescent childbearing
Homework	◆ Higher achievement test scores ◆ Higher grades ◆ Greater homework completion and accuracy ◆ Improved scientific literacy ◆ Less marijuana use ◆ Fewer conduct problems
Bonding to School	◆ Better attendance ◆ Higher academic self-concept ◆ More time on homework ◆ Increased college attendance ◆ Greater use of "deep" study techniques ◆ Greater feelings of support at school ◆ Greater feelings of support at home ◆ Less drug use ◆ Less adolescent childbearing
Reading for Pleasure	◆ Increased time on homework ◆ Increased reading achievement ◆ Better grades

Compiled from *P.C. Scales and N. Leffert*, Developmental Assets: A Synthesis of the Scientific Research on Adolescent Development *(Minneapolis, MN: Search Institute, 1999).*

cultural and socioeconomic backgrounds. Schools that work to increase students' levels of those developmental assets are likely to have a positive impact on diverse students' success.

But not all students experience those assets to the same degree. In general, girls report much higher levels of the Commitment-to-Learning assets than boys do. And, with the exception of School Engagement, reports of these assets decline from the 6th grade to the 12th grade (reports of Achievement Motivation decline significantly for both boys and girls across middle school, but only boys experience further decline; and reports of Homework decline precipitously between 11th grade and 12th grade).[5]

Schools and Achievement

Building the Commitment-to-Learning assets involves understanding how those assets are affected by many other assets—some that schools can most easily influence directly, and others that schools can influence only indirectly. In order to better understand how the developmental assets work together, we need to ask a basic question: How do schools help students to achieve?

The answer to this question is more than "by teaching students." Search Institute researchers' synthesis of more than 800 scientific studies on child and adolescent development suggests that the assets are related to—and may well help contribute to—students' academic success through these collective effects:

- ◆ Promoting supportive and caring relationships among students, and among students, teachers, and other school staff;
- ◆ Increasing student motivation and engagement;
- ◆ Increasing the value that students attach to education;
- ◆ Increasing the effectiveness of students' study habits;
- ◆ Strengthening social norms and expectations that promote achievement; and
- ◆ Increasing parent involvement and student attendance.[6]

An academically successful school—an effective school—actually achieves those objectives. And when schools use the asset framework, it can help them organize their efforts to get there.

Integrating the Asset Framework

Clearly, students need more than direct instruction in specific subjects in order to achieve academic success. What the developmental assets framework can do is show how school staff can organize their work, structure their school, and give students consistent messages so that all students really learn.

It might be tempting at this point to say, Well, then, the thing to do is work on building the Commitment-to-Learning assets, which certainly are a core group of assets for schools to build. But there are also indications that the 40 developmental assets are interrelated, so that raising the levels of, for example, Support and Empowerment assets may have effects on the levels of some Commitment-to-Learning assets. So it would be a mistake for schools to narrow their efforts too much.

Search Institute researchers' synthesis of research on adolescent development shows that data are plentiful and convincing on the workings of some assets and sketchier on others. Some developmental assets seem to work more powerfully and directly to help young people live healthier and make better choices, while others seem to provide more indirect help. But despite the variation in our knowledge of their effects and in the amount each developmental asset contributes, the research suggests that *practically all the assets play some role in helping to create and sustain a climate for improved student learning.*

The point is, the framework as a whole serves as an organizing model, helping schools recognize what they're already doing, find out what they need to begin doing, and gain a new sense of how all the pieces—the curriculum, the caring, the after-school activities, the leadership roles for young people—all fit together.

Like any other action that is intended to have far-reaching results, building developmental assets cannot be just a new responsibility added on to scores of other things that already-overloaded teachers, administrators, and other school adults have to do. It must become an integral part of *all* those basic responsibilities, a way of getting current jobs done, and even done better, rather than an additional job to do. In a real sense, building developmental assets is a means of moving beyond school reform to education reform, a means of "connecting the dots" in the complex world of modern schools, a philosophy that recognizes that children's school performance depends on their health, development, and well-being, which in turn hinges on the well-being of their families and communities.[7]

All children and youth need to repeatedly experience as many as possible of the 40 developmental assets in their daily lives, throughout all the places they go in their communities, and within all their relationships. But no single institution or relationship—family, friends, schools, neighbors, congregations, youth programs—can by itself provide high levels of all the assets. As schools begin to see themselves as asset builders, in partnership with other community sectors like youth organizations, businesses, and families, they will bring to the task their own needs, their ideas, and their own unique ways of building assets. As we describe later in this book, some schools choose to work on building as many as they can of the 40 assets each school year. Other schools emphasize the 40 assets over the course of two to three years but give most of their attention to a smaller number each year. Still others focus on a small number of assets that they feel they can do the most about, or that are most lacking for their students, or that their students, parents, and staff want to focus on. All of these choices have merit. What's best depends on your school, your students and parents, and your community. As you choose, though, be sure to think about how the various developmental assets may interact.

For example, the asset of Cultural Competence doesn't appear to have a direct relationship to students' academic success, but a focus on building students' cultural competence will also involve reinforcing and strengthening teachers' and staff's cultural competence. We can speculate that such a focus might help raise some teachers' expectations of racially and ethnically diverse students. It might improve school staff/parent relationships, so that the involvement in school affairs of racially and ethnically diverse parents is strongly welcomed. And it might make it easier for students of all races and ethnicities to have both caring relationships with adults and a sense of fairness and equality in the boundaries they experience at school. Those experiences might in turn help them feel more bonded to school and encourage greater school engagement, each of which is related to greater academic achievement.

One thing we'd like to stress, whatever path you choose, is that you walk down it conscientiously and intentionally. Working on all 40 assets can amount to far less impact if asset-building actions are haphazard and largely a matter of accident. And focusing on even a small number of assets can make a huge impact when you choose the assets for good reasons and when personal and program actions are intentional, effective, and sustained.

So, which assets should schools focus on? One strategy is to intentionally build a smaller number of assets that can more directly be influenced in a school setting *and* that research has shown are related to increased school success. The developmental assets that research has shown best explain variations in students' grades are Achievement Motivation, School Engagement, Youth Programs, Positive Peer Influence, School Boundaries, and Self-Esteem. In fact, in one analysis of our data, three assets were among the most important contributors to good grades for students in all the cultural groups we've studied: Achievement Motivation, School Engagement, and Youth Programs.[8]

Does that mean that schools should focus only on these assets? Not by any means! First, we believe that schools can directly affect many more assets that research shows have moderate to strong relationships with different measures of academic success. And second, despite thousands of studies on issues related to student achievement, researchers' concrete knowledge of exactly how different influences work, and to what degree, is modest. For example, the developmental assets account for some but not all of the explanation for why some students get good grades and other students don't. The level of explanation found by the Search Institute researchers was in line with most educational and social science research, but it means that much of what contributes to students' grades was "unexplained." Although the institute identified a handful of assets as having the most influence on grades, numerous other assets also made smaller contributions, suggesting that many assets affect how well students do. A focus on too few assets would leave untapped the full power of all the assets, as well as the potentially important interconnections among the assets.

Working to build any number of the assets, such as the 22 we label as the ones schools can most directly affect, invariably will help build other assets that aren't being targeted. For example, the more youth subscribe to the value of refraining from using alcohol or other drugs or from having early sexual intercourse (the Restraint asset), the more they feel bonded to their school (the Bonding to School asset). In turn, other research shows that students who feel bonded to school are more likely to behave well and get good grades.[9] We can't always identify the cause and effect of these relationships, and in many cases it likely goes in both directions (e.g., bonding to school might lead to students getting good grades, and getting good grades also might lead to students feeling more bonded to school), but that simply reinforces the basic point: Focusing on some developmental assets may often contribute to having an impact on additional assets.

In Handout 3.2, we present what we believe are the developmental assets that research suggests schools can most directly affect through the relationships in the school, the environment of the school, and the programs and practices that occur in the school community. Numerous research studies conclude that these assets can have important positive effects on students' school attendance, sense of bonding to school, effort, conduct, and performance.[10]

From the list in Handout 3.2, we can draw several clear conclusions.

1. **Schools can have a direct impact on more than half the developmental assets,** including 13 assets that research suggests are very important in promoting academic success. Schools can't directly affect all 40 assets. For example, many schools make much of their commitment to various values such as honesty, responsibility, and integrity. But evaluations of character education programs suggest that the impact schools can have on basic values is limited.[11] Schools usually can at best reinforce values already learned at home, through religious teachings, and in everyday interactions with peers. And although Self-Esteem and Personal Power have also been found to be associated with school success, those Positive-Identity assets are also a result of years of accumulated experience in various areas of life, not only school. Despite the many curricula and classroom exercises designed to "raise self-esteem" among students, most experts believe that self-esteem and other aspects of identity are far too stable and broadly caused to be easily affected by direct exhortations and exercises. Self-esteem may indeed improve as a result of changes such as improved academic performance, new leadership opportunities, or

Percentage of Youth Who Report Experiencing the Developmental Assets That Schools Can Most Directly Affect

Assets Schools Can Most Directly Affect	Percentage of Youth Experiencing Asset
School Engagement*	64%
Achievement Motivation*	63%
Positive Peer Influence*	60%
Youth Programs*	59%
Safety	55%
Bonding to School*	51%
Service to Others	50%
School Boundaries*	46%
Homework*	45%
Peaceful Conflict Resolution	44%
Interpersonal Competence*	43%
Other Adult Relationships*	41%
High Expectations*	41%
Resistance Skills	37%
Parent Involvement in Schooling*	29%
Planning and Decision Making	29%
Adult Role Models	27%
Caring School Climate*	25%
Youth as Resources	25%
Reading for Pleasure*	24%
Community Values Youth	20%
Creative Activities	19%

N = 99,462 6th- to 12th-grade students in public and independent schools surveyed in 213 U.S. communities during the 1996–1997 school year.

*Assets that research suggests are most important to academic success.

Statistics from P.L. Benson, P.C. Scales, N. Leffert, and E.C. Roehlkepartain, A Fragile Foundation: The State of Developmental Assets among American Youth (Minneapolis, MN: Search Institute, 1999).

better relationships with teachers and peers, but this is not the result of a specific, targeted program to raise self-esteem.[12]

Keep in mind, of course, the interconnectedness of all the developmental assets. Here's an example: Establishing a family resource program at school might be intended as a means of increasing Parent Involvement in Schooling, but as staff and parents grow in their relationships, it may provide opportunities to affect Positive Family Communication, an asset that school staff normally would be unable to affect directly. Another example is the Religious Community asset. Public schools can't build this asset directly, but they often collaborate with community groups, such as religious organizations, that offer after-school programs providing secular activities such as academic enrichment or recreation programs.

As a final example, a community volunteer might work at the school by supervising an after-school arts program for 6th-grade students. On the surface, that activity certainly helps build time in Youth Programs and time spent in Creative Activities. But because the adult volunteer cares about those youth and spends considerable time talking with them about their personal interests, and because sometimes one of the school custodians stops by to say hello and see what the students are doing, it also builds Other Adult Relationships. In the context of that program and those relationships, a student might seek advice on how to deal with a situation involving a friend, which might lead to an impact on values such as Honesty, as well as insight into an Interpersonal Competence such as communication skills. During a school year of having similar experiences within genuine and authentic relationships, that student might even gain a clearer Sense of Purpose in life. None of those specific possibilities is a certainty, of course, but it *is* a certainty that when schools focus on assets they can most directly affect, they'll also find opportunities to build assets they can *in*directly affect. All members of the school community should be ready to make the most of those moments.

2. **Only 7 of the 22 developmental assets that we believe schools can directly influence are experienced by half or more of students.** Most students do not experience most of these key assets. And as we've seen, students in the higher grades usually report fewer of these assets. So, just as their schooling is becoming more demanding, more advanced, more "academic," with more at stake, students are likely to experience fewer of the assets that can help them academically succeed! Specifically, 10th-grade students report lower levels

than 6th-grade students of 17 of the 22 assets schools can more directly affect, and 12th-grade students report lower levels of 15 of those 22.[13]

3. **The majority of the key developmental assets related to academic success involve relationships more than they do programs.** They are about how students are treated as individuals, how much they feel valued and cared about, the kinds of positive models they have, and how connected they feel to their school. Researchers have repeatedly found that schooling is as much social—how students relate to each other and to the adults around them—as it is intellectual,[14] and the list of assets in Handout 3.2 underscores that observation. These data show that only a minority of students experience school as a caring place—where students care about each other, and where students get care and encouragement from their teachers. The handout suggests that only a minority of 6th- to 12th-grade students experience school as a place where lots of adults are interested in them, where adults and peers consistently express high expectations for each other's performance and behavior, where parents are genuine partners in children's schooling and learning, where students have plentiful and systematic opportunities to learn key interpersonal and decision-making skills, and where the great majority of young people are excited about learning and consistently put forth great effort on their schoolwork.

Even the impact of what appear to be curriculum and instruction issues may turn on how they're perceived by students in terms of relationships. For example, giving students demanding work challenges their skills and encourages them to develop high levels of competency. And for some students, having high standards also says that teachers care enough about them to be tough with them and to expect the best from them. This is exactly what researchers found in a study of male African American students in middle and high school. Teachers who set high standards were also considered to be caring and supportive.[15]

Setting high standards in general may be more important for boys, since girls report valuing education more than boys do and in middle school decline less in their perception that education is valuable.[16] However, in specific subjects, teacher expectations may be critical for girls' performance. For example, some research has found that girls' belief in their science ability may decline over the school year, not because their actual ability declines, but because some teachers don't expect as much of them as they do of boys in science, and don't give girls as much hands-on experience with lab equipment.[17]

Strategies throughout the School Community

The responsibility for building each particular asset is widely distributed across the major areas of school life:

- ◆ Curriculum and instruction (what's taught and how it's taught);
- ◆ Organization (the structure of the building and the school day);
- ◆ Cocurricular programs (after-school and before-school programs, or what used to be called "extracurricular" programs);
- ◆ Community partnerships (relationships with families, neighbors, volunteers, and community organizations and businesses); and
- ◆ Support services (health care, counseling).

In Handouts 3.3–3.15, we briefly list some examples of what school communities can do to build each of the developmental assets important to academic success. These range from inviting community businesses to partner with your school in providing internships and experiential learning opportunities to refocusing health education on personal wellness and responsibility.

Consider two additional points: First, the developmental assets and the activities that can build them often blend into each other. For example, using team teaching and theme-based, integrative curriculum organized around student projects not only has an impact on students' interest in the content of schoolwork (School Engagement), but it may also affect their Bonding to School, their potential circle of relationships with caring adults other than parents (Other Adult Relationships), the consistency of High Expectations they're surrounded with, and the kinds of Interpersonal Competence they can develop in that setting as compared to a setting where a single teacher tries to "pour" knowledge into the "student-as-empty-vessel." And second, although many of these activities are already being done by some schools, they are not always *intentionally* done, that is, deliberately carried out to build specific assets. Having an awareness of the assets as you plan, teach, mentor, and otherwise work with young people means you'll be alert to the moments when you can expand an activity to really aid a young person's positive development. *Intentionally* building assets in all your activities increases the likelihood that students will benefit.

All the other assets that schools can most readily affect are less directly related to academic success but have some bearing on it. They include the four Empowerment assets (Community Values Youth, Youth as Resources, Service to Others, and Safety), three Social-Competencies assets (Planning and Decision Making, Resistance Skills,

Handout 3.3

Building the Assets Most Directly Connected to Academic Success: School Engagement

School Engagement: 64% of students report having the asset.

Area	Strategies
Curriculum and instruction	◆ Develop integrative and interdisciplinary curricula. ◆ Use team teaching with adequate common planning time. ◆ Initiate projects that involve more than "skill and drill." ◆ Implement exploratory programs that keep students interested. ◆ Use student-led activities and group learning.
Organization	◆ Arrange large schools into small "houses" or teams so that more intimate learning communities can foster interpersonal connections. ◆ Use advisor-advisee or teacher-based guidance programs to foster close teacher-student relationships.
Cocurricular programs	◆ Offer a variety of clubs and after-school activities based on inclusion more than interscholastic competition.
Community partnerships	◆ Engage businesses and other community organizations to provide internships and experiential education that connects students to the "real" world. ◆ Invite community people into school as resources.
Support services	◆ Have extensive articulation programs to ease building transitions from elementary to middle school and middle school to high school. ◆ Maintain a low student-to-counselor ratio.

and Peaceful Conflict Resolution), one Boundaries-and-Expectations asset (Adult Role Models), and one Constructive-Use-of-Time asset (Creative Activities). The interconnections among the assets that we described earlier suggest that, in doing many of the sample strategies suggested in Handouts 3.3–3.15 for building those assets, students may well experience positive effects in these other assets, too.

All the developmental assets are built across multiple school community functions, not just through curriculum and instruction or just through community partnerships. This is the essence of a *schoolwide* approach—all school staff (custodians, bus drivers, food-service staff, support staff, health-care staff, faculty, and administrators), all students, and all community partners (parents and other family members,

Handout 3.4

Building the Assets Most Directly Connected to Academic Success: Achievement Motivation

Achievement Motivation: 63% of students report having the asset.

Area	Strategies
Curriculum and instruction	◆ Provide ungraded units and courses to stimulate learning for its own sake.
	◆ Use heterogeneous grouping whenever possible and minimize tracking.
	◆ Add "authentic" assessment, e.g., student portfolios.
	◆ Evaluate students' personal progress, not only their standing relative to their peers.
Organization	◆ Use flexible scheduling that allows greater depth of content and more opportunity for teacher aid to individual students.
Cocurricular programs	◆ Provide tutoring alternatives.
	◆ Offer after-school homework programs.
Community partnerships	◆ Offer experiential education, including service learning.
Support services	◆ Offer ways of engaging students as leaders in the community (such as youth members of school boards or community planning boards).

businesses, youth organizations, congregations, neighborhood groups, and other civic organizations) have important roles to play. This is a key foundation of the developmental assets approach. In fact, research on how schools respond to external standards and accountability systems indicates that schools and students respond better to performance standards in those school communities where members have a strong sense of collective responsibility for student success.[18]

With all this, we don't want to overshadow a less easily seen piece of the academic success puzzle: Young people are more likely to stay in school if they *like* it there.[19] In the mid-1980s, in her groundbreaking book *Successful Schools for Young Adolescents*, Joan Lipsitz chose students' *joy* in school as one of the "nonnegotiable" criteria for selecting successful schools to study. She wrote that "laughter, vitality, interest, smiles, and other indications of pleasure are reasonable expectations for schools" and that "happy experiences in school are central to well-being and should be so recognized by policy setters, practitioners, and researchers."[20] No dry list of concepts and "action steps" adequately describes that condition of joy that exists in a successful school.

Building the Assets Most Directly Connected to Academic Success: Positive Peer Influence

Positive Peer Influence: 60% of students report having the asset.

Area	Strategies
Curriculum and instruction	◆ Use cooperative learning strategies to provide constructive group interaction.
Organization	◆ Keep students in the same teams for several years, to enable deeper relationships.
Cocurricular programs	◆ Provide rotating leadership opportunities in clubs and activities to enable leadership by more than the usual student leaders.
Community partnerships	◆ Involve students with community organizations as leaders and trainers in skill-building activities with other children.
Support services	◆ Train numerous children and youth—and not only the highest-achieving students—to be peer tutors and educators in areas of their interest.

Building the Assets Most Directly Connected to Academic Success: Youth Programs

Youth Programs: 59% of students report having the asset.

Area	Strategies
Curriculum and instruction	◆ Ensure that all students are actively recruited for participation in school-sponsored after-school programs.
Organization	◆ Keep the school building open for activities more hours in evenings and on weekends.
Cocurricular programs	◆ Ensure that all students are actively recruited for participation in school-sponsored after-school programs.
Community partnerships	◆ Collaborate with a wide range of community resources to expand the variety and the duration of school- and nonschool-sponsored youth programs.
Support services	◆ Assess each student's talents and interests in order to make appropriate recommendations of constructive after-school activity programs.

Building the Assets Most Directly Connected to Academic Success: Bonding to School

Bonding to School: 51% of students report having the asset.

Area	Strategies
Curriculum and instruction	◆ Provide extensive health and sexuality education that focuses on fostering personal and social health and wellness. ◆ Use service learning and other types of experiential education that give students opportunities to feel valuable and make contributions.
Organization	◆ Use advisor-advisee or teacher-based guidance programs to foster close teacher-student relationships. ◆ Ensure staff and student safety (freedom from harassment as well as violence) through consistent rule enforcement. ◆ Provide encouragement and opportunities for school staff to model healthful habits of exercise, nutrition, and conflict resolution. ◆ Ensure widespread student input to school rules and sanctions. ◆ Keep the same students and teachers together for several years ("looping") to maximize the strength of relationships.
Cocurricular programs	◆ Offer a variety of clubs and after-school activities based on inclusion more than interscholastic competition.
Community partnerships	◆ Provide extensive health and sexuality education that focuses on fostering personal and social health and wellness. ◆ Use service learning and other types of experiential education that give students opportunities to feel valuable and make contributions.
Support services	◆ Maintain a peer mediation program with student participation from all achievement levels. ◆ Teach students and staff how to express their caring for each other. ◆ Provide school health services. ◆ Have extensive articulation programs to ease building transitions from elementary school to middle/junior high school and from middle/junior high school to high school.

Building the Assets Most Directly Connected to Academic Success: School Boundaries

School Boundaries: 46% of students report having the asset.

Area	Strategies
Curriculum and instruction	◆ Provide clear guidance on standards for performance that earn different grades, along with plentiful assistance in meeting those standards, and give students the grade they earn.
Organization	◆ Develop with widespread student input, and regularly communicate, clear school rules and sanctions. ◆ Enforce violations with consistency and certainty.
Cocurricular programs	◆ Enforce the same expectations for behavior as are the norm during the school day.
Community partnerships	◆ Expose all students to community resources and business through experiential education, and encourage those resources to teach students about the rules and consequences of their operation.
Support services	◆ Maintain a peer mediation program as a visible part of a program to enforce school rules.

Building the Assets Most Directly Connected to Academic Success: Homework

Homework: 45% of students report having the asset.

Area	Strategies
Curriculum and instruction	◆ Use teacher teams so the amount and type of homework can be better coordinated.
Organization	◆ Provide times within and outside the school day for tutorial assistance from peers or adults.
Cocurricular programs	◆ Provide after-school homework programs, such as student or parent volunteer mentoring/tutoring.
Community partnerships	◆ Ensure that parents understand expectations of students for doing homework. ◆ Provide an ongoing centralized system for responding to questions from parents and addressing their ideas about homework.
Support services	◆ Provide regular mini-courses on learning skills—for students and for parents—emphasizing hands-on technology for students and parent involvement strategies for parents.

Building the Assets Most Directly Connected to Academic Success: Interpersonal Competence

Interpersonal Competence: 43% of students report having the asset.

Area	Strategies
Curriculum and instruction	◆ Include communication, decision-making and planning skills, and other emotional intelligence skills (e.g., self-control, stress management, nonviolent conflict resolution) as formal content throughout the curriculum.
	◆ Emphasize cross-cultural understanding by an emphasis on studying the contributions of experts from a wide range of cultures.
Organization	◆ Keep the same students and teachers together for several years ("looping") to maximize the strength of relationships.
Cocurricular programs	◆ Provide after-school programs that focus on emotional intelligence skills, especially opportunities for young people to help others.
Community partnerships	◆ Provide after-school programs that focus on emotional intelligence skills, especially opportunities for young people to help others.
Support services	◆ Assess individual students' various interpersonal skills and emotional intelligence as regularly as you assess their cognitive progress or occupational interests.

Building the Assets Most Directly Connected to Academic Success: Other Adult Relationships

Other Adult Relationships: 41% of students report having the asset.

Area	Strategies
Curriculum and instruction	◆ Use team teaching to maximize the extent to which teachers can get to know individual students.
Organization	◆ Use teacher teams and interdisciplinary "care teams" of school adults to deepen personal relationships with students.
Cocurricular programs	◆ Train adult after-school program leaders in mentoring.
Community partnerships	◆ Recruit numerous community adult volunteers.
	◆ Provide specific support and training for volunteers in the instructional strategies being used in classrooms.
	◆ Invite neighborhood residents to school functions.
Support services	◆ Use advisor-advisee or teacher-based guidance programs to foster close teacher-student relationships.

Handout 3.12

Building the Assets Most Directly Connected to Academic Success: High Expectations

High Expectations: 41% of students report having the asset.

Area	Strategies
Curriculum and instruction	◆ Provide challenging curricula to all students as an expression of high expectations.
Organization	◆ Minimize grouping of students by ability (tracking).
	◆ Use various forms of flexible grouping strategies to support student progress toward expectations.
Cocurricular programs	◆ Encourage young people to set, and help them meet, "personal best" goals in sports, clubs, or other organized activities.
Community partnerships	◆ Recruit sufficient mentors (one for every few students) so that every student has an opportunity to benefit from a mentor from the community.
Support services	◆ Have counselors explicitly talk about students' short- and long-term plans with every student several times a year.

Developmental Assets and Current Educational Issues

The potpourri of issues facing parents, teachers, administrators, other school adults, and community members should not obscure one simple, overarching fact: Whatever shape school improvement may take, the primary mission of our schools is still to help all students succeed academically. The research suggests that building developmental assets can help schools fulfill that mission. But we should be clear: "Schools" don't really build assets—individuals do. Teachers, administrators, other school staff, students' peers, parents, and community members build assets directly: in the hallways, classrooms, playgrounds, and lunchrooms of individual school buildings; and in homes, neighborhoods, and community organizations. District leadership, including superintendents, curriculum coordinators, and boards of education, build assets indirectly, through how they shape policies and programs. Ultimately, as the National Research Council points out, "changes in policy are important only if they contribute to more effective school and classroom environments in which students are strongly motivated to work hard at challenging learning tasks."[21] The Council review concluded that the practices that for so many years have been staples of schools—grouping by ability (tracking), dropout prevention programs, and grade retention, among others—have been shown to exacerbate the problems of underachieving students, not relieve them. In emphasizing basic skill-and-drill teaching, and in labeling some students as academic underachievers, those practices seem to have engaged neither stu-

56

Handout 3.13

Building the Assets Most Directly Connected to Academic Success: Parent Involvement in Schooling

Parent Involvement in Schooling: 29% of students report having the asset.

Area	Strategies
Curriculum and instruction	◆ Make curriculum content, student standards, and descriptions of grade level or course content available to parents. ◆ Assign homework involving parents. ◆ Provide ongoing, hands-on experiences with both content and process for parents to better understand classroom work.
Organization	◆ Give parents opportunities to volunteer. ◆ Recruit parents for committees and task forces.
Cocurricular programs	◆ Recruit parents as advisors and adult mentors for after-school programs.
Community partnerships	◆ In communications to parents, provide suggestions for supporting learning at home (e.g., talking about what goes on at school, expressing the value of education, reading some of what students read). ◆ Encourage employers to permit periodic workday involvement at school without employees having to take time off.
Support services	◆ Provide on-site family resource centers. ◆ Have extensive articulation programs to ease building transitions from elementary school to middle/junior high school and from middle/junior high school to high school.

dents nor teachers. The National Research Council flatly states that they "have not been effective" in raising academic achievement.[22]

We hope it's clear that systematically and intentionally building developmental assets among students is a different approach that's likely to change the teaching and learning environment in positive ways for school staff, students, their families, and the community. But does a commitment to building developmental assets really help schools respond to the most critical issues, complex forces, and expectations that they experience?

The answer is that building developmental assets can't respond to all pressures, all issues. It's not intended to stand alone as a schoolwide reform or restructuring framework, but rather to be part of other schoolwide efforts that are already demonstrating success or have shown promise, such as the School Development Program,

Handout 3.14

Building the Assets Most Directly Connected to Academic Success: Caring School Climate

Caring School Climate: 24% of students report having the asset.

Area	Strategies
Curriculum and instruction	◆ Offer challenging curricula with lots of exploratory opportunities.
	◆ Integrate service learning throughout the curriculum.
Organization	◆ Arrange large schools into small "houses" or teams so that more intimate learning communities can foster interpersonal connections.
	◆ Establish teacher teams.
	◆ Provide opportunities for physical activity throughout each day.
Cocurricular programs	◆ Emphasize participation more than competition.
Community partnerships	◆ Invite community resources to teach interpersonal skills.
Support services	◆ Ensure that staff know and greet all students by their first names.
	◆ Give all students opportunities to be problem solvers and contributors to the school community, such as through peer-mediation teams, other kinds of peer helping programs, or expanded student governance programs.

Success for All, or the Coalition of Essential Schools.[23] Building developmental assets will not by itself improve students' success, but it can be tremendously helpful in organizing and planning responses to a number of critical issues. Handout 3.16 provides an overview of how the developmental assets framework connects with a number of important educational policy issues.

The Rationale for Building Developmental Assets

The "why" of asset building is relatively straightforward:

- ◆ Building developmental assets is associated with not only academic achievement, but also a host of other behaviors and qualities that most people desire for students.
- ◆ Building assets can easily be incorporated into schools' missions and standards; in fact, the effort to build assets often clarifies how those missions and standards will be fulfilled.

Building the Assets Most Directly Connected to Academic Success: Reading for Pleasure

Reading for Pleasure: 24% of students report having the asset.

Area	Strategies
Curriculum and instruction	◆ Emphasize reading in all classes, as well as a sharing of favorite things to read related to various curriculum themes. ◆ Read aloud in the classroom. ◆ Have students demonstrate different levels of information about the same topic retrievable from reading off the Internet, and from reading newspapers, magazines, and books. ◆ Provide training in reading for teachers in all content areas, specifically on the role of reading for both meaning and pleasure.
Organization	◆ Consistently ask for suggestions from students and parents for materials to acquire for the school library.
Cocurricular programs	◆ Encourage parents to read and have plentiful material to read at home. ◆ Suggest that community resource people involved in after-school programs or other school collaborations share their favorite relevant readings with students.
Community partnerships	◆ Encourage parents to read and have plentiful material to read at home. ◆ Suggest that community resource people involved in after-school programs or other school collaborations share their favorite relevant readings with students.
Support services	◆ Designate a reading corner in guidance; provide comfortable chairs and current reading for all reading levels.

◆ Building assets is something that most school adults who care about students already do to some extent; *intentionally* building assets increases the scope and effectiveness of what they do and encourages expansion of what they do.

We're now going to turn our attention to the "who" and the "how" of asset building. If you accept the rationale for building students' developmental assets, then who's going to be doing the building? And how do those people build assets?

The Relationship between Current Educational Issues and Building Developmental Assets

Current Educational Issue	Connection to Building Developmental Assets
Accountability and test scores (the pressure on schools to raise standardized achievement test scores)	◆ The more students experience the developmental assets, the more their grades improve.
	◆ Research shows[24] that various assets, especially those we've identified as ones schools can most directly affect, are associated with higher achievement scores and with greater levels of other personal traits and environmental conditions that lead to higher performance, such as family support, high expectations, bonding to school, and greater effort.
Closing the achievement gap (between white, African American, Asian, Native American, and Hispanic students; and between poor and more affluent students)	◆ Search Institute's research shows that, in general, higher levels of assets seem to exert an even more powerful positive effect on vulnerable youth who are already at higher risk of lower achievement and other negative experiences.[25]
	◆ The top assets predicting school success (Achievement Motivation, School Engagement, and Youth Programs) are the same across all racial/ethnic groups Search Institute has studied.[26]
	◆ Other research[27, 28] shows that when schools use practices such as interdisciplinary curricula, team teaching, advisor-advisee guidance, heterogeneous grouping rather than tracking, and other practices that help build youth's developmental assets, grades and achievement test scores among underachieving and higher-achieving youth become more similar—because under-achievers do better, not because high-achievers do worse.
Connecting school with real world needs (preparing students for work)	◆ Among the most important employability skills are motivational attributes and interpersonal skills that enable employees to work hard and to understand and work with many types of people in different positions.
	◆ Asset development encourages the use of experiential education approaches such as service-learning that widen young people's circle of relationships with other adults.
	◆ Done well, there is evidence that such approaches are associated with greater caring about others' welfare, greater commitment to doing schoolwork, and other positive outcomes.[29, 30] Build-ing assets also promotes the school success and sustained adult contacts envisioned in various work readiness blueprints.
Site-based management (increasing teachers' voices in school decision making)	◆ Building developmental assets is everyone's responsibility, not just superintendents and members of boards of education, not only principals or teachers, but all school adults.

Current Educational Issue	Connection to Building Developmental Assets
	◆ The developmental assets framework reinforces the notion of those closest to students having strengthened hands in school decision making, but also works against "dumping" of responsibilities (e.g., teachers shouldn't suddenly add the role of guidance counselor to their jobs, but teachers, counselors, and all other school adults *should* more intentionally express care and support to students).
	◆ A study of 11,000 students in more than 800 high schools found that in schools in which staff have a strong *collective* responsibility for student success, "students learn more, and learning is more equitably distributed."[31]
	◆ According to the researchers, what makes the difference in these schools is a commitment to building strong caring relationships among staff, among staff and students, and among school, family, and community—exactly the kind of relationships that are the foundation of the developmental assets framework.
"Back to basics" (cutbacks in arts, health, and "extra"-curricular activities)	◆ In the attempt to focus more on "core" curricula, too many schools have chosen to cut back in recent years on art, music, health, physical education, and "extra"-curricular programs.
	◆ Search Institute's research shows that time spent in youth programs truly is cocurricular, in that Youth Programs is one of the three assets that most strongly predict school success
	◆ Recent reports also show that students' participation in art and music—expressed by the Creative Activities asset—can also have positive effects on their school achievement.[32]
	◆ Health education, too, is generally associated with a host of important outcomes and is specifically the discipline in which students gain the most experience with the assets in the social competencies category.[33] Building developmental assets reinforces all these curricular and cocurricular areas.
Schools' role in community partnerships (connections between schools and community)	◆ "Community" and "full-service" schools connect—in one location—education, health, social services, recreation, and other activities in support of the healthy development of children and youth, and they usually do so through arrangements that keep school buildings open and used for extended hours in the evenings and on weekends.

The Relationship between Current Educational Issues and Building Developmental Assets (cont.)

Current Educational Issue	Connection to Building Developmental Assets
	♦ In addition to student achievement, other positive outcomes include improved health, personal growth, social development, and community improvement.[34]
	♦ This simultaneous attention to multiple parts of young people's worlds is paralleled and supported by the breadth of the developmental assets framework and its attention to family, school, peer, and community influences on children and youth, as well as its specific addressing of strategies such as youth programs and service-learning.
Safe and drug-free schools and communities, school violence (reducing students' involvement with violence and drugs)	♦ As assets go up, experiencing or committing violence goes down, as does problem use of alcohol and other drugs.[35]
	♦ Students in schools that enforce clear values, rules, and expectations, and that are perceived by students as caring schools, experience less violence.[36, 37]
	♦ The assets explicitly include a focus on reinforcing students' values against drinking alcohol or having sexual intercourse while still a teenager, and developing effective, nonviolent conflict resolution skills.
	♦ According to the Principles of Effectiveness adopted by the U.S. Department of Education,[38] school districts receiving or pursuing funding under the Safe and Drug-Free Schools and Communities Act may now also use data associating developmental assets with reduced risk behaviors to demonstrate that building developmental assets "shows promise" as an effort to reduce drug use and violence.
"Values education," "moral education," "character education" (schools and morality)	♦ Asset development names six values often emphasized in values education, moral education, or character education programs—Caring, Equality and Social Justice, Integrity, Honesty, Responsibility, and Restraint.
	♦ More importantly, positive norms and values are implied throughout the 40-asset framework. For example, the Cultural Competence asset implies that youth *should* respect the experiences, values, and beliefs of people who are of a different race or culture from their own; the Caring School Climate asset implies that students *should* care about each other, and the High Expectations asset implies that teachers *should* push students to be the best they can be. Building the developmental assets is consistent with school promotion of such norms and values.

Notes

1. Reviewed in Scales, P.C., & Leffert, N. (1999). *Developmental assets: A synthesis of the scientific research on adolescent development.* Minneapolis: Search Institute.

2. Wentzel, K.R. (1991). Relations between social competence and academic achievement in early adolescence. *Child Development,* 62, 1066–1078.

3. Johnson, J.H., Jason, L.A., & Betts, D.M. (1990). Promoting social competencies through educational efforts. In T.P. Gullota, G.R. Adams, & R. Montemayor (Eds.), *Developing social competency in adolescents* (pp. 139-168). Newbury Park, CA: Sage. (p. 141)

4. Bowman, B.T. (1994). Home and school: The unresolved relationship. In S.L. Kagan & B. Weissbourd (Eds.), *Putting families first: America's family support movement and the challenge of change* (pp. 51–72). San Francisco: Jossey-Bass. (p. 69)

5. Benson, P.L., Scales, P.C., Leffert, N., & Roehlkepartain, E.C. (1999). *A fragile foundation: the state of developmental assets among American youth.* Minneapolis: Search Institute.
   See also Leffert, N., Benson, P.L., et al. (1998). Developmental assets: Measurement and prediction of risk behaviors among adolescents. *Applied Developmental Science,* 2, 209–230.

6. Scales & Leffert, op. cit.

7. Lawson, H., & Briar-Lawson, K. (1997). *Connecting the dots: Progress toward the integration of school reform, school-linked services, parent involvement and community schools.* Oxford, OH: The Danforth Foundation and the Institute for Educational Renewal at Miami University.

8. Scales, P.C., Benson, P.L., Leffert, N., & Blyth, D.A. (in press). The contribution of developmental assets to indicators of thriving among adolescents. *Applied Developmental Science.*

9. Scales & Leffert, op. cit.

10. Ibid. (see especially pp. 119–147)

11. Damon, W., & Gregory, A. (1997). The youth charter: Towards the formation of adolescent moral identity. *Journal of Moral Education,* 26, 117–130.

12. Kohn, A. (1994). The truth about self-esteem. *Phi Delta Kappan,* 76, 272–283.

13. Benson et al., op. cit.

14. Ryan, R.M., Stoller, J.D., & Lynch, J.H. (1994). Representations of relationships to teachers, parents, and friends as predictors of academic motivation and self-esteem. *Journal of Early Adolescence,* 14, 226–249.

15. Davis, J.E., & Jordon, W.J. (1994). The effects of school context, structure, and experiences on African American males in middle and high school. Special issue: Pedagogical and contextual issues affecting African American males in school and society. *Journal of Negro Education,* 63, 570–587.

16. Roeser, R.W., & Eccles, J.S. (1998). Adolescents' perceptions of middle school: Relation to longitudinal changes in academic and psychological adjustment. *Journal of Research on Adolescence,* 8, 123–158.

17. Dreves, C., & Jovanovic, J. (1998). Male dominance in the classroom: Does it explain the gender difference in young adolescents' science ability perceptions? *Applied Developmental Science,* 2, 90–98.

18. Olson, L. (1999). Shining a spotlight on results. *Education Week,* 28(17), Jan. 11, 1999, 8–10.

19. Scales, P.C. (1996). *Boxed in and bored: How middle schools continue to fail young adolescents and what good middle schools do right.* Minneapolis: Search Institute.

20. Lipsitz, J. (1984). *Successful schools for young adolescents.* New Brunswick, NJ: Transaction Books. (p. 15).

21. National Research Council. (1993). *Losing generations: Adolescents in high-risk settings.* Washington, DC: National Academy Press. (p. 205).

22. Ibid., 141.

23. Viadero, D. (1999). Who's in, who's out. *Education Week,* January 20, 1999, 28(19), 1, 12–13.
24. Scales & Leffert, op. cit.
25. Benson et al., op. cit.
26. Scales et al., op. cit.
27. Felner, R., Jackson, A., Kusak, D., Mulhall, P., Brand, S., & Flowers, N. (1997). The impact of school reform for the middle grades: A longitudinal study of a network engaged in Turning Points-based comprehensive school transformation. In R. Takanishi & D. Hamburg (Eds.), *Preparing adolescents for the twenty-first century: Challenges facing Europe and the United States* (pp. 38–69). Cambridge: Cambridge University Press.
28. Lee, V.E., & Smith, J.B. (1993). Effects of school restructuring on the achievement and engagement of middle-grade students. *Sociology of Education,* 66, 164–187.
29. Melchior, A. (1997). *Interim report: National evaluation of Learn and Serve America school and community-based programs.* Washington, DC: Corporation for National Service.
30. Scales, P.C., Blyth, D.A., Berkas, T.H., & Kieslmeier, J.C. (in press). The effects of service-learning on middle school students' social responsibility and academic success. *Journal of Early Adolescence.*
31. Lee, V.E., Smith, J.B., & Croninger, R.D. (1995). Another look at high school restructuring. *Issues in Restructuring Schools* (Wisconsin Center for Education Research), Issue Report No. 9, 1–10.
32. Weitz, J.H. (1996). *Coming up taller: Arts and humanities programs for children and youth at risk.* Washington, DC: President's Committee on the Arts and Humanities.
33. Scales, P.C. (1993). The centrality of health education to developing young adolescents' critical thinking. *Journal of Health Education,* 24(6), S10–S14.
34. Dryfoos, J.G. (1998). School-based health centers in the context of education reform. *Journal of School Health,* 68(10), 404–408.
35. Benson, et al., op. cit.
36. Anderman, E.M., & Kimweli, D.M.S. (1997). Victimization and safety in schools serving early adolescents. *Journal of Early Adolescence,* 17, 408–438.
37. Gardner, D. (1995). Improving our schools 1995: *The first annual report of student and parent perspectives on Broward's public schools.* Fort Lauderdale, FL: Broward County Board of Education.
38. U.S. Department of Education. (June 1, 1998). Safe and drug-free schools program notice of final principles of effectiveness. Federal Register, 63(104), 29902–29906.

4

⚜

Preparing to Build Assets

Who Builds Assets

Who *are* the people who can build assets in a school community? In Susan Lindgren Intermediate School, grades 3–6, in St. Louis Park, Minnesota, the students decided to give a monthly "Golden Apple" award to the adults in school they felt did the most for them. According to special education teacher Lisa Sloan, the students chose the nominees and discussed their qualifications without any adult input. Who won the first Golden Apple Award? Who was surprised with the award at the end of an assembly, at which point the entire student body stood and wildly cheered? The first Golden Apple Award at Susan Lindgren Intermediate School went to the two janitors. Why? Because they were nice people who helped them a lot without getting credit for it, and, as one student said, "Because they clean up our messes!"

Who are the people who build assets in a school community? The answer is both simple and complex, both obvious and overlooked. The answer is—everyone *can* build assets. Everyone who interacts with young people, everyone who *could* interact with young people, and everyone who does anything that affects young people is in a position to build assets. Regardless of who is doing what at Susan Lindgren Intermediate School, kids value the janitors. Regardless of the janitors' knowledge of developmental assets, they are in a position to help build children's assets. Shouldn't they be encouraged to build assets systematically? Shouldn't they be encouraged to do even more of what they're already apparently doing? And shouldn't they be encouraged to set an example for other adults in the school community?

Look at the following list:

- Teachers
- Students
- Aides and paraprofessionals
- Librarians
- Coaches
- Principals
- Assistant principals
- Secretaries and administrative assistants
- Counselors
- Nurses
- Cafeteria workers
- School psychologists and social workers
- Bus drivers
- Janitors

If you're a student, you might look to any of these people—not just your teacher—for relationships. If you have a run-in with a bully, you want to be able to talk with someone you *trust*, someone you believe cares about you; it doesn't matter to you how much that person is paid or where that person figures in the school hierarchy. That's why, when we talk about positive, caring relationships with students, we're talking about *every* potential relationship.

Handouts 4.1–4.5 display numerous asset-building ideas that teachers, administrators, student support staff, school support staff, and school bus drivers can use to build assets in each of the eight asset categories. The strategies that school staff—and for that matter, students themselves—use are limited only by imagination.

Now let's add the following to our list:

- Superintendents
- Members of school boards
- Curriculum directors
- Prevention coordinators

What we have in this combined list are people who can affect the environment of the school. Is the environment one that fosters building assets? How do I *feel* when I enter the school's corridors? How do I think the students and school adults feel? Intimidated? Glum? Resigned? Or welcome, happy, energetic? What kinds of systems are in place that show students the school community cares about them? What kinds of policies protect students, and how were they derived? Which curricula actually

Asset-Building Ideas for School Teachers

Asset Building in General

- Post the list of assets in your classroom.
- Devote a bulletin board in your classroom to asset-building messages.
- If your community has an asset-building initiative, get involved.
- Orient all volunteers and support staff you work with to the asset model.
- Plan asset-building learning activities as part of the curriculum (for example, service learning projects, social skills training, or setting aside time to read for pleasure).
- Put an asset-building message on your computer screen saver. One school used the slogan, "Wrap Your Arms around Cherry Creek Kids . . . Build Assets!"

Support

- Greet students by name when you see them.
- Send a letter to parents about the idea of asset building, and then use assets as springboards for discussions in conferences with parents and students.
- Meet with other teachers and brainstorm ways to help students succeed. A school in Wisconsin set up DATES (Developing Assets To Encourage Success) meetings that are designed to help students who are struggling academically.
- Encourage access to at least one caring adult for each student in the building. Home-rooms can facilitate this.

Empowerment

- Teach students about the 40 assets and help them set goals for assets they want to develop.
- Provide opportunities for service-learning. Help students plan and make decisions about providing service to others.
- Empower students by encouraging them to tell their stories through written and visual autobiographies.

Boundaries and Expectations

- Work with students to set school boundaries or rules, to set school standards or behavior goals, and to help create norms of caring, honesty, and respect.
- Post a written set of the rules and standards in conspicuous places: hallways, class-rooms, the lunchroom, the gymnasium, and other common areas.
- Create copies of the rules and standards, and have an agreement form for students and parents to sign, indicating their willingness to stay within the boundaries and try to live up to the standards.
- Set high and clear expectations for student behavior and learning outcomes.

Constructive Use of Time

- Create visual symbols of assets. For example, cooperative murals can show the importance of working together to strengthen the community. Art students can create self-portraits that reflect their assets.
- Praise other teachers, staff, and students when you catch them building assets.

Asset-Building Ideas for School Teachers (cont.)

◆ Demonstrate sensitivity with respect to student involvement in cocurricular activities. Some teachers make it a practice to always allow at least two nights for students to complete assignments.

◆ Read biographies or view videos or films about musicians and other artists. Discuss the assets students see in these people's lives.

◆ Discuss current music, movies, or arts and entertainment and the messages they send. How are these messages consistent or inconsistent with assets?

Commitment to Learning

◆ Use assets as the focus for assignments.

◆ Choose a quote of the day with an asset focus and ask students to talk about it.

◆ Introduce students to Web sites that have asset-building themes.

◆ Read biographies of people who have realized their dreams. Talk about the assets that helped those people succeed.

Positive Values

◆ Ask students to gather information about people they look up to or admire—their heroes, famous or not. Then have small-group or class discussions about what values these heroes seem to have and how those values guide who they are and what they do.

◆ As a class, create a list of shared values. See the Positive-Values assets (#26–31) as a place to start. Talk about what it takes to uphold these values. Set boundaries and expectations based on these values.

Social Competencies

◆ Provide a process in the classroom for mutual goal setting and evaluation. Such a process empowers students and actively engages their learning.

◆ Encourage planning through the use of student agendas and calendars.

◆ Use resources in your community to help you learn about and teach Cultural Competence (asset #34). Consider having students organize a diversity-awareness week, a cultural fair, or some other way for the whole school community to learn about each other's backgrounds and cultures.

Positive Identity

◆ Use "strength interviews" with students to help them identify their assets and their sources of support.

◆ Attend concerts, programs, and activities your students are involved in.

◆ Congratulate successes with a written note, a call home, or verbal praise.

◆ Create life-planning portfolios that follow a student from the end of one school year to the beginning of the next school year and include goals, dreams, and hopes. They can be an important tool for the student—and for teachers—to keep track of accomplishments and challenges.

Asset-Building Ideas for School Administrators

Asset Building in General

◆ Provide professional development for staff members in asset building.

◆ Dedicate a few minutes at each staff meeting to share asset-building stories, information, strategies, and ideas.

◆ Encourage your school board to proclaim an asset-building week within the community.

◆ Include asset building in your school's mission and goals.

◆ Add an assets column to the school newspaper. Include students as writers, editors, and reviewers.

◆ If your community has an asset-building initiative, get involved.

◆ Create a fax cover sheet that has an asset-building message on it (for example, "You have the power to build assets for kids").

◆ Leave a message about asset building on your voice mail (for example, ". . . please leave your name, number, and a brief message, and remember, you can build assets for kids today").

◆ Train teachers and other staff in asset building and use the assets as part of performance planning and evaluation.

◆ Print asset-building tips on paycheck envelope inserts.

◆ Support and underwrite the cost of Search Institute's *Profiles of Student Life: Attitudes and Behaviors* survey in your district so that the community has an accurate assessment of young people's assets, deficits, and risk behaviors.

◆ Distribute information about the assets to all teachers. Consider purchasing asset-building resources for each employee or for a resource library.

◆ Take advantage of grant opportunities that could support asset-building initiatives in the district. Engage parents with skills in grant writing to help with the process.

◆ If your school or community has an asset-building initiative, paint the logo on buses, create a banner to hang on school buildings, or run messages about the initiative on the school marquee.

Support

◆ Create mentoring programs for staff as well as students. It can increase school bonding and provide needed support.

◆ Share information about developmental assets with parents. (One resource for this is the *Ideas for Parents* newsletter from Search Institute.)

◆ Create an environment that welcomes students, staff, and visitors. Have student and staff greeters at the doors. Keep the building clean. Invite parents and other community members to visit. If safety is an issue, work with your local law enforcement to keep the building as secure as possible without giving it the feel of a prison.

Empowerment

◆ Recruit community groups and individuals to volunteer time to build assets in your school(s).

◆ Praise staff and students whenever you see them building assets.

◆ Include students on interview teams for selection. Students can provide tours to informally assess candidates and/or take part in the official interview.

◆ Include students on school-improvement management teams, disciplinary teams, and other working groups.

Boundaries and Expectations

◆ Clearly state rules for appropriate behavior and consequences for violating those rules. Post them in visible places.

◆ Work with staff and students to develop positive standards and expectations, too.

Constructive Use of Time

◆ Make cocurricular activities like theater, sports, music organizations, clubs, and academic teams a priority.

◆ Celebrate success. Whether it's a commendation in the announcements, a personal letter to a student, or a pat on the back, catch staff and students doing things well.

Commitment to Learning

◆ Encourage scholarship contributors to establish criteria and select recipients based on students' asset-building efforts as well as other achievements.

Positive Values

◆ Work with parents, teachers, board members, and others to create a list of shared values for the school. See the Positive-Values assets (#26–31) as a place to start. Integrate these values into lesson planning, external communication, and boundaries and expectations for behavior.

Social Competencies

◆ Provide agendas and calendars for students to help them with planning and decision making.

Positive Identity

◆ Support and attend recognition banquets and other ways of honoring students.

Asset-Building Ideas for Student Support Staff

◆ Post the list of developmental assets in your office or work area.

◆ Greet students whenever you see them—in or out of school.

◆ Use the asset language when talking with students, parents, or other staff.

◆ Use the asset model as part of any assessment and goal setting you do with youth.

◆ Whenever you talk with parents, be sure to tell them what you like about their kids.

◆ When dealing with students who are struggling, work as many sincere compliments into the conversation as possible (even if it's just one).

◆ If your community has an asset-building initiative, get involved.

◆ Build your own assets; you'll be better able to deal with your students if you take care of yourself.

◆ Praise students when you see them building assets for their peers.

◆ Help coordinate information nights and orientations to help students and parents locate classrooms, meet staff, learn about the services you provide, and ask questions before school begins in the fall.

◆ Start a peer-helping program. For example, offer new student support groups to help students adjust to a new environment. Those who graduate from the group can lead the group the next year.

◆ Offer student-assistance programs that reflect an asset-building focus. For example, when working with recovering chemically dependent students, focus as much on future plans and goals as you do on staying sober.

◆ Involve students in strength interviews as they process challenges in their lives. Ask questions such as: Who protects you? What protects you? What inner resources do you have to draw on? Who can you turn to when you need extra support?

◆ Serve as liaison with the local radio and television stations to share with your community the good news about your school.

◆ When discussing specific students with other staff, focus as much on their personal strengths as on challenges. If you believe in students, others will start to believe in them as well.

◆ Work with teachers to incorporate asset assessment and development into group and classroom guidance activities. For example, a career unit could include an interview where students talk about which assets they think they most need for on-the-job success.

Asset-Building Ideas for School Support Staff

- ◆ Post the list of the developmental assets in your work area or office.

- ◆ Learn about the assets and talk about them with others. Speak well of students, and speak warmly to them.

- ◆ Do at least one intentional asset-building action a day.

- ◆ Ask your supervisor if you can attend professional development opportunities related to asset building.

- ◆ View visits from students not as interruptions but as your most important work. It may not always be efficient, but taking the time to talk with and help students will make your school a better place.

- ◆ See yourself and your colleagues as part of a web of support for young people. Be flexible with time and duties so that students feel comfortable approaching you for help, advice, or other kinds of support.

- ◆ View your activities within the asset framework. If you are supervising the study skills laboratory, for example, help students develop the Commitment-to-Learning assets (#21–25).

- ◆ When supervising the hallways or lunch area, focus on positive values. If students cut in line, remind them of the importance of being a role model (#15), being honest (#29), having integrity (#28) as you uphold school boundaries (#12).

- ◆ Show genuine enthusiasm for a job that allows you to work closely with and for young people. If you don't like your job, talk to your supervisor or a trusted colleague about what you can do to make it better.

- ◆ Laugh a lot. While anyone can complain, it takes a creative person to rescue difficult situations with humor.

- ◆ Notice what's working. Tell a student directly when he or she does something right. Send a note to a teacher when he or she does something you admire.

- ◆ Greet students by name.

- ◆ Attend student activities and tournaments.

- ◆ Get involved with other organizations that build assets for and with children and youth.

- ◆ Send notes to young people commending their efforts, whether the efforts lead to failure or success.

- ◆ Call parents with news of positive and helpful behavior you see in their children.

- ◆ When participating in or observing a student activity (such as track or band), take pictures. Get double prints and give the students the second copy.

Handout 4.5

Asset-Building Ideas for School Bus Drivers

- ◆ In addition to paying attention to safely transporting students, think of yourself as an adult role model for them.

- ◆ Post the list of assets on your bus.

- ◆ Praise young people when you "catch them doing something right."

- ◆ Be clear from the first time students ride your bus about the behavior you expect from them. Know what consequences you can enforce and who you can go to for support.

- ◆ Get to know the names of the young people who ride on your bus. Greet them when they get on and off the bus.

- ◆ If you regularly drive for the same team or group of young people, get to know them. For example, if you drive the swim team whenever it has a meet, drop in on a meet and watch the young people swim. Talk with them afterward about how it went.

- ◆ Hang up newspaper clippings and pictures of young people who ride your bus in front of the bus. One bus driver plastered the area above his windshield with photographs, mementos, and news clippings about students. The riders loved seeing their pictures. Some even drew pictures for the bus driver to hang up in the bus.

- ◆ Make the atmosphere on the bus supportive and fun within safety limits. Talk with the kids, play music that is appropriate for young people, tell them jokes.

- ◆ Get to know the bullies on the bus. Take a course in Peaceful Conflict Resolution (#36), and—based on what you learn—talk with the bullies about alternative ways to act around other young people. Let them know you won't tolerate bullying. Talk to the other young people, too, about standing up for themselves and working together to set higher standards.

- ◆ Talk with other drivers about creative solutions to problems and how to make buses places to build assets.

promote learning, as opposed to memorizing? Which programs help students think for themselves, as opposed to thinking what they believe others want them to think?

Finally, add the following to the list:

- ◆ Youth-serving organizations
- ◆ Businesses
- ◆ Religious and spiritual congregations
- ◆ Community centers
- ◆ Media outlets
- ◆ Parent groups
- ◆ Neighborhood organizations

Members of these groups also can build assets in school communities. When schools reach out to these individuals and organizations, when they share the philosophy of identifying and building on students' strengths, and when they coordinate their efforts, the *extended* school community can lend full force to building assets.

One group has been left off our list, perhaps the most important group of all: families. In a way, "families" should top the list, because members of young people's families transcend all the initial lists we looked at. Parents and extended family members who work in schools—whether as volunteers or staff—are in primary positions to forge caring relationships. Older siblings can lend guiding hands to younger brothers and sisters wending their way through schools' social strata. Parents, grandparents, and aunts and uncles who work on curriculum committees, school boards, and the like have a great deal of influence on how the school treats its students. And family members throughout the larger community all have a stake in incorporating activities into the asset-building philosophy, because how students behave affects the entire community. It brings us full circle: *Everyone* can be an asset builder.

To summarize:

◆ Building assets is everyone's job.
◆ When students get consistent, repeated asset-building messages and opportunities from a variety of sources, they benefit.

How to Build Assets

Now let's turn our attention to the "how" of asset building. Here's where it gets a little tricky, because there is no one "how." Every school community is different— different students, different histories, different politics, different socioeconomic realities, different needs, different goals. We can't present you with a single picture and say, here, draw this, and you'll be doing fine. What we can do, though, is show you pictures that people from around the country have drawn. We can give you the best paints we know of, and we can even tell you what we think is the best way to paint. But the canvas is your own, and so is the final picture. So, think of the rest of this book as a combination art gallery and art school. When you emerge—when you finish reading the book—we think you'll be ready to start painting in a new way.

One of the nice things about talking to people about building assets is that it's an easy sell, because to some extent everyone *is* already doing it. And just as we'd like you to acknowledge students' strengths while you give them guidance and opportunities, we'd like to acknowledge *your* strengths while we give *you* guidance and opportunities. Most of you reading this book may have already begun building assets in school communities, even if you haven't called it that.

We want to do two things in the remainder of this book that will help you build on what you've *already* done:

◆ Suggest a process to make your asset-building efforts intentional, directed, and more effective, and

◆ Present what other school communities across the country are doing.

There is always more to do, and there are always ways to do it better. You can always reach more young people, you can always reach young people more deeply. That's what we'd like you to keep in mind as you read what others have done and think about how you can incorporate some of these ideas into your own school community.

An Organic Process

Suppose you were in charge of effecting some systematic change in your school. You know what you need to do, but you're not quite sure about how to do it. Let's talk it through.

The first thing you'd probably do is gather about you a core group of people to help you make the whole thing work. You'd talk to them about the nature of the change you envision, explore the major issues, brainstorm additional people to enlist, and maybe even consider some initial strategies. You'd realize that the more people buy in early, the more they'll be vested in the effort. As you proceed with your plans, you involve more and more people in an ever-widening circle. You'd generate as much awareness as you could.

Next, you'd probably determine the status quo. Who's being served? How are they being served? What are their needs? What are their strengths? You'd look over your resources, perhaps make an inventory of what you had on hand—and what you *could* have on hand—to meet the needs: people, programs and practices, funds, political backing, time, and energy. What are you already doing? What can be adapted? What must be added? You'd realize that assessing the situation accomplishes at least two objectives: It motivates people to action. And it directs them to the arena. Besides, it's always helpful to figure out where you are before you can begin to go somewhere else.

Now you'd be ready to follow through with your plans. This is the big step: It entails coordination. It suggests cooperation, dedication, and persistence. This is where the enterprise rises or falls—or fades away unnoticed. How would you follow through? You might choose three different spheres of action in order to effect real change:

◆ A personal level;
◆ A schoolwide level; and
◆ A programmatic level.

You'd conclude that any change needed to work person to person, that individuals in your school needed to *believe* in the change. You'd also want to create an environment throughout the school that encouraged the change. And you'd take a look at what programs you could use—or adapt—to help the change along.

Finally, you'd work at keeping the efforts going. You'd want the change to take root, to grow and thrive, to become the *norm*. There are many ways to do this: incorporate previously secondary yet positive attitudes and behaviors into the norm; celebrate successes; train the people involved in the effort; network with others who do asset building to share ideas, strategies, difficulties, and solutions; evaluate frequently and make the appropriate changes. All these actions help to *sustain* the change.

This is the basic process we're recommending for incorporating asset building into school communities. We think it's intuitive: You gather supporters, you assess your strengths and needs, you take action, and you keep your efforts going. Here's the process in its entirety:

Incorporating Asset Building into School Communities

- Generate awareness of the asset framework.
- Conduct assessments of your students' asset levels and of the resources you have to build assets.
- Form relationships to build assets.
- Create an environment that fosters asset building.
- Use programs and practices to build assets.
- Sustain asset building.

There's an important reason that the preceding statements aren't numbered: The process isn't chronological. Although assembling a core team of supporters is an essential early step, you'll continually be generating awareness, first among the people in your school, then to an ever-widening circle of members of the community. Assessment needs to come early in the process, but since your students and staff change throughout the years, so will the assessment. You can simultaneously form relationships, create an environment, and use programs and practices to build assets; in fact, that's probably the best way to do it. And sustaining the framework requires a constant effort. Think of this process not as the steps of a ladder but rather as the arms and legs of something organic and growing, each appendage necessary to further the well-being of the organism.

A Vision for Schools

We've talked with hundreds of people involved in building assets around the country. Each is currently at a different place in the process. Many have made their school community aware of the asset framework. Some have assessed the asset levels of students and have then made people in the community aware of the results of that assessment. And some—but not many—have assessed their resources, determining which people have asset-rich relationships, which activities in school provide opportunities for students to build assets, and which programs and practices build which assets for whom.

What we'd like to see more of is *intentional* asset building. We'd like to see school communities not only talking about assets and conducting assessments, but following through with the rest of the process as well. We'd like to see schools nurturing relationships, creating environments, and using programs and practices to build assets. We'd like to see schools sustaining their efforts and even becoming leaders in their communities to build assets. Our vision is for school communities to be constantly, deliberately building assets in a variety of ways for all their students.

Consequently, we're going to spend most of the rest of this book showing you how schools and communities across the country have gone about doing this—from generating awareness to conducting assessments to building and sustaining assets.

5

❧

Generating Awareness

The Core Team

The primary audience for building awareness about asset building in a school community is—the school community. The entire school community—students, teachers, administrators, parents and extended family, support staff, counselors, other school adults (including volunteers)—should be a primary focus for awareness and embracing of the developmental assets framework.

Earlier, we spoke to the fact that "you" can't incorporate an asset-building framework into a school community all by yourself. You need allies, supporters—people who are as passionate and committed as you are. When you generate awareness of the asset framework in the school community, you start with a core team.

Who constitutes this core team? Consider the following criteria:

- ◆ They're familiar with and are respected by students.
- ◆ They're respected by the adults in the school community.
- ◆ They represent a wide range of roles in the school community, e.g., teacher, student, administrator, support staff, school board.
- ◆ Their philosophies are consistent with that of the asset framework.
- ◆ They're competent and reliable.
- ◆ They work well in diverse groups.
- ◆ They have influence.

Having a mix of people on the core team adds credibility to your efforts, builds youth buy-in early on, sends the message that every part of the community is valuable to the effort, provides a forum for concerns to be raised and addressed, and helps distribute the responsibilities for action.

Together with the core team, you can shape a vision for your school or district, identify potential obstacles, get buy-in from leaders and decision makers, and determine first steps for increasing awareness about the developmental assets and inspiring the whole school community to get involved.

Awareness in the School Community—and Beyond

Once the core team is in place, people in school can become aware of asset building in a variety of ways—some formal, such as awareness presentations, and some informal, such as conversations about the success a teacher is having using students as resources.

School Staff and Parents

Here's one way Belleview Elementary School, in Englewood, Colorado, begins to bring staff on board: They give a certificate and silver pin to all teachers and other staff. The certificate is personalized, dated, and signed by the "Belleview Building Assets Committee," and this is how it reads:

> Many factors influence why some young people have successes in life and why others have a harder time. While economic circumstances, genetics, trauma, and many other factors seem difficult to change, they aren't all that matter. Research by the Search Institute has identified 40 concrete, positive experiences and qualities—"developmental assets"—that have a tremendous influence on the lives of young people.

You Are One of Those Assets!!

> As people working with young people, you play a critical role in the lives of our children. Belleview has embraced the asset-building initiative since 1996. We are not alone. Assets for Colorado Youth is a 5½-year statewide initiative, funded by The Colorado Trust, designed to help Colorado's children and adolescents gain the developmental building blocks they need to become healthy, caring, and responsible citizens. The silver pin is the logo for Assets for Colorado Youth and is given to you by Belleview's Asset Building Committee during our annual "Asset Awareness Week" to thank you for your hard work and dedication to the children of Belleview.

Our Children Need Each of You!!!

> "Wrap your arms around Cherry Creek kids . . . build assets."

Newsletter #50

ideas for parents

Practical Suggestions for Building Assets in Your Child

FAST FACTS

ASSETS: The Power of Parenting

Youth are more likely to grow up healthy when they experience more assets— and parents can help build them.

100%
Aim to build all 40 assets in your child.

What Are Assets?

Assets are 40 key building blocks to help kids succeed.

You Are Your Child's Compass

Any hiker knows the most important tool to take on a journey is a compass. It's a guide when you know where you're going. It's also a guide when you don't.

As children journey through life, they must step into unfamiliar territory. Sometimes they'll try paths we'd rather not have them take while ignoring others that we think they should follow.

No matter where they go, we as parents are their compasses. As compasses, we don't tell them which path to take (even though it's tempting at times), but we serve as a resource—a guide. We can help, suggest, question, encourage. We can also point out other useful guides when our children wish to take a path we're not equipped to navigate.

The 40 assets help us be good compasses. The first 20 assets, known as external assets, come from the people and institutions that surround our children. We as parents play a critical role in the development of these first 20 assets.

The other 20 assets, known as internal assets, are the commitments, attitudes, values, and skills that support our youth from within. While we as parents can't control these assets, we can intentionally nourish them.

As parents we can have a tremendous impact on building assets in our children and teenagers. Building assets truly is a journey, a journey that reaps great rewards and brings out the best in our children—and in ourselves.

Quick Tip:
Building assets is easier than you think.

time together

Three ways to build assets with your child:

1. Spend time together. Asset building requires building relationships.

2. Plan and do fun things together as a family. Focus on enjoying your time together.

3. Give children meaningful opportunities to contribute to your family.

One way Belleview works to bring its parents on board is with newsletters like Search Institute's *Ideas for Parents* newsletter above. The newsletters highlight different assets, give tips on what parents can do for children of any age, cite statistics, and offer resources.

A parent-teacher organization was the conduit for generating awareness of asset building in one school: In Fort Collins, Colorado, Ruth Lytle-Barnaby is director of community and foundation development at Poudre Valley Hospital. She became fascinated with the developmental assets framework and talked to her local PTA representatives about it. They in turn gave the information to teachers at Lopez Elemen-

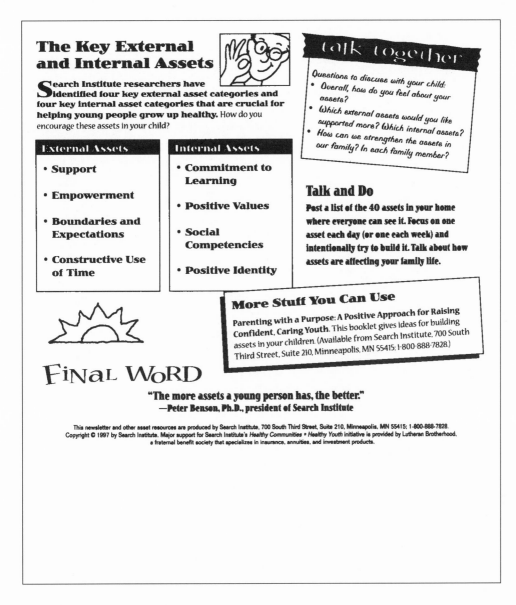

The Key External and Internal Assets

Search Institute researchers have identified four key external asset categories and four key internal asset categories that are crucial for helping young people grow up healthy. How do you encourage these assets in your child?

External Assets

- **Support**
- **Empowerment**
- **Boundaries and Expectations**
- **Constructive Use of Time**

Internal Assets

- **Commitment to Learning**
- **Positive Values**
- **Social Competencies**
- **Positive Identity**

talk together

Questions to discuss with your child:
- Overall, how do you feel about your assets?
- Which external assets would you like supported more? Which internal assets?
- How can we strengthen the assets in our family? In each family member?

Talk and Do

Post a list of the 40 assets in your home where everyone can see it. Focus on one asset each day (or one each week) and intentionally try to build it. Talk about how assets are affecting your family life.

More Stuff You Can Use

Parenting with a Purpose: A Positive Approach for Raising Confident, Caring Youth. This booklet gives ideas for building assets in your children. (Available from Search Institute, 700 South Third Street, Suite 210, Minneapolis, MN 55415; 1-800-888-7828.)

FiNaL WoRD

"The more assets a young person has, the better."
—Peter Benson, Ph.D., president of Search Institute

This newsletter and other asset resources are produced by Search Institute, 700 South Third Street, Suite 210, Minneapolis, MN 55415; 1-800-888-7828. Copyright © 1997 by Search Institute. Major support for Search Institute's *Healthy Communities • Healthy Youth* initiative is provided by Lutheran Brotherhood, a fraternal benefit society that specializes in insurance, annuities, and investment products.

tary School, the teachers told their students about it, and one result was that teacher Judy Harris's 4th-grade students came up with two ideas based on the Safety asset: If you eat lunch in the school cafeteria these days, you'll hear music in the background; the students thought it would have a calming effect. And if you wander out to the playground, you'll notice that some children have "buddies"; the students thought that every child who tended to be picked on should have another student to rely on or to mediate in case of trouble. From parent to PTA to teacher to student to implementation: That's building on everyone's strengths to generate awareness.

Community Partners

But what about the greater community? What about the buy-in from anyone else who cares about young people or who is in a position to affect young people? That may be a pretty wide spectrum, but think about what you're doing with young people: You're focusing on *all* of them, encouraging *all* of their strengths. You don't know how students will shine until you turn the light on them. It's the same with the community. You need to turn the light on everyone to see how they will shine—all the socio-economic levels, all the cultures, all the people who "give you trouble" as well as the people who support you. In fact, you need to reach out especially to the people who are initially skeptical or even hostile. They are the ones who, once convinced of the soundness of your approach, may be your staunchest backers. Delve into your community; look for people who influence other people. Take advantage of organizations that already exist—particularly educational organizations—and give them the opportunity to take up the standard.

These partnerships may need to start small, for example, with a business-sponsored after-school mentoring program "staffed" by employee volunteers. But as you continue to build awareness and additional partnerships, you may find the momentum and passion for asset building increasing. Schools can take advantage of that momentum by taking a leading role in creating a community-wide asset-building initiative. If that's where you're headed, Handout 5.1 provides some principles for getting started. But you don't have to go community-wide right away; there are plenty of opportunities for increasing awareness of asset building in your classroom, your hallways, your building, and your district.

Spreading the Word

Sometimes awareness can be generated by the implementation of asset building and by making frequent use of the common language of developmental assets.

⚘

"Kids are taking a better look at what they're doing," says Connie Wirz, a teacher at Kenai Middle School in Kenai, Alaska. She integrates building assets into her curriculum anyplace she can and has seen results that extend beyond the walls of her classroom. Wirz does a lot of work in cooperative teams, and has had some of her students create a pamphlet describing the different ways their community cares about them. The pamphlet is then distributed in the community.

In this manner, Wirz is building assets on several different levels: First, she's involving students in a fun, creative activity (School Engagement, Creative Activities). Second, in the context of cooperative teams, she's giving students responsibility for completing an assignment (Responsibility, Planning and Decision Making, Interpersonal

Eight Principles for Starting a Community-Wide Initiative for Asset Building

One of the exciting, though challenging, aspects of launching a community-wide asset-building initiative is that each community goes about it in a slightly different way. Keeping the following principles in mind will help guide your efforts.

1. **Engage people from throughout the community.** Because the asset-building vision calls for community-wide responsibility for youth, involving many different stakeholders is important from the outset. Many communities have developed a "vision team" with representatives from all sectors (e.g., schools, government, law enforcement, congregations, service agencies, business, health care) along with young people, parents, and other citizens, including senior citizens and people from various racial/ethnic and socioeconomic groups.

2. **Start with a positive vision.** A positive vision can energize a community for the long term. It can also help groups lay aside political and ideological agendas to work together because of their shared commitment to the well-being of children and adolescents.

3. **Build on quality information.** Many communities find that surveys of young people can be an important catalyst for creative and sustained action. Quality information gives people a shared reference point for reflecting on the needs, realities, and resources in the community as they shape their vision for the future.

4. **Resist the temptation to create new programs.** Because most responses to youth issues in recent decades have been programmatic, intentional effort will be needed to avoid simply developing another program to respond to a specific need. The most important tasks for the "vision bearers" of asset building are to keep the vision of a healthy community alive and prompt individuals and institutions to discover ways that they can integrate asset building into their own mission and commitments.

5. **Take time to motivate and educate.** Because asset building represents a new way of thinking about communities and youth, it is important not to assume that everyone automatically understands the framework and its implications. Unless people internalize the many dimensions of the asset framework, asset building risks becoming a shallow campaign to "be nice to kids."

6. **Celebrate commitments and success.** Asset building is a long-term vision, not a quick fix. But as communities embark on this journey, it is important to notice, celebrate, and talk about the landmarks along the way. These stories renew energy and refocus commitment.

7. **Embrace innovations from the community.** Once people are aligned with the vision of asset building, their creativity in finding ways to nurture assets can be startling. Encouraging this innovation is key to breaking out of old patterns and discovering fresh approaches.

8. **Network with other communities.** While many communities have begun asset-building initiatives, the vision is only in its infancy. No one knows all the answers, and no one knows how everything will work. But each community is learning something new each day.

Adapted from P.L. Benson and E.C. Roehlkepartain, Healthy Communities • Healthy Youth *(Minneapolis: Search Institute, 1996).*

Competence). And finally, she's getting students to acknowledge the ways their community cares about them (Community Values Youth). According to Wirz, activities like these, and efforts to make the community aware of the asset framework, have brought the community together. In this case, the means—getting the community on board—was also the end.

⚜

Suzanne Siler is coordinator of Safe and Drug-Free Schools in the Hickman Mills School District in suburban Kansas City, Missouri. For the past few years, when her student assistance family empowerment teams have identified students for whom they want to develop an improvement plan, they also identify those students' strengths, and incorporate into the plan an effort to bring out those strengths. Since the adoption of this philosophy, Siler has seen decreases in the number of behavior referrals for these students and improvements in grades, attendance, and positive attitudes. "When you see kids turn around," she says, "it makes it worthwhile." Again, the cycle continues: The school builds assets for students, students' families become aware of the effort, they work to build assets themselves, and others become aware.

⚜

Another coordinator of Safe and Drug-Free Schools, Michael Kerosky works for the Anchorage School District. Once he secured the acceptance of the asset framework from the school board—a "major breakthrough," in his words—he set about "infusing" the framework throughout the district with:

- ◆ Teacher training;
- ◆ Bus-driver training;
- ◆ District improvement plans;
- ◆ Grants given to schools that focus on assets; and
- ◆ Classes for continuing education that focus on assets.

In addition, some schools in the district pick an asset every month and focus activities on that particular asset, trying to raise the level of that asset for their students.

Kerosky's efforts are instructive, in that he searched for any connections that would generate awareness of the asset framework in Anchorage schools. A major gatekeeper was apparently the school board, but that's also instructive. The effort can gain momentum every time it traverses another gatekeeper, every time it garners another endorsement, every time it picks up new names and organizations.

⚜

Alaskans have taken another step to spread the word about assets. In cooperation with Search Institute, the Association of Alaska School Boards and the Alaska Department of Health and Social Services developed a book called *Helping Kids Succeed—Alaskan Style* (1998). The book contains ways that people in Alaskan communities can build each asset, and it cites each of the 114 villages, towns, and cities that contributed the ideas.

For example, under Asset 1, Family Support, there are sections on how parents and extended family can build the asset (from the village of Hoonah—"Tell your children that you love them. Tell them often. Show them in many ways."), how school staff can build the asset (from the town of Kotzebue—"Begin the school year with a unit on 'family' to help children appreciate all types of families."), how faith communities can build the asset (from the town of Soldotna—"Sponsor activities all family members can join in."), how any community member can build the asset (from the city of Fairbanks—"Talk with young people about their families, and notice ways that kids are supported and loved by their family members."), and how people can build the asset in the traditional ways (from the village of Elim—"Make kuspuks [traditional blouse] with your daughters. Spend the time with them to learn the work, practice the stitching, and just be in each other's space.").

Helping Kids Succeed—Alaskan Style is a good example of *infusing* the asset framework into the community—indeed, into many communities. Because so many people had a part in coming up with the ideas, they all have a part in operationalizing them.

꽃

PEAK is a community-based asset-building initiative in Portage County, Ohio, with its own web site—http://www.peak-assets.net. "PEAK" is an acronym for "Portage Elevates Assets in Kids," and its mission is to "facilitat(e) and mobiliz(e) the collective energies, commitments, and creativity in Portage County individuals, leaders, organizations, and institutions in building assets to promote healthy lives and bright futures for our children and youth." Each school district in Portage County has the freedom to design and implement its own asset-building initiative, and many of the programs and practices are similar to those cited in this book. For example, one of the school districts, Streetsboro City Schools, is creating a character development handbook based on the asset framework; it's called Promoting Assets through Character Education in Streetsboro—PACES. The district committee consists of school personnel, youth, parents, and community members.

But what we want to highlight here is an example of how awareness can spread through a community by means of networking. Currently, PEAK consists of six county organizations, five school districts, three libraries, two university-based organizations, two health departments, and almost a dozen other public and private organizations. Colleen Mahoney, assistant professor of health education and director of the Center for Health Promotion at Kent State University, is the leader of the PEAK initiative. Mahoney says that schools and agencies are now "thinking assets" when they apply for grants, the Portage County Network for Young Adults is using the asset philosophy to guide their decisions, and parenting groups throughout the county are incorporating the asset framework into their sessions.

"It is an ongoing challenge," says Mahoney, "promoting a philosophy rather than a program. . . . What I have observed and heard is that the asset framework/PEAK initiative is providing a common language both at an inter- and an intra-agency level. Some school districts are 'getting it' and in turn living it quicker than others. Their successes appear to be linked to many things. Two key factors that I have noticed are the commitment level of the superintendent to the initiative and the district's willingness to pursue technical assistance . . ."

Many successful community initiatives can boast connections like PEAK. That's because connections like these—to schools, to universities, to social-service organizations, to libraries, to congregations, to industry, to city government, and most important, to families—produce an ever-widening circle of people who will join the effort to build assets.

Reaching Out

How do you reach the community? You hold awareness presentations (and you try to provide transportation, childcare, and food), you send out newsletters (and you try to keep them concise), you contact people who can influence or persuade others to join in (e.g., respected community spokespeople, political leaders, presidents of businesses, heads of congregations), and you involve young people as your spokespeople as much as possible. This last point is critical: It's young people that this whole effort is based on; who better to solicit buy-in? Who better to recruit other youth volunteers? to form a speakers bureau? to offer a realistic perspective? to bring enthusiasm and new ideas to the process? to persuade adults, gatekeepers, and especially those who are skeptical or disengaged? to comprise panels for awareness presentations? to create text and artwork for brochures? to conduct research on the Internet? And involving young people as resources is a foundation for building assets.

Consider the following groups in your community, and think about how to reach them: young people, adults, elderly people, retired people, parents, adults without children, people with disabilities, employed people, unemployed people, other schools, congregations, youth-serving organizations, businesses, health-care systems, civic organizations, government agencies, foundations, media organizations, libraries, labor unions . . . . The list could be endless, once you start thinking about all the potential asset builders in your school, district, and wider community!

Making awareness presentations is a very direct way of reaching people—once you can get them to come to the presentation. Here is an example of an agenda for an awareness presentation to parents:

1. Welcome to participants.
2. Introduction of hosts and dignitaries (e.g., superintendent, school board members, civic leaders, students).
3. Description of developmental assets, including research base, connections to achievement, philosophy of building on strengths (using a speaker or one of Search Institute's videos).
4. Student discussion of the importance of caring adults in their lives.
5. Discussion of what members of the community, including the school and parents, are already doing to build assets.
6. Discussion of what members of the community, including the school and parents, can still do to build assets.
7. Solicitation of volunteers to work in various phases of the effort.

*

There are many venues for presentations on asset building. Patsy Roybal, family resource coordinator at Denver's Cheltenham Elementary School, says that "at our school, every parent involvement program begins with an assets presentation." She says that the PTA, learning support program, and Los Padres—a program for Spanish-speaking parents—all incorporate asset building into their work. Parents are asked to focus on the Achievement Motivation, Homework, and Reading for Pleasure assets.

*

Here is an example of an article you might place in a local newsletter. It was written by Nancy Ashley, owner of a consulting business in Seattle called Heliotrope. Ashley donates her writing services on behalf of the Seattle asset-building initiative—"It's about Time for Kids."

About What Kids Need to Succeed:
The 40 Developmental Assets

Whether or not you are a parent, you are probably too familiar with headlines about kids using guns, drugs, and alcohol. You worry that kids you care about and kids in your neighborhood aren't as caring or strong as you would like them to be. You may believe there is little you can do, or you may be confused about what to do.

That's partly because, for the last 25 years, we've tended to focus on why kids go wrong, instead of working on what it takes for things to go right for them. Recent research by Search Institute in Minneapolis has boiled down the formula to 40 "developmental assets" that work. The more of them a young person has, the more likely he or she is to be a leader, help others, and succeed in all areas of life. Better yet, young people with more assets avoid school problems, substance abuse, violence, and making poor decisions.

The 40 assets represent the common sense that's been lying dormant in many of us—buried as we are in bombardments about increasingly specialized programs to fix kids. "Asset" is a convenient label to help us express an idea. If you call to mind the good things you do for kids (your own children, nieces, nephews, the child you tutor, the kids on the block), they are probably all assets. Assets include such things as caring neighborhoods, adult role models, good family communications, and feeling valued by the community.

Ideas for Neighbors

There are hundreds of things neighbors can do to help build assets for the kids that live around them. Here are ten to get you started:

1. Hire a neighborhood kid to help with yard and household chores on the weekend and work alongside him or her.
2. When you organize a block party or a meeting of your block watch group, involve young people in planning and carrying out the event.
3. Learn the names of the children on your block. Say hello and call them by name every time you see them.
4. Offer to watch your neighbor's children once in awhile. Have fun playing games with them, reading with them, or helping to clean up the neighborhood.
5. Talk to young people at your bus stop, or as you go by them waiting for their school bus.
6. Send a note to a young person in your neighborhood when you hear about one of their achievements or kind acts.
7. Encourage young people to join neighborhood groups, such as gardening clubs or graffiti paint-outs.
8. Start an informal system of connecting youth and adults in the neighborhood who have similar interests—music, birds, computers. Perhaps a local store would put up a bulletin board to help.
9. If you have a home business, consider hiring kids in the neighborhood to collate, staple, address mailings, and more.
10. Encourage parents in the neighborhood when you see them enjoying and spending time with their children. Order an extra pizza every once in awhile and take it over to their house.

Newsletters like the ones Ashley writes can be sent to many of the groups in your community we listed above. They also can serve as a weekly column for the local newspaper (a low-cost way to spread the word).

꞊

In Virginia, the Hampton Coalition for Youth distributes a brochure with the stated goal to involve everyone in their asset-building initiative. They offer ideas of what people in the community can do to build assets:

What YOU Can Do:

◆ get to know the kids in your neighborhood
◆ volunteer as a tutor, mentor, or coach in a youth-serving program, or place of worship
◆ challenge people who say negative things about young people

What YOUR ORGANIZATION Can Do:

◆ encourage your employees/members to become involved in children's lives
◆ contribute time, talent, or resources to community asset-building efforts
◆ offer activities that build assets, such as training, service learning, the arts, and recreation

What YOUR COMMUNITY Can Do:

◆ develop support for neighborhood asset-building activities
◆ create opportunities for youth to contribute to the community
◆ celebrate youth and the commitment of people who dedicate their lives to children and youth

Slogans and Logos

Many asset-building initiatives have done something else that has helped their awareness campaign. They've created slogans. In Colorado, Cherry Creek School District's slogan is "Wrap your arms around Cherry Creek kids." In Virginia, the slogan for the Hampton Coalition for Youth is "What kids need to succeed." In Traverse, Michigan, the slogan is "Give 'em 40 24-7." In North Branch, Minnesota, the slogan for the Community Partnership with Youth and Families is "Working together to promote healthy lifestyles." As we noted earlier, the slogan for the Seattle initiative is "It's about Time for Kids." In Chicago, the slogan for the Chicago Safe Schools and Communities Initiative is "Safety in Numbers." And the name of the organization behind building assets in St. Louis Park, Minnesota, is a slogan all by itself: "Children First."

A visual reminder of an asset-building initiative is a logo, and students in Georgetown, Texas, had a strong hand in designing the logo for their initiative. A contest was held to select the best logo designs from the two local middle schools, and winners spent a day with a local artist designing the logo.

When schools use the slogan and logo of the asset-building initiative, they're increasing its visibility, and they're reinforcing the message—short though it is—for those who already know about it. There's probably no better example of such an effort than the one orchestrated by Brenda Holben, prevention coordinator of Cherry Creek Schools, in partnership with the Cherry Creek Community Prevention Project Board. Holben is a walking, talking awareness campaign for building assets. Her office in Englewood, Colorado, is festooned—literally from top to bottom—with photographs, letters, ribbons, bumper stickers, dolls, and all manner of products advertising the asset framework. She began in 1994 to spread the word in the third largest school district in Colorado—42 schools, 37,000 students. Today there are very few people in her district who aren't familiar with at least the "Wrap your arms around Cherry Creek kids" slogan.

The message shows up everywhere: banners and posters, stickers for car windows and businesses, stationery, fax sheets, brochures, community newspapers, school/PTO newsletters, reports, training workshops, presentations, an Asset Awareness Week, a town meeting, the sides of school buses, and events like a "24-Hour Relay Challenge."

Holben's latest effort, in her own words:

> This is our 3rd Annual Asset Awareness Week—A Celebration. We joined with the Colorado Children's Campaign—a statewide effort to celebrate children and build environments where children succeed, with many specific programs and events. One is their doll campaign held each spring. They hand out cardboard dolls to organizations, have them decorate them and then put them out in the community—in offices, businesses, coffee shops, retail stores, etc. They get great TV coverage. Well . . . my dream . . . We just distributed 10,000 of these dolls yesterday to the majority of our elementary schools. Our K–3rd-graders are decorating the dolls this week and next and then taking them home. It will be the responsibility of the families to put the dolls into the community. The children are learning about assets, supporting a community effort, and the families are joining the project by distributing them throughout the community. WOW!!!

Outside the School Walls

Another, critical type of awareness raising is getting the message to families that they can build assets for and with their children. Look at Handout 5.2, and consider sharing it with families in your community. Working together with families using the asset language and common goals can strengthen home life and school life for students.

What follows are some examples of what other people are doing around the country to make their communities aware of asset building. Again, take what makes sense for you. Adapt what looks like it might fit. Talk to other people who might be able to use these ideas. And be creative: let these ideas be a springboard for your own.

Asset-Building Ideas for Parents, Guardians, and Extended Family

- Post the list of 40 developmental assets on your refrigerator door. Each day, do at least one asset-building thing for each family member.

- Connect with other parents who are interested in asset building. Form relationships in your neighborhood, on the job, through a congregation, or through a parent-education organization.

- Regularly do things with your child, including projects around the hours, recreational activities, and service projects. Take turns planning activities to do together as a family.

- Eat at least one meal together as a family every day.

- Negotiate family rules and consequences for breaking those rules, and talk about expectations for positive behaviors and attitudes.

- Develop a family mission statement that focuses on building assets. Then use it to help you make family decisions and set priorities.

- Talk about your values and priorities, and live in a way that is consistent with them.

- Give your children lots of support and approval while also challenging them to take responsibility and gain independence.

- If you are parenting alone, look for other adult role models of both genders who can be mentors for your children.

- Nurture your own assets by spending time with people who care about you and are supportive. Also, take opportunities to learn new things, contribute to your community, and have fun. You'll take better care of your children if you take care of yourself.

- Think about the way you were parented and how that affects your relationships with your children. If there are parts of your relationship with your parents that were very difficult or that get in the way of your parenting, consider talking with someone about these issues.

- Don't let anyone in your family (including you) watch too much television. Find other interesting and meaningful activities for your children to do—some with you, some with their friends, some by themselves.

- Learn as much as you can about what your kids need at their current ages.

- Recognize that children need more than just financial support. They also need emotional and intellectual support. Balance family time with other priorities like work, recreation, and hobbies.

- Don't wait for problems to arise before talking with your children's teachers. Keep in regular contact with them abut how your children are doing and what you can do to help your children learn.

- Think of teenagers as adults in training. Teach them something practical, such as how to change a tire on the car, prepare a meal, or create a monthly budget.

- Be aware of differences in how you relate to your children. Are you more comfortable with one gender? If so, why? What impact does that have in your family?

- Talk to your children about the 40 developmental assets. Ask them for suggestions of ways to strengthen their assets.

> ## Asset-Building Ideas for Parents, Guardians, and Extended Family (cont.)
>
> ◆ Do intergenerational activities with extended family and with other neighborhood adults and families.
>
> ◆ Be an asset builder for other young people in your life.
>
> ◆ Remember that you are not alone. Other asset builders in your children's lives may include coaches, child-care providers, religious education teachers, club leaders, and neighbors. Work with these people to give kids consistent messages about boundaries and values.

⅃⅄

If you are employed by one of the businesses in North Branch, Minnesota, you might receive something extra in your pay envelope: an insert on asset building. Each insert is different, but they all feature a story like this one:

School Tip Sheets Help Parents "Catch-22"

"We are always talking about the importance of parental involvement," said Karen Atkinson, coordinator of Children First in St. Louis Park, Minnesota. "But sometimes we need something concrete to build upon." That's why the team developed tip sheets suggesting activities for parents and their children, hoping this would increase the amount of time parents spend with their children. Dubbed "Catch-22," parents were invited to "catch" 22 minutes each day with their children. The tip sheets found their way into kids' backpacks, report cards, and school conference material throughout the entire school year.

You'd also see on the insert the following lists:

- ◆ The 40 developmental assets;
- ◆ The eight categories of assets, i.e., Support, Empowerment, Boundaries and Expectations, Constructive Use of Time, Commitment to Learning, Positive Values, Social Competencies, and Positive Identity;
- ◆ Categories of people who are potentially involved in building assets, e.g., educators, parents, policy-makers;
- ◆ Developmental stages of young people who are potentially affected by building assets—infants through 12th grade; and

◆ Groups of young people who are potentially affected by asset-building efforts.

The items on each list that are illustrated by that particular insert's story are checked.

Community Partnership with Youth and Families developed these paycheck inserts to make people in the business community aware of building assets. Executive Director Tom Koplitz increases awareness in other ways, too, for example, giving out cards that provide tips for young people to make healthy decisions and tips for parents when talking with their children. "We are always trying to attach the practical application to this," says Koplitz, "which is much of what my organization does in promoting healthy lifestyles."

Schools, of course, are employers, too, and the idea of attaching "assets inserts" to paychecks can be transferred to many different locales and situations.

❧

One way to get the asset message into the community is to use a speakers bureau. And a great way to set up a speakers bureau is to staff it with students. Judi Edwards, program coordinator for the Linn-Benton-Lincoln Educational School District in rural Oregon, helped set up a speakers bureau comprising 40 middle school and high school students. Students take a 9-week leadership course and are then paired with an adult of their choosing to raise awareness in the community about the asset framework.

❧

Colorado Springs Public School District 11—called D-11—is the fourth-largest school district in Colorado, with over 32,000 students and almost 3,500 employees. The district incorporates assets into not only its curricula but also its calendar. Here's part of what you'd read about assets even before turning to the first month:

"Forty assets and the need to provide them for all children have been embraced by our community and more than 200 others nationwide. We at D-11 have prioritized nine of the 40 assets to concentrate on this school year. Schools are encouraged to include one or more of these nine assets in their School Improvement Plans or to emphasize an asset throughout the year. The Division of Instruction will support them with resources, including staff development, training educational opportunities, specific expertise, and materials."

You'd then read about the nine assets. Each succeeding page of the calendar features information about activities that are consistent with the assets, for example:

◆ "Fourth-graders at Monroe worked all semester studying the Anasazi and Pueblo Indian cultures. Students constructed an Anasazi village complete with cornfield, kiva, matates and manos, dried food, and a three-story dwelling with ladders. The class also completed a Pueblo community that included handmade pots and adobe brick, and they lunched on traditional foods of the Anasazi and Pueblo cultures." (Cultural Competence)

◆ "A student at Mitchell earned a Youth Citizenship Award from Soroptimist International of Colorado Springs for her contributions to home, school, and community. She is a volunteer with Court-Appointed Special Advocates and a student member of the CASA board. She also has worked at Colorado Springs Child Nursery Centers and Marian House Soup Kitchen." (Service to Others)

◆ "Twenty-five schools have after-school study centers, and seven schools operate before-school centers through the Breakfast Buddies program. Two churches operate tutoring centers." (Achievement Motivation)

You'd also read tips on how to build assets for—and with—young people:

◆ "Get to know the names of teenagers in your neighborhood. Greet young people with a smile when you pass them on the street. Hire young people to mow your lawn, shovel snow, or rake leaves."

◆ "If you are a parent, ask your child to help you with a project. Explain what you are doing, why, and how."

◆ "If you are an employer, hire a teenager to work in your office two afternoons a week. Offer plenty of training, support, and encouragement."

◆ "If you are a young person, find one special adult, other than your parent(s), to spend time with regularly."

That is one way the Colorado Springs community—parents, young people, businesses, youth-serving organizations, and the rest—have become aware of building assets.

❧

Handout 5.3 begins with several general ways that school communities can build assets. It then identifies other ways that school communities can build developmental assets in each of the eight asset categories—Support, Empowerment, Boundaries and Expectations, Constructive Use of Time, Commitment to Learning, Positive Values, Social Competencies, and Positive Identity. Many of these ways accomplish two important objectives: They build assets *and* they build awareness of the asset framework.

All the while you're generating awareness about building developmental assets, you can also be—building assets. Lots of people learn best and are most persuaded by successful examples. And while you're doing that, you can also be determining a baseline. To what extent do your students report experiencing the assets? And to what extent is your school prepared to help build them? Those are the questions we'll examine in the next chapter.

Asset-Building Ideas for Schools

Asset building in general

- ◆ Support administration of the *Profiles of Student Life: Attitudes and Behaviors* survey in your district.

- ◆ Encourage your school board to pass a resolution supporting asset building and to make a commitment to promote it within the school system and the community.

- ◆ Include information on asset building in each school newsletter.

- ◆ Educate parents about the assets and use the asset language when talking with them about their children.

- ◆ Share the asset-building model with coaches and other extracurricular leaders. Make asset building part of the philosophy guiding extracurricular programs.

Support

- ◆ Keep class sizes small to give teachers and staff more time with each student.

- ◆ Encourage teamwork.

- ◆ Offer parents easy and convenient ways to get involved in their children's education (asset #6). For example, one-time activities such as tutoring high school students right before exam time can be perfect for a parent who wants to volunteer but cannot commit to regular involvement. For parents who never come to conferences, have an educator call them or go to their homes to meet with them.

- ◆ Create a parent education program that starts by serving breakfast to families. When the students start their class day, invite the parents to stay for a message on parenting or child/adolescent development. Also offer learning opportunities during evenings or following conferences. Consider offering bus rides to parents who do not have transportation.

- ◆ Invite senior citizens to have lunch with students. It's a wonderful way to "civilize" a cafeteria and it helps students to connect with adults in the community.

- ◆ Work with your parent/teacher organizations to build an educational component into their activities. Encourage them to bring in speakers on parenting and child/adolescent development.

- ◆ Assign each class a building-maintenance or cleaning project that requires them to work with the custodians. It will sensitize the students to the care of the building and build bridges between the custodial staff and the students.

Empowerment

- ◆ Engage students as leaders and decision makers, including getting their input on school board decisions.

- ◆ Seek learning opportunities that take students out into the community and bring community resources into the classroom as well.

- ◆ Invite students to discuss their school experiences with the school board.

Boundaries and Expectations

- ◆ Expect everyone to do their best.

- ◆ Set high standards for student and staff behavior. Be consistent about following through with consequences when these standards are not met.

Constructive Use of Time

◆ Work with congregations and cultural groups in your community to avoid scheduling school events that conflict with families' religious or cultural commitments. Find out if your community has a calendar of events to help with this planning. If not, consider creating one.

◆ Provide constructive before- and after-school programs for young people who would otherwise spend the time unsupervised (and probably lonely). One way to do this is to link with existing programs and help expand them through financial, human, or in-kind resources.

Commitment to Learning

◆ Have administrators greet students and staff at the door each morning. The connection will create a caring environment (asset #5) and reinforce the commitment students and staff have to one another (asset #24).

◆ Create a visual reminder of asset building. For example, one school made an assets quilt that they hung in a prominent central location.

Positive Values

◆ Work with parents, teachers, board members, and others to create a list of shared values for the school. See the Positive-Values assets (#26–31) as a place to start. Integrate these values into lesson planning, external communication, and boundaries and expectations for behavior.

Social Competencies

◆ Train all students and staff in cultural competence and nonviolent conflict resolution.

◆ Open your building to community groups and organizations during nonschool hours.

Positive Identity

◆ Focus on students' long-term goals as well as short-term assignments and projects. Help students develop plans and visions for the future and the skills to make those dreams come true.

6

٭

Conducting Assessments

Assessing Levels of Assets

Profiles of Student Life: Attitudes and Behaviors is a self-report survey developed by Search Institute expressly to measure to what extent students in grades 6–12 have the 40 developmental assets. The survey asks students 156 questions about what they think, what they do, what positive things are in their lives, and what is missing. When you decide to use the survey to gain a "portrait" of your school community's young people, the first part of the process is fairly simple and standard: You confer with Search Institute survey services staff to determine how many surveys you need, the institute sends them to you, students complete them, you send the institute the completed surveys, and some time later the institute gives you the results.

The rest of the survey process is less standard. You can decide how you involve your community, how you communicate the survey results, and what you decide to do about the survey results—and this sets the tone for your subsequent efforts to build assets.

Think about it: You get your survey results back from Search Institute, and, if your students are anything close to being typical, they report having fewer than half the assets. What's the most likely reaction to these results if, say, you copied a fact sheet with all the percentages and sent it out to everyone in the community? Let's see:

- "You're doing a terrible job."
- "What's wrong?"

- ◆ "These kids aren't satisfied with anything."
- ◆ "This can't be true; the test is (biased) (unreliable) (invalid) (irrelevant)."
- ◆ "What do these kids want?"

Numbers are dry, without personality, and sometimes not very illuminating. That's why you need to *discuss* the results. The best people to have that discussion with—and probably among the *first* people—are the people responsible for the results in the first place: your students.

Terry Knisler is the superintendent of schools in Philomath, Oregon. After he got the survey results back, he facilitated two six-hour meetings, during the day. Participating in these meetings were Philomath High School and Philomath Middle School students, who took the surveys; principals, teachers, and other adults from those schools; and representatives from families, the police, and other community agencies and organizations. During the meetings, people calmly discussed what the survey results really meant, determined from those discussions which assets to focus on, and devised strategies for raising asset levels. One of the striking findings was that even though the students scored low on the Caring School Climate asset, the reason, according to the students, was not dissatisfaction with the behavior of school adults, but rather with the behavior of students. It was the lack of civility and caring of fellow *students* that they saw as the problem. Without this discussion, the schools might have adopted a misguided strategy that focused only on modifying adult behavior.

Phil Heath, prevention education coordinator of the Northwest Iowa Alcoholism and Drug Treatment Unit, based in rural Algona, is involved with promoting understanding of student development through the asset framework. He works with 9th-grade students at Bishop Gerrigan High School. Using the list of developmental assets as a discussion starter, the students first go through the list to mark off which assets they perceive as present or missing in their lives. The students' parents or guardians then rate their children on how they believe their children would respond. Then students and adults compare their ratings; usually, a fascinating talk ensues.

This is an excellent method for teaching about the assets and helping parents and children communicate. For example, imagine a discussion that might take place when a student says her school does not have a caring climate, but her parents think it does. It can go far beyond the usual 10-second "How was school today?" check-in and become a meaningful talk about the student's expectations about school adults and what they could do to help her feel valued and to learn more.

These types of discussions between young people and their families are happening with more frequency around the country. Bev Lackey, president of Albuquerque Assets, facilitates asset-building trainings for teachers, administrators, and parents in New Mexico. She says that more than once students have surprised members of their families by revealing, for instance, that they had very low levels of the Positive

Peer Influence asset, and that, in fact, they had no friends they could count on for modeling responsible, positive behaviors. Discussions like these pave the way for effective, targeted strategies to address the barriers to learning and school engagement that students have identified. And you can expect them to be full of surprises—and rewards.

"It's an interesting dance that we're all trying to learn how to do," says Rick Jackson. Jackson has been involved with assets almost since its inception at Search Institute, and he's talking about the coordination—and cooperation—necessary between his organization and schools. As vice-president of the Greater Seattle YMCA, Jackson has been a key player in assessing levels of assets for students in Seattle and in neighboring Bellevue and Bainbridge Island. Jackson considers the survey "a report card filled out by kids about the community." He, along with others, emphasizes how critical it is to identify and involve a cross section of the community in the entire process; those representatives can then secure support from their constituencies, and the asset initiative will truly become a community-wide effort.

Jackson has welcomed the asset framework. He's glad to get away from what he calls "teen baby-sitting"—merely making sure that teens don't get into trouble—and says that asset building is "not only good for kids—it's good for us." He incorporates the framework into his trainings and presentations with youth workers. He says that the framework is always looked upon as "commonsensical" and therefore embraced. "There's a renewed sense of possibility," he says. "It's more hopeful."

Jackson has also seen firsthand what a difference students can make to the assessment process. One of the teachers at Bainbridge High School, Eric Hoffman, teaches a class in contemporary issues, and his students became excited about the survey. They attended the public meeting to discuss the results of the survey, and Jackson found that the adults were routinely deferring to the students to explain the results. For their part, the students were eager to contribute. "We never get a chance," one of them said, "to be taken seriously by adults."

Involving young people in the assessment process makes sense: They're the ones with the information. They're the ones with whom you're trying to build good relationships. They're the ones on whom you're depending as resources. And they're the ones you'll be depending on to help effect change in your school community. Young people are the focus of the effort; they should also be the focus of the process.

Working in groups with both young people and adults can be a challenge; that's largely because many young people and adults aren't used to working together as colleagues. Handout 6.1 offers some tips for getting along in "mixed company."

Communicating Survey Results

There are many ways to interpret and communicate survey results. The important thing is to look genuinely at what the results mean, look for "strengths" in the results

Tips for Meetings with Youth and Adults

Part of "walking the assets talk" is having both youth and adults participate in leadership and decision making. But how do you make sure this is a good experience for everyone involved?

Getting started

◆ Be creative and sensitive about meeting times and places. For example, if evening meeting times interfere with teenagers' after-school jobs, and Saturday times are bad for Jewish youth, meet on a weekday at lunch time in the school cafeteria.

◆ Understand the needs of participants. If they come to a meeting straight from school, you might need to serve snacks. Most youth don't carry calendars with them, so you might need to make reminder phone calls a day or two before each meeting. (If you don't know the young people's needs, ask them! Then ask again after you've had a meeting or two.)

◆ Remember that young people may not feel comfortable as the sole representative of their peer-group; try to include more than one or two youth from different social groups.

Communication and language issues

◆ Talk openly about language issues. Will you all go by first names? Is the term "kids" offensive to some participants?

◆ Become aware of and confront adult bias. Watch for unconscious stereotyping of youth by age, by appearance or clothing style, or by gender, race, ethnicity, or economic class.

◆ Be intentional about taking youth seriously and be ready to redirect the conversation if adult participants talk too much, interrupt or ignore youth, or are critical or scolding.

◆ If youth are hesitant to speak up or tend to respond "I don't know" to questions you're sure they have an answer for, help them identify the reasons for their reticence (e.g., difficulty telling when people are done talking).

Training, support, and process

◆ Make sure to bring new people—youth or adult—up to speed. Review the group's goals and provide pre-meeting training for newcomers about basics such as meeting structures, discussion ground rules, and agendas and reports.

◆ Be aware of the developmental needs of young people and accommodate the preferred learning styles of all group members. This may mean adding more experiential meeting elements, augmenting written and verbal communication with visual aids, and breaking into small groups.

◆ Start off with a game or other fun activity that helps all participants with the transition from other activities to the meeting.

◆ Plan concrete projects, give youth responsibilities early, and expect achievement. Let youth learn from their own mistakes, too.

◆ Be clear about each participant's role and level of authority, the time and number of meetings, and the expected duration of the commitment.

◆ Have youth and adults periodically evaluate the role of youth (e.g., are youth being given only insignificant or peripheral tasks?).

(for example, it may be that students have rated Positive Family Communication low but Family Support high; what this could mean is that students feel their parents are receptive to their needs but neither the students nor the parents have the skills to discuss them, which points to a skill-building strategy), and translate the data into relevant, appropriate strategies. Some of the data may be disturbing or confusing, but they provide useful information. And with the right emphasis and context, low scores on particular assets can inspire involvement and guide future action. What you do with the information is the key.

People in the field who have been through this process of communicating survey results offer some intriguing suggestions about communicating survey results: Avoid using school stationery in the letters to the community inviting them to attend. Hold the "survey results" meeting someplace other than on school grounds. Be sure to involve young people in the presentation and allow plenty of time for small group discussions. Take a low profile. If a community organization has launched an asset-building initiative, give the organization the reins. If the school has launched an initiative, then give the reins to an asset-building team within the school—with its own stationery, slogan, and logo.

Why not have the meeting at the school, you may ask. If the school—or the school district—presents itself as the main player in this effort, then the bulk of the responsibility for action will probably fall on the school. But the school can do only so much, and one school can't be responsible for low scores on the survey or solely responsible for working to raise student levels of assets. As we previously pointed out, schools, for the most part, can most directly affect 22 of the 40 assets so far identified. The issue of building developmental assets for and with young people is one that the entire community—families specifically included—must own. You may get the best results by pointing out (or having students point out) that young people in your community need these assets, that none of them have enough, and then ask the question: "What can each of us do?"

Assessing Resources

The companion activity to assessing the strengths and needs of your students is assessing the strengths and needs of the resources (e.g., people, budgets, programs, partnerships) in your school community. In many ways, this latter activity is more difficult. Why? For many people, it's first nature to begin looking for quick, targeted solutions once a need is identified. Students are using drugs, so they need to have a drug education program. Students are being mean to each other, so they have to learn skills to resolve conflicts peacefully. Students aren't reading at the appropriate grade level, so they have to be subjected to intensified instruction.

People sometimes think this way about the asset framework and their survey results, too. Particularly because most survey results will indicate low levels of many assets, the inclination is to immediately create or import new solutions. But often the solutions are already in place. Maybe they need to be redirected a bit, or enhanced, or restaffed, or reorganized and connected into the bigger picture, but it's prudent for schools to look at what they're already doing before they start writing the checks for brand-new programs. This is the flip side of the "We're already doing that" misconception: the "We're not doing any of that" misconception. The answer generally lies in between those two extremes.

This is a good time to issue two caveats: First, don't do too little. And second, don't do too much. The first caveat arises from the tendency to choose just one or two assets to address and ignore the rest. But asset building is a "way of life," not merely an effort to raise levels of discrete qualities as one would try raise test scores in math or science. When all the members of the school community adopt the philosophy of being healthy, caring, and responsible, and when they go about examining and improving their relationships with others in order to help *them* be healthy, caring, and responsible, that's when the effects of asset building can truly be seen.

The second caveat arises from the tendency to be overwhelmed. How can a few people accomplish so much change? The counter to this tendency is the same as to the first: Don't think of this as a series of dozens of tasks, several for each asset. Think of it as a way of life, a way that you're going to try to relate to others, think about things, and organize activities. Start with something simple and informal, like learning the names of young people in your school and making intentional efforts to greet them in the hallway. Then go on to learn something about their lives—what matters to them, what their strengths are, what sorts of leaders they might be. Finally, think about how you can provide them opportunities—either individually or as a group, e.g., a class—to raise their asset levels.

LeAnn Bauer, coordinator of Youth First, an initiative in Hastings, Minnesota, made an inventory of the activities in her local middle school and high school. A committee including a student, school board member, principal, counselor, parent, and teacher solicited descriptions of all noncurricular activities in the two schools. They then rated them as to what assets those activities likely build and for whom.

Information like this is invaluable. Taking a long, hard look at what resources you already have avoids needless restructuring, needless expenditures, and a contradiction in philosophy: The whole point of building assets is to capitalize on the strengths of young people. Shouldn't you also be capitalizing on the strengths of your own resources?

Too often one of the most important resources in your school community is overlooked: students. Which of your students seem to have high levels of assets? Which of them are resilient? Which of them are influential? Which ones are involved in activities, and which ones need to be invited to participate more? Interviewing students—involving them in the process of determining your strengths, perhaps as a class project—benefits you, them, and the school.

Assessment Tools

In order to help you work through this process of assessment, we have provided a variety of assessment tools at the end of this chapter. Don Draayer, former national superintendent of the year, from Minnetonka, Minnesota, and currently an educational consultant, has helped to develop several tools for taking stock of how the developmental assets framework is being addressed in school communities. His tools are not means of measuring assets, but they can provide a clear picture of what ought to be happening in an asset-rich school. Handouts 6.2 and 6.3 are inventories adapted from Draayer's tools; you can complete them for your own school as a way to consider what you're currently doing to build assets and what more you may need to be doing.

Both of these tools are starting points. They can form the impetus for fruitful discussions about where your school is in terms of building assets, where it needs to go, and how it can get there. The discussions of the results from administering these tools are as important as the tools themselves. Consider: Are all representatives of the school community—including students—on hand to interpret the results? Based on those results, what is the ideal plan? What is the most reasonable plan?

You can construct your own inventories, too, especially for students, who can give you significant feedback about what's working and not working for them at school. Handout 6.4 is a sample inventory for high school students.

John Preston works for an Area Education Agency in Iowa; he consults with two dozen school districts about how to improve their schools, especially in the area of health education. Preston finds that the asset framework fits nicely with the desires of superintendents, principals, and teachers to reduce the incidence of substance abuse, teenage pregnancy, and other problem behaviors. Along with Vickie Trent of the University of Northern Iowa, he developed exercises that schools and other organizations can use to inventory how they're doing in terms of building assets. Handout 6.5 is an adaptation of one of these exercises, tailored specifically for schools.

Preston suggests meeting with students—or training students to meet with other students—to ask them the questions about each of the 15 statements: "If this were a perfect school, what would [e.g., receiving high levels of care and support] look like?" "What would it sound like?" "What would it feel like?" Again, students need to take part in the inventory of their school's strengths; they're the ones with the most relevant perspective. You may *think* that a program or practice is building assets when in fact students perceive it quite differently. Many a teacher or administrator has been surprised to hear from students that a particular activity or program is not nearly as effective as they thought.

Finally, Handout 6.6 is a tool for taking stock of what is going on in your school community. This tool is tied both to individual assets and individual programs and practices that are being facilitated in your school. You can complete this worksheet for each of the main programs and practices you use, resulting in a profile of how your current activities relate to building assets. What's important to note is that the tools we present in this chapter—as well as the *Search Institute Profiles of Student Life: Attitudes and Behaviors* survey—are not ends in themselves, but rather means by which you can gather information for designing strategies to build assets for your students.

It's not quite accurate to say that after you've made people aware of assets, after you've surveyed your students, and after you've inventoried your resources, now you have to *do* something. Developing assets is certainly about "doing," but it's also about "being." Asset building is not another thing to "do." When you implement the asset framework, you don't just add programs to an already overloaded curriculum, and you don't just add tasks to the schedule of already overworked school adults. You infuse whatever else is happening with a way of being, a philosophy, a lens with which to view the learning and development of students. What do you see through this lens?

We think that you see the following:

- Relationships, especially between school adults and students, that are mutually respectful, caring, and genuine;
- An environment in the school that encourages asset building; and
- Programs and practices that provide specific opportunities for asset building.

We're going to discuss and give examples for each of these categories in the next three chapters. Most of the strategies you use to build assets will fall in at least one of these categories.

Inventory of School Practices Consistent with the Developmental Assets Framework

Check either 1=well done, 2=needs work, or 3=don't know.

ORGANIZATION

1 2 3

☐ ☐ ☐ The **vision** includes the developmental assets framework.

☐ ☐ ☐ The **goals** are clear, achievable, and appropriate.

☐ ☐ ☐ The **objectives** are measurable.

☐ ☐ ☐ The **structure** promotes relationships, e.g., intergenerational associations.

☐ ☐ ☐ **Teacher/Pupil assignments**—e.g., multi-year assignments—promote relationships.

☐ ☐ ☐ **Planning** sets benchmarks.

☐ ☐ ☐ **Data** are collected in a variety of ways from a variety of sources.

☐ ☐ ☐ **Participation** is universal.

☐ ☐ ☐

☐ ☐ ☐

☐ ☐ ☐

ENVIRONMENT

1 2 3

☐ ☐ ☐ **Safety** concerns are clearly identified and publicly addressed.

☐ ☐ ☐ **Positive values**—e.g., health, responsibility, and caring—are articulated and constantly nurtured throughout the school.

☐ ☐ ☐ **Boundaries** are clearly communicated to everyone in the school.

☐ ☐ ☐ **Rewards** for exceeding expectations are fair, consistent, and communicated to everyone in the school.

☐ ☐ ☐ **Discipline** for transgressing boundaries is fair, consistent, and communicated to everyone in the school.

☐ ☐ ☐ **Peaceful conflict resolution** processes are in place and adopted as a norm.

☐ ☐ ☐ **Staff development** is accessible and appropriate.

☐ ☐ ☐ Peer and cross-age **support** is available.

☐ ☐ ☐

☐ ☐ ☐

INSTRUCTION

1 2 3

☐ ☐ ☐ **Expectations** are set high for achievement and social responsibility.

☐ ☐ ☐ **Supervision** includes feedback, encouragement, and support.

☐ ☐ ☐ **Bloom's Taxonomy of Educational Objectives** is a part of all instruction.

Check either 1=well done, 2=needs work, or 3=don't know.

☐ ☐ ☐ **Cooperation**—e.g., by using cooperative team learning—is practiced in classrooms.

☐ ☐ ☐ **Relationships with adults** other than the teacher are strengthened by team teaching.

☐ ☐ ☐ **Relationships with other students** are strengthened by combining students of various ages in classes.

☐ ☐ ☐ **Individualized instruction** is promoted by a manageable class size and opportunities for tutoring.

☐ ☐ ☐ Peer and cross-age **mentorships** are available.

☐ ☐ ☐

☐ ☐ ☐

☐ ☐ ☐

CURRICULA

1   2   3

☐ ☐ ☐ Both the **content and the format** of curricula relate to students' lives.

☐ ☐ ☐ Curricula are **integrated** into many disciplines.

☐ ☐ ☐ **Homework** is relevant to objectives and includes parent involvement.

☐ ☐ ☐ **Assessment** of students is frequent and shared as constructive feedback.

☐ ☐ ☐ Curricula promote **intergenerational activities**.

☐ ☐ ☐

☐ ☐ ☐

☐ ☐ ☐

COCURRICULAR ACTIVITIES

1   2   3

☐ ☐ ☐ Activities are **plentiful and diverse**.

☐ ☐ ☐ Activities are **accessible**, i.e., at a reasonable time, in a reasonable place, and for a reasonable price.

☐ ☐ ☐ Activities are **supervised** by competent and caring adults.

☐ ☐ ☐

☐ ☐ ☐

☐ ☐ ☐

PARENT PARTNERSHIPS

1   2   3

☐ ☐ ☐ **Communication** between the school and families is accessible, open, frequent, two-way, and evident to students.

> **Inventory of School Practices Consistent with the Developmental Assets Framework (cont.)**

Check either 1=well done, 2=needs work, or 3=don't know.

☐ ☐ ☐ Families are apprised of students' **curricula and activities**.

☐ ☐ ☐ Families are given opportunities to learn **parenting skills**.

☐ ☐ ☐ Families are encouraged to participate in school **decisions** affecting their children.

☐ ☐ ☐ **Parent/Teacher conferences** include students.

☐ ☐ ☐ Parents are invited to volunteer at the school and otherwise **participate in school events**.

☐ ☐ ☐

☐ ☐ ☐

☐ ☐ ☐

COMMUNITY ENGAGEMENT

1   2   3

☐ ☐ ☐ The school **reaches out** to the community in positive ways.

☐ ☐ ☐ Residents are asked to be **mentors, resources, and volunteers**.

☐ ☐ ☐ School leaders are active and visible in **community activities**.

☐ ☐ ☐ **Service-learning** that includes reflection is promoted.

☐ ☐ ☐ **Resource people** are used frequently, and their services are communicated to everyone in the school.

☐ ☐ ☐

☐ ☐ ☐

☐ ☐ ☐

Inventorying Asset Building in School

Indicate how important each item is to you and how well your school does it by circling 1, 2, 3, 4, or 5 for each question.

1. **Build a shared vision and commitment to asset building.**

   Involve everyone in developing a vision for asset building; develop concrete plans for building assets in the school and community.

How important is this? (1=not important; 5=top priority)	1 2 3 4 5
How well do we do this? (1=not well at all; 5=very well)	1 2 3 4 5

2. **Assess current needs, structures, and resources.**

   Collect data on student needs through surveys, focus groups, etc.; know and celebrate what is currently being done to build assets; assess current organization, structures, and strategies in light of asset building.

How important is this? (1=not important; 5=top priority)	1 2 3 4 5
How well do we do this? (1=not well at all; 5=very well)	1 2 3 4 5

3. **Encourage individual commitment to asset building.**

   Highlight ways individuals already take time to build assets in the school; encourage and reward asset-building actions by students and school adults.

How important is this? (1=not important; 5=top priority)	1 2 3 4 5
How well do we do this? (1=not well at all; 5=very well)	1 2 3 4 5

4. **Create a positive, safe school environment.**

   Create a sense of collegiality among school adults; provide opportunities for students to develop caring, supportive relationships with school adults and with one another.

How important is this? (1=not important; 5=top priority)	1 2 3 4 5
How well do we do this? (1=not well at all; 5=very well)	1 2 3 4 5

5. **Engage parents in their children's learning.**

   Communicate regularly with parents about school activities, goals, and expectations; offer resources to parents to enhance learning at home; provide opportunities for parents to volunteer; engage parents in school decision making and planning; provide parent education opportunities to strengthen and nurture families.

How important is this? (1=not important; 5=top priority)	1 2 3 4 5
How well do we do this? (1=not well at all; 5=very well)	1 2 3 4 5

6. **Establish and enforce consistent boundaries.**

   Develop clear norms in areas such as respect, studying, responsibility, etc.; name and enforce discipline policies for negative student behavior; work with parents and community members to develop consistent messages through the community regarding students' behavior.

How important is this? (1=not important; 5=top priority)	1 2 3 4 5
How well do we do this? (1=not well at all; 5=very well)	1 2 3 4 5

7. **Involve students in constructive activities.**

   Make a variety of activities available to all students; cooperate with community groups and congregations to facilitate involvement in arts, sports, recreation, or educational enrichment programs; reach out to uninvolved students.

   How important is this? (1=not important; 5=top priority)   1 2 3 4 5
   How well do we do this? (1=not well at all; 5=very well)   1 2 3 4 5

8. **Foster a commitment to learning in all students.**

   Set challenging expectations of learning for all students; use educational methods that actively engage students in the learning process; assign and monitor home-work daily; offer challenging course work to all students; guide and encourage all students to continue their education beyond high school.

   How important is this? (1=not important; 5=top priority)   1 2 3 4 5
   How well do we do this? (1=not well at all; 5=very well)   1 2 3 4 5

9. **Articulate and nurture positive values.**

   Identify and articulate positive, commonly held values as norms for the school; engage students regularly in service projects that integrate learning and service; encourage students to talk with their parents and other caring adults about their values and beliefs.

   How important is this? (1=not important; 5=top priority)   1 2 3 4 5
   How well do we do this? (1=not well at all; 5=very well)   1 2 3 4 5

10. **Develop social competencies and positive identity.**

    Integrate life skills into the curriculum for all grades; provide opportunities for all students to have leadership roles in the school; be sure that all students are sensitive to those from other cultures.

    How important is this? (1=not important; 5=top priority)   1 2 3 4 5
    How well do we do this? (1=not well at all; 5=very well)   1 2 3 4 5

11. **Build bridges with the community.**

    Become a partner in a community-wide partnership on behalf of youth; collaborate to provide a variety of after-school programs for youth; involve community members in school policy and decision making; promote volunteerism, e.g., as tutors.

    How important is this? (1=not important; 5=top priority)   1 2 3 4 5
    How well do we do this? (1=not well at all; 5=very well)   1 2 3 4 5

Adapted from D. Draayer and E.C. Roehlkepartain, Learning and Living *(revised edition) (Minneapolis: Search Institute, 1998).*

Asset Inventory for High School Students

We're interested in your views about how the school is building developmental assets. Please circle the most appropriate response; your answers will be confidential.

1. How familiar are you with developmental assets?

    a) I've never heard of them.

    b) I've heard of them, but I'm not quite sure what they are.

    c) I'm familiar with developmental assets and what the school is doing to build them.

    d) I'm actively involved with the school's efforts to build developmental assets.

2. How have you participated in the school's efforts to build developmental assets?

    a) I'm not aware of participating at all.

    b) I've taken a survey to measure my developmental assets.

    c) I've discussed the results of the survey with people in school.

    d) I've taken an active part in planning how to build assets in school.

3. In general, to what extent are positive behaviors—showing respect, being caring and honest, giving support to others, e.g.—encouraged and acknowledged in school?

    a) Not at all.

    b) They might be acknowledged, but only in passing.

    c) They're encouraged, but not acknowledged.

    d) They're both acknowledged and encouraged; efforts are made to encourage similar behaviors among all students and staff.

4. On the whole, how would you characterize the relationships between adults in school?

    a) Adults don't seem to respect each other.

    b) They seem to tolerate each other.

    c) They seem friendly enough.

    d) They seem supportive and respectful of each other.

5. On the whole, how would you characterize the relationships between students in school?

    a) Students don't seem to respect each other.

    b) They seem to tolerate each other.

    c) They seem friendly enough.

    d) They seem supportive and respectful of each other.

6. On the whole, how would you characterize the relationships between adults and students in school?

   a)   Adults and students don't seem to respect each other.

   b)   They seem to tolerate each other, but mostly stay in their own groups.

   c)   They seem friendly enough.

   d)   They seem supportive and respectful of each other.

7. How would you characterize the discipline policies in school?

   a)   I don't know what they are.

   b)   The policies are inconsistently enforced.

   c)   The policies are consistently enforced, but they're not always good policies.

   d)   The policies are consistently enforced, and students have opportunities to change them.

8. How available are arts, music, sports, recreation, or educational enrichment activities to students in school?

   a)   Not many are available that I know of, at least that I would like.

   b)   There are some activities like those available, but not everyone has access to them.

   c)   There are many different kinds of activities available, but not everyone has access to them.

   d)   There are many different kinds of activities available, and people try hard to make them accessible to all students.

9. How committed do you think the school is to giving every student a good education?

   a)   I don't think the school is very committed at all.

   b)   I think the school is committed to some students, but not all of them.

   c)   I think the school is committed to some extent, but it does only what seems to be required.

   d)   I think the school is very committed; people in the school all work together and try hard to help all students succeed academically.

10. How much do you hear about "positive values" in school?

   a)   I don't hear much at all.

   b)   People tell us about the importance of being honest, caring, and responsible, but they don't walk their talk.

   c)   The school encourages service projects that help students learn firsthand about positive values.

   d)   The school actively encourages students to act in positive ways—e.g., by doing service projects—and to influence others to do the same.

11. How common is the teaching of social skills—e.g., resistance, decision making, self-control, communication, or conflict resolution skills—in school?

    a) I'm not aware of having been taught any skill like those.

    b) I've been taught some of those skills, but only in the sense of watching a video or talking about them.

    c) I've role-played skills like those in class.

    d) I've learned skills like those, and my teachers have encouraged me to use them outside the classroom.

12. How easy is it for students to have leadership roles in school?

    a) It's impossible for most students; only certain ones are included.

    b) There are "positions" of leadership, but they're meaningless.

    c) Some students have influential leadership roles.

    d) Lots of students are encouraged to take meaningful leadership roles.

13. How well do you think students and staff in the school do at learning about and understanding people from various cultural or racial backgrounds?

    a) Not well at all.

    b) People talk about it, but they don't do anything about improving things between different groups.

    c) There have been some decent efforts to help students and staff learn about all the different cultures represented in the school.

    d) The school has provided programs and activities to help everyone learn about their own and other people's cultural and racial backgrounds.

14. How active a role do parents play in school?

    a) I'm not aware of parents being involved.

    b) Some parents occasionally volunteer for activities and some come to teacher meetings.

    c) Parents have a continual presence in school.

    d) Parents are an essential part of the activities in school.

15. How active a role do other members of the community play in school?

    a) I'm not aware of other members of the community being involved.

    b) Other members of the community occasionally volunteer for activities.

    c) Other members of the community have a continual presence in school.

    d) Other members of the community are an essential part of the activities in school.

Asset-Building Activity

Step 1: Review the following statements and list all of the ways your school is responsive to each:

1. Students receive high levels of care and support.

2. Students communicate positively with school adults, and they're willing to seek their advice and counsel.

3. Students receive support from three or more school adults.

4. Students experience a caring, encouraging environment.

5. School adults are actively involved in helping students succeed.

6. Students perceive that school adults value them.

7. Students are given useful roles.

8. Students feel psychologically and physically safe.

9. Behavioral expectations are clearly communicated to students.

10. Students receive clear "guidelines for success," i.e., they know what it takes to be successful.

11. School adults model positive, responsible behavior for students.

12. Other students model positive, responsible behavior.

13. School adults encourage young people to do well.

14. Students spend three or more hours per week in activities like band, chorus, academic clubs, or sports.

15. Students receive numerous opportunities for meaningful involvement with the school.

Step 2: Indicate whether students think your school is reponsive to each statement and how you know or could find out.

Step 3: Compare your answers from Step 1 with your answers from Step 2. Brainstorm additional measures your school could take to further build assets in students' lives.

Step 4: Narrow your focus to a few things your school could start or continue doing immediately.

Step 5: Develop a matrix of other things your school will do in the future, e.g.:

What we'll do	When we'll do it	Who's primarily responsible for doing it	How we'll know we're having a a positive effect

Step 6: Implement your plan, review it periodically, and update or modify it as needed.

Inventory of Programs and Practices That Help Build Developmental Assets

Take some time to think about each category of the developmental assets: Are you building assets from each category in your school community? Are you *intentionally* building them? How are you doing it? Which assets *aren't* you building? This is an inventory, a starting point for you to take stock of your efforts. Under "Program or practice," list any curriculum, project, event, or action occurring in the school community, ranging from the informal ("teachers greet students by name every morning") to the formal ("peer-helping or peer-mentoring program"). Then write in the assets in each asset category that are addressed (or could be addressed) by that program or practice.

Program or practice: _____

Assets and other criteria   _____

Primary target audience

The audience for whom the program or practice is primarily intended, e.g., "all third-grade students," "40 high school teachers"

Duration

How long the program or practice lasts, e.g., "every school day," "once in November and once in April"

Focus

Whether the primary focus is on relationships ("R"), school environment ("E"), or a formal program or practice ("P")

Ease of implementation

The ease of beginning and carrying through with the program or practice

easy   hard
1   2   3   4

Prominence of assets

The degree to which assets have been addressed in the implementation of the program or practice

yes   no
1   2   3   4

Effectiveness

The degree to which the
program or practice meets   yes   no
the purpose for which it   1   2   3   4
was intended

Support

Empowerment

Boundaries and Expectations

Constructive Use of Time

Commitment to Learning

Positive Values

Social Competencies

Positive Identity

7

꧰

Forming Relationships:

Stories from the Field

When we talk about relationships that build assets, we're talking about two things: First, these relationships in and of themselves are often assets, e.g., in the "Support" category. They're assets because they provide the caring, the listening, the "empowering" that young people need to succeed. But second, relationships are often vehicles by which other assets can be built. If you're a student trying to build the asset of School Engagement, it helps if you know some school adults who value you. If you're trying to build the asset of Time at Home, it helps if you have good relationships with the members of your family. If you're trying to build the asset of Positive View of Personal Future, it helps if someone close to you, someone you respect, repeatedly assures you that you have the capability to succeed.

The implications of this are profound: No matter who you are or what your position is, you can potentially form a caring, respectful, genuine relationship with a young person and build assets for that young person. Regardless of the policies of your school, the status of the larger community, or the many programs that may come to bear on this person, you can do your part, unfettered.

That's why the following stories are so important. They all have as their centerpiece a relationship, and they all hold out the promise that anyone can make a difference—which is, after all, why people choose to be educators. David Fischer, a principal whose school we'll highlight a little later, maintains that building relationships with students engenders accountability, and he's right. When you know a student, when you know that student's name and history and personality, then it helps make you accountable to the student. It's much easier to remain passive in front of a name on a list than a person with whom you've built a relationship. It's almost too simple: Knowing a student makes you care more about that student. If you're a principal, consider this image: Fischer, an energetic, smiling man who seems always to be putting his arm around a student or laughing with a staff member about some recent event, abruptly approaches a visitor and says with genuine excitement, "Don't we have just the greatest kids?" If you're a principal, can you do that?

In Peter Benson's book *All Kids Are Our Kids* (San Francisco: Jossey-Bass, 1997), he offers a description of the "characteristics of asset-building adults." (See Handout 7.1.) His suggestions about the attitudes, qualities of character, and actions of asset-building adults can serve as a guide to begin forming—or expanding—"asset-rich" relationships.

It's important to remember that these relationships have many benefits, and not only to students.

- They engage students in learning, because students believe that someone cares about their achievement.
- They promote bonds between students and school adults, between students and other students, between school adults and other school adults, and between everyone and the school.
- They foster a norm of caring, in which everyone has a stake in everyone else's success and well-being.
- They offer a foundation for the social skills that students will use in school and beyond.
- They give everyone energy, which often translates into a motivation to succeed and an inspiration to exceed goals.

In short, relationships are the basis for building assets. The *type* of relationship—even a mutually caring, respectful relationship—depends on the individuals. For example, consider the following personalities:

- Someone who is nervous about meeting new people
- Someone who demands a lot of attention
- Someone who shuns physical contact
- Someone who is always serious
- Someone who is always cheerful
- Someone who uses humor as a defense
- Someone who argues about everything
- Someone who avoids hard work
- Someone who enjoys being alone
- Someone who has irritating personal habits

Characteristics of Asset-Building Adults

"Being" Characteristics

Attitudes toward Youth	◆ Values young people for who they are, not just who they will become
	◆ Has a sense of hope and optimism for young people and the future
	◆ Recognizes personal responsibility for children and adolescents in the community
	◆ Celebrates the gifts, commitments, and zeal of the adolescent years
Character and Competencies	◆ Has a personal foundation for healthy growth and development
	◆ Personally experiences assets (e.g., support, appropriate boundaries, self-restraint, self-esteem)
	◆ Has relational skills (conversation skills, skills for dealing with conflict, etc.)
	◆ Is trusting and trustworthy

"Doing" Characteristics

Relationships with Children and Adolescents	◆ Takes the initiative in building relationships with young people
	◆ Respects and affirms young people; seeks to understand them
	◆ Spends time with young people; is actively engaged
	◆ Builds long-term relationships with young people
	◆ Balances protecting the young person with need for independence in ways that are appropriate to the young person's age and development
	◆ Models healthy attitudes and choices, including service, lifelong learning, civic involvement, and self-restraint
	◆ Never violates or takes advantage of a young person's trust
Other Actions	◆ Makes caring for children and adolescents a lifelong priority
	◆ Looks out for the best interest of children and adolescents in the community and the nation through advocacy, civic engagement, and political action

Reprinted with permission from P.L. Benson, All Kids Are Our Kids *(San Francisco: Jossey-Bass, 1997), p. 160.*

Any of those personal traits—and obviously many more—could belong to a student or a school adult. Think of the myriad types of relationships that could be formed! The truth is that if you're a teacher, for example, you're not going to like every student. Not every student will like you. You may be a "warm, fuzzy" type, and the student you're concerned about may be a dry intellectual. You may feel uncomfortable about behaving impulsively, and the student whose assets you'd like to help build is a spontaneous extrovert. To form a relationship with someone very different from you means you have to establish common ground, gently work through differences, and create a give-and-take based on mutual respect. This process holds not just for relationships between school adults and students, of course; it is integral to any good relationship.

The process may not always be easily accomplished, though. You may need to brush up on some of your own social skills, and learn not to take an initial "brush-off" too seriously. You may need to take the lead in early conversations, or become more comfortable letting silences linger. And you may have to try a variety of techniques; for example, some students will feel more comfortable talking when they don't feel stared at, so talking while walking together might make a chatterbox of a formerly quiet fellow.

One more note: You may want to make a special effort to connect with the boys. According to data from Search Institute, boys score much lower on the Social-Competencies assets than girls. For example, 60 percent of girls report having the Interpersonal Competence asset (which includes empathy, sensitivity, and friendship skills), as opposed to only 26 percent of boys.[1] What this means is that forming an asset-building relationship with boys might at the same time be a little more difficult, but highly beneficial.

Are the difficulties worth the effort? Sure. And the difficulties become easier to work through the more people form asset-building relationships; experience helps, and the rewards of creating a few asset-building relationships can sustain you through further attempts. So even though the following stories are primarily about individual relationships, start with one relationship, then think about setting the norm in your school for *numerous* individual relationships.

⚹

At the Bus
Seattle, Washington
featuring the following asset: Caring School Climate

Every morning, when Zachary Laster-Hazzard got off the school bus and prepared to enter the doors of Hawthorne Elementary School in Seattle, he could be assured that at least one person would be on hand to greet him, by name, with a question or a comment or a hug, no matter what the weather. That person was the school's principal, John Morefield. While he was principal, Morefield made it a practice to know every one of the 525 kids in his school by name. And every morning—rain or shine—students could count on starting their school day with a feeling that their principal cared about them.

These days, Morefield teaches classes at the University of Washington that prepare people to become teachers, principals, and superintendents. He also facilitates training workshops that help people who already are teachers, principals, and superintendents become better at what they do. Morefield is emphatic about relationships; he believes that relationships between school adults and students must be "real, ongoing, meaningful, and deep." According to Morefield, greeting students as they entered the school every day gave them essential messages: "You are important." "You count." "I love you."

꽃

Checklists for Parents, Writing for Kids
Minneapolis, Minnesota
featuring the following assets: Positive Family Communication, Caring School Climate,
Parent Involvement in Schooling, High Expectations

"I just live assets," says Helene Perry, who teaches math and communication to 7th- and 8th-grade students at Clara Barton Open School in Minneapolis. She relates to students the way adults related to her when she was a child: She has high expectations for all of them. Perry uses the developmental assets framework in a number of ways; for example, she gives checklists of assets to students and their parents. That way, the families can discuss the meaning of each of the assets as well as whether those assets seem to be present or missing in their lives.

Perry also has her students create and produce "Teen Pages," a bimonthly compilation of original articles, essays, and art with a different asset-related theme each time. Recent issues contained the following pieces, among others: "Do People Accept Your Sense of Fashion?," "How Drugs and Money Can Destroy Families," "Girls with Low Self-Esteem," "Healthy Snacks for Teens," "Amount of Money 7th- and 8th-Graders Spend on a Valentine for Valentine's Day," and "Diversity in Movies."

꽃

From Homeless to Collegiate
Stamford, Connecticut
featuring the following assets: Other Adult Relationships, High Expectations,
Achievement Motivation, Responsibility, Planning and Decision Making,
Personal Power, Positive View of Personal Future

Nancy Heishie (not her real name) was an 11th-grade student at Westhill High School, in Stamford, Connecticut. The oldest of eight kids, with chemically dependent parents and an abusive grandmother, Nancy was also occasionally homeless. If you asked virtually any adult in her school about Nancy's chances for academic success—or indeed for any type of success—the answer would probably have been "none."

Judith O'Leary, however, looked for and saw something that apparently no one else—except perhaps Nancy—did: potential. O'Leary is the executive director of Communities in Action, one of the many community groups around the country whose mission it is to build assets for young people. She met Nancy while bringing together teams of adults and students to work on developing assets; Nancy was part of a peer-mediation group from her high school. O'Leary thought it was "criminal" that the people who were supposed to be encouraging students like Nancy were instead discouraging her, and in effect giving up on her.

O'Leary got to know Nancy, gave her counsel and advice, supported her efforts, and stood by her as she used every means possible to study for her SAT's and apply for college. O'Leary drove her to Purchase, New York, the home of Manhattanville College, where Nancy not only interviewed for admission but also—only by chance—met the president of the college and evidently made quite an impression on him. O'Leary relates that the interview took place on a Saturday, and on the following Monday she walked into a room with a stunned Nancy on the phone, saying, "I've been accepted." Today Nancy is a full-fledged student at Manhattanville College with a 3.0 average. One caring relationship, a determination to find and support a student's strengths, plus the internal resources of a determined young woman, made the difference.

❧

The Bus Driver
Rochester, New York
featuring the following asset: Other Adult Relationships

Desiree Voorhies is a health education specialist, and she speaks glowingly of an asset builder she's very close to: her mother, Mary Yagel. Yagel is 62 years old and has been driving a school bus for 30 of those years in upstate New York. As Yagel picks up new children in the morning—either because it's the beginning of a new school year or because a child has just transferred into the district, she does something very special. She introduces herself, asks about them, and takes their pictures. And on Christmas or other holidays, those children receive hand-designed cards with their photographs on them. During the year, they're also likely to get "Mary-made" pins or pendants, constructed from pipe cleaners, beads, twine, or whatever else was handy. Mary Yagel obviously does more than drive students to and from school; she forms relationships with them.

🌿

The Boy Who Became a Mentor
Englewood, Colorado
featuring the following assets: Youth as Resources, High Expectations, School Engagement, Caring, Responsibility, Interpersonal Competence, Personal Power, Self-Esteem, Sense of Purpose

Sometimes it doesn't take much. Hilde Newman, social worker at Dry Creek Elementary School in Colorado, tells the story of a boy ("Max") who had all kinds of emotional, learning, and motor problems. He was becoming increasingly difficult to teach—or even have in a classroom. But something happened; somebody found the "positive" in the boy. One of the teachers told Newman that Max did great in her room. Asked what was different about the situation there, the teacher revealed that the other students in the room were younger than Max, and he seemed to really enjoy working with them and being a leader. So Max was given the opportunity and responsibility of teaching several kindergarten students, and he became a mentor. The improvement in Max was dramatic. He began to walk taller, to show more tolerance for behaving in class, and to concentrate on his own work. "He loves helping out," says Newman, smiling. "He told me, 'I've got it worked out, I've got a plan for the kids.'" He was being treated as a resource, not as a problem, and as a result he more than fulfilled people's expectations and blossomed.

🌿

The Girl Who Became a Mentor
Bismarck, North Dakota
featuring the following assets: Youth as Resources, High Expectations, School Engagement, Caring, Responsibility, Interpersonal Competence, Personal Power, Self-Esteem, Sense of Purpose

Rick Heiden, assistant principal of Bismarck High School, in Bismarck, North Dakota, remembers one young, very defiant student who was constantly in his office for discipline problems. She would frequently tell him off, even in front of her mother. One day, Heiden, who tries to translate the asset-building message into practice as much as he can, asked the student if she'd be willing to work with students with mental disabilities. She agreed, she tried it, and she became an excellent mentor. The girl graduated, something that was clearly in doubt before Heiden looked to her as a resource.

٭

The Basketball Players
Colorado Springs, Colorado
featuring the following assets: Other Adult Relationships, Adult Role Models,
Community Values Youth, Service to Others, Adult Role Models, School Engagement,
Caring, Responsibility, Interpersonal Competence, Sense of Purpose

Mentoring programs focus on forming "deliberate relationships." Most mentoring programs pair a student with an older student or adult, the goal being to give academic and emotional support to the student. Of course, what often happens in most mentoring programs is that a strong bond is formed between the student and the mentor, and the mentor derives as much—or more—benefit from the relationship as does the student. For example, a program out of Colorado Springs paired women basketball players from Colorado College with struggling 5th-grade girls from Monroe Elementary School. The idea was that the athletes would act as role models for the children. But much more than that happened. College students and elementary students became close friends, and the relationships continued well beyond the bounds of the program. The younger girls learn about leadership, team building, and goal setting. The older girls learn about responsibility, personal power, and caring. One of the college students, Molly Calhoun, says, "It gives us a chance to give something to the community."

٭

School-Plus Mentoring
Minneapolis, Minnesota
featuring the following assets: Other Adult Relationships,
Community Values Youth; School Engagement

A program out of Minneapolis combines this mentor relationship with community participation and asset building. The program is called School-Plus Mentoring, and it's a collaboration of The Pillsbury Company, Big Brothers Big Sisters of America (BBBSA), and schools around the country. School-Plus Mentoring places Pillsbury employees with elementary school students in—currently—five sites around the country (all with Pillsbury plants): Allentown, Pennsylvania; Cedar Rapids, Iowa; Joplin, Missouri; Vineland, New Jersey; and Minneapolis.

The program started in Richard Green Central Park School in Minneapolis. Pillsbury employees had been getting paid leave to read to 3rd- and 4th-grade students, but the company wanted more of a long-term commitment and started the program with BBBSA. Barb Alfrey, manager of volunteer programs at Pillsbury, was involved from the beginning, and, she says, so was the asset model: "The school was behind it, and Pillsbury was behind it."

How does the collaboration work? Pillsbury provides a coordinator to develop and manage the program, funding to BBBSA, and the employees (and retirees) who want to be mentors. BBBSA provides staff to work with the coordinator, training for the mentors, and case managers to supervise the relationships. The schools provide staff to help develop and manage the program, assistance in identifying the students to be matched with mentors, and opportunities for the mentors to meet with the students at school and to communicate with the children's teachers. The mentors provide personal contacts with their students at least two to three times a month during the school year; phone calls, mail, and E-mail to supplement the contacts; and optional contacts over the summer.

Alfrey points to a benefit not immediately obvious: Pillsbury sets a standard for other companies in communities. The business/social service organization/school collaboration works to everyone's advantage, and more collaborations can only help a community. As she says, and as Pillsbury has evidently expressed as a policy, "A healthy business needs a healthy community."

✺

DO-IT

Seattle, Washington
featuring the following assets: Other Adult Relationships, Creative Activities, Achievement Motivation, School Engagement, Homework, Planning and Decision Making, Personal Power, Self-Esteem

Another community-based mentoring program that reaches out to a school population is DO-IT. "DO-IT" stands for "Disabilities, Opportunities, Internetworking, Technology." Based at the University of Washington in Seattle, DO-IT aims to increase the participation of students with disabilities in challenging academic programs and careers. Among the components of DO-IT:

- ◆ "DO-IT Scholars" are high school students with disabilities who have strong leadership potential and who are provided with "loaner" computers, modems, software, and adaptive technology for use in their homes. They communicate with "DO-IT Mentors"—college students, faculty, and professionals in a wide variety of career fields, many also with disabilities—about college life, employment, and careers.

♦ "DO-IT Campers" attend a summer camp to learn Internet and college-transition skills.

♦ DO-IT sponsors programs and delivers presentations and workshops to enhance the lives of people with disabilities around the world. Its activities are hosted at conferences, universities, K-12 schools, corporations, state agencies, and professional organizations.

Deb Cronheim is a research coordinator at DO-IT. She tells about physically disabled high school students creating a videotape that illustrated how they need access to science labs. The video, entitled *Working Together: Science Teachers and Students with Disabilities,* is now distributed to schools across the country.

⚘

Special Students
St. Louis Park, Minnesota
featuring the following assets: Caring School Climate, Youth as Resources, Service to Others, School Engagement, Caring, Interpersonal Competence

The idea of pairing students with complementary needs, strengths, or backgrounds isn't new, but pairing them intentionally to build assets *is* relatively recent. Sally Goddard, a 3rd-grade teacher at Aquila Primary Center, in St. Louis Park, Minnesota, selects some of her students who have trouble socializing and pairs them with special education students from St. Louis Park High School for about 45 minutes a week; the results are beneficial to both groups: The third-grade students, in Goddard's words, "get that extra boost they might not otherwise get all week," and the high school students get a renewed sense of purpose from helping others. Goddard tells of one high school mentor who was approached on the playground by a classmate of one of the third-grade students being mentored; the high school mentor was told, "I wish I had you for *my* buddy." Said Goddard, "It made her feel just wonderful."

⚘

Invisible Mentoring
St. Louis Park, Minnesota
featuring the following assets: Other Adult Relationships, Caring School Climate, Religious Community, Bonding to School, Caring, Self-Esteem

Bob Tift, principal of Benilde-St. Margaret's, a Catholic school of 1,035 7th- to 12th-grade students in St. Louis Park, Minnesota, runs an "invisible mentoring program": The Student Support Team—including the principal, counselors, deans, and school psychologist—identify students who they feel would especially benefit from mentoring; many of these are students with whom the adults already have a working relationship. Faculty and staff are asked if they're interested in mentoring, and those interested are matched with students. The adults—with assets in mind—then assertively pursue improving those relationships. The students aren't told that they have mentors; the relationships are formed quietly and casually.

The students, says Tift, typically don't need a support group, but they do benefit from a relationship to an adult. What do the mentors do? They might sit down with a student in the cafeteria to ask how things are going. They might attend an event that a student is participating in, like a ball game or a play. Tift points out that the goal is to "foster connections"—to find out students' interests and try to direct them to activities that meet those interests. To this date—after three years of "invisible mentoring"—adults report that their experiences and those of the students are overwhelmingly positive. "We don't always talk the language of assets," says Tift, "but they are really the basis for what we do."

The key to all these examples is that individuals are forging relationships with students that let those students know someone cares about them and expects a lot from them and will be straight with them. This kind of relationship—a relationship that builds assets—*looks* different from other relationships: The adult considers the student a resource and consequently *listens* to what the student has to say, seriously considers the student's suggestions, and seeks out the student for ideas. This kind of relationship hinges on mutual respect.

These relationships don't just happen. Teachers, principals, cafeteria workers, administrative staff, and bus drivers we've spoken with all work at it. And for some people, it takes a real shift in the way they think and act to lift their everyday interactions with young people into asset-building relationships. It means taking the risk of knowing yourself and knowing the students, and it means continuing to learn more and better interpersonal skills. It means being willing to try new ways of speaking, listening, believing, and mentoring; and it means letting go of being in control of the relationships and sharing the power.

These asset-building relationships are both means and ends. They're means because establishing these relationships can help students succeed in school—academically, emotionally, and, in the case of being protected from risky behaviors, physically. They're ends because successful relationships are at the core of socialization: A person who can sustain mutually respectful, caring relationships is successful in life.

Handout 7.2

Create Your Own Stories: Asset-Building Relationships

The Story	Some Things You Can Do
"At the Bus"	◆ Know as many students' names as you can. ◆ Greet them by name when they enter the school or whenever you see them.
"Checklists for Parents, Writing for Kids"	◆ Give checklists of assets to students and their parents, so families can discuss them. ◆ Have your students create and produce their own magazine.
"From Homeless to Collegiate"	◆ Be on the lookout for students who are discouraged about achieving. ◆ Make a special effort to encourage those students and remind yourself never to give up on a student.
"The Bus Driver"	◆ Take an interest in students' lives. ◆ Note students' birthdays and celebrate with them.
"The Boy Who Became a Mentor"	◆ Give students opportunities to teach others.
"The Girl Who Became a Mentor"	◆ Look to students—especially "problem" students or other students you don't know well—as resources.
"The Basketball Players"	◆ Enlist college students to be mentors with elementary school students.
"School-Plus Mentoring"	◆ Find partners in the business community to build assets and foster students' achievement.
"DO-IT"	◆ Make Internet technology available to students. ◆ Be sure that disabled students have opportunities to participate in challenging academic programs.
"Special Students"	◆ Form mentor relationships with students who have trouble socializing and special education students.
"Invisible Mentoring"	◆ Identify students who will particularly benefit from mentoring, and pair them with interested school adults who already have relationships with them.

Notes

1. Benson, P.L., Scales, P.C., Leffert, N., & Roehlkepartain, E.C. (1999). *A fragile foundation: The state of developmental assets among American youth*. Minneapolis: Search Institute.

128

8

✤

Creating an Environment:
Stories from the Field

When we talk about environment in school communities, we're talking about comfort, warmth, and caring; we're also talking about challenge, expectations, limits, and boundaries. An asset-rich environment is one in which students—and, indeed, school adults as well—feel safe and secure. They're confident that people care about them and that they'll be looked after. They know that they're valued as resources and that people will not only listen to what they have to say but also come to them for advice or support. They receive an effective balance of structure and freedom, appropriate to their level of development. They're held accountable for their own actions or lack of actions. And they feel challenged—that they'll be pushed to excel, to make the most of their own inner resources. Schools with asset-rich environments have *infused* asset building throughout the community.

Some of the stories that follow highlight programs. In fact, asset-rich schools usually have many programs that help students build assets. These stories are here because they illustrate how entire school environments are changed—when the asset framework is infused through a school. What you'll discover from reading these stories is that some activities and actions transcend their initial purpose and help change the entire school community. That's our criterion for "environment": When you make changes that affect how students and school adults in general *feel* about their school community, then you're changing the environment.

✤

Asset Building Everywhere
New Richmond, Wisconsin
featuring the following assets: Caring School Climate, Parent Involvement in Schooling,
Youth as Resources, High Expectations, Achievement Motivation,
School Engagement, Bonding to School

Which assets do you feel you're strong in? Which assets present a challenge to you? Entering 9th-grade students at New Richmond High School, in rural New Richmond, Wisconsin, can tell you which assets *they* feel strong in and which present a challenge to *them;* it's part of their year-long orientation, along with an overview of all the programs and opportunities available to them in the school. Their parents can tell you about assets, too: At the same time that the students are receiving the first part of the orientation, their parents are discussing how they can become active in the school and how they can build developmental assets to help their children succeed.

How might the tragedy of *Romeo and Juliet* have been averted had the principal players had higher levels of developmental assets, say, Family Support, Honesty, Youth Programs, and Restraint? Again, New Richmond freshmen can tell you, because they discuss it in English class. And prospective staff at the school can witness first-hand the responsibility that's given some of the students: Students escort them on a tour of the school, observing how the prospective staff interact with them and with other students. Only later do the interviewees find out that the students are on the selection team. Even the report cards at New Richmond High—computerized to reflect continual changes—contain comments about students' strengths. You can hardly go anywhere in the school without being reminded about building assets.

Much of this is the result of applying what is known about the asset-building process. While one individual can make a difference, the ripple effect is tremendous when a core team of supporters is identified. Marilyn Peplau, a guidance counselor, had waged a long and sometimes lonely campaign to get the school community to trust youth and to see them as resources. Before hearing about the framework of developmental assets, she "felt like Pollyanna, alienated. But," she says, smiling, "I knew I was right." The framework validated her belief in the worth of students and gave her a tool and a research base to guide her efforts. Looking for a core team of supporters for the framework, she found fellow guidance counselors Wayne Whitwam and Kelly Curtis, who became essential to the change process. A study group of 14 mostly school personnel evolved over four years into the Health Communities • Healthy Youth Team and has effectively transformed the environment into one that gives students opportunities to build assets, to contribute, and to succeed. Not everyone has jumped on board; some teachers use the asset language, while others don't. But little by little, the initiative has gained supporters. The school norm is becoming "everyone's job is to build assets."

Now, assets are everywhere. Here is a New Richmond form for a memo introducing a new student to the high school:

From: Kelly Curtis
To: _____
Date: _____
Subject: new student

Hello! _____ is a new student at New Richmond High School, and I would like to introduce her to you.

_____ is a sophomore who attended New Richmond Schools until 7th grade. Since then, she has been in various school districts, most recently the Eau Claire Academy. She is happy to be back in New Richmond, and one of her goals is to graduate from here and attend a four-year university (Achievement Motivation).

_____ likes to read and write and indicates that some of her greatest assets include Planning and Decision Making, Interpersonal Competence, and Cultural Competence.

Sometimes a challenge for _____ is Peaceful Conflict Resolution. When she experiences a conflict with staff, it's helpful for both the staff person and her if another person is there to help work through the conflict. _____ is also working to improve her assets in the category of Support.

The following is her schedule . . .

It's important to note that none of these events—the discussion of *Romeo and Juliet*, the parent orientation, the students on the hiring committee, the comments about assets on the report cards, the memo accompanying new students, and a multitude of other events reflecting the philosophy of asset building—none of these is a formal *program*. A school doesn't have to have formal asset-building programs to create an environment that encourages asset building. To be sure, New Richmond High School facilitates programs throughout the school and the greater community. But even without these programs, it still would characterize an asset-rich environment. And providing the asset-rich environment in which students can succeed helps fulfill the school's mission.

❦

The Architecture of Schools
Minnetonka, Minnesota
featuring the following assets: Caring School Climate, Bonding to School

Mark Scharenbroich, of Scharenbroich & Associates, an educational consulting firm, is a motivational speaker who's interested in the antecedents of school performance. He has visited schools in every U.S. state and every Canadian province, investigating what contributes to (and what detracts from) an asset-rich environment. One of the things he's noticed is that the architecture of a school often reflects—deliberately or not—an attitude about students. Some schools are intimidating, others friendly; some are cold, others warm. Short of rebuilding, Scharenbroich suggests decorating walls with photographs of role models, projects that students have created, words and pictures and anything else that will foster a connection between student and school. He uses the example of a teenager's bedroom, which is often an extension of that teenager's personality and which is almost always a comfortable, secure place for that teenager to be. How many schools look like places that young people would want to spend a lot of time in? Ask *your* students: What is it about *your* school that welcomes, repels, or even threatens them? What would make it better? Brightly colored walls? Cleaner bathrooms? Plants and pillows in the library?

❧

The Spaceship
Minneapolis, Minnesota
featuring the following assets: Caring School Climate, Adult Role Models, Creative Activities, Youth Programs, Achievement Motivation, School Engagement, Bonding to School

In Minneapolis, Kayleen Bonczek, the principal of Franklin Junior High School—a school that is decidedly not architecturally friendly—likens school to a spaceship. "Kids fuel it," she says, "and then they take off." These days, the 740 students in the school are taking off in a variety of directions. Under the auspices of the YWCA Beacons program, a variety of free after-school activities are available to Franklin students, for example:

- Y Scholars, which matches Franklin students with volunteer student-tutors from the University of Minnesota;
- The Gospel Choir;
- Sisters Who Read, coordinated by a group of women from General Mills, Inc., who select books for girls to read, help them check the books out of the library, and then discuss the books with them;

- Board Games Bonanza, which focuses on not only games but also social interaction, mathematics, and reading skills;
- The Internet club; and
- The Afro-centric Academy—a class focusing on history, math, and English from an African American perspective.

Other programs include an email mentoring partnership with corporations like Reliastar and Norstrand (students learn to use computer software while they're getting valuable information from adults) and Gamma Sigma, which is an exclusively African American version of Girl Scouts (the Girl Scouts of America sponsors the group, which focuses on teaching girls about college life).

One unique program at Franklin is the Junkyard Band. Created and led by music teacher Tim Buzza, the band makes use of a hodgepodge of drum-like percussion instruments, including five-gallon water jugs and dozens of huge plastic pails and buckets. Students learn notation, compose and arrange music, write programs, and study and play rhythms from around the world. Most important, they have a great deal of fun. The band performs nearly 20 times a year in such places as school basketball games, elementary schools, and in a partnership with the St. Paul Chamber Orchestra.

The point here isn't just that Franklin Junior High School has a lot of activities for kids. They do. More important is that the environment at Franklin gives students numerous opportunities to participate, lead, and succeed. That may constitute an attitude greater in the long run than the sum worth of all the individual activities.

❧

The Garden of Assets
Denver, Colorado
featuring the following assets: Caring School Climate, Youth as Resources, Adult Role Models, Positive Peer Influence, Creative Activities, School Engagement, Bonding to School, Responsibility, Planning and Decision Making, Interpersonal Competence, Peaceful Conflict Resolution

Suppose you wanted to impress upon a young student that a virtue—an *asset*—like honesty or integrity had to be nurtured and nourished to grow. What metaphor might you use to get that idea across? Many people would use the metaphor of a seed growing into a plant or flower. At Denison Elementary School in Denver, they go the metaphor one better: Students in this public, Montessori-based school actually *plant* the seeds in their "Virtue Garden." They water the seeds, tend to the growing flowers, and wait expectantly for them to blossom. The Virtue Garden is part of a larger

"Global Garden": Each room in the school has a plot to tend, and shifts are rotated. During any given sunny spring day, you can go out to the garden and see students from kindergarten through sixth grade watering, raking, hoeing, and otherwise operationalizing the assets of Youth as Resources, School Engagement, Bonding to School, Responsibility, Planning and Decision Making, and Interpersonal Competence, among others.

Operationalizing assets is normal for Denison Elementary, one of only a few public Montessori schools in the country. Under the leadership of principal Martha Urioste, psychologist Gayle Hamlett, and nurse Marleen Yaniglos, Denison students experience assets firsthand, whether it's working in the garden, kicking off their shoes and putting on slippers to sit in a circle and discuss the life and philosophy of Gandhi as part of a weeks-long focus on peaceful conflict resolution (the school was recently visited by Dr. Arun Gandhi, Mahatma Gandhi's grandson), or seeing to the needs of some of the pre-kindergarten students who also go to school at Denison.

A visitor to Denison Elementary School can almost immediately see, hear, and feel that the environment is asset-rich. When the students emerge from their buses at about 8:15 in the morning and walk through either of two entrances to the school, many of them are holding hands—frequently, older children with younger children. People are smiling, curious, and welcoming. Music reverberates through the open doors of the gym, over which the sign reads, "Are you ready to play?". A tiny store located just inside the main entrance offers supplies to students; it's also staffed by students. Hamlett says that "the school is like a family," and it's evident in the way students greet "strangers" with a smile, eagerly offer them directions to rooms, and engage them in conversation.

The environment certainly shines through the eyes of Urioste, Hamlett, and Yaniglos: Each of them speaks with a passion about the school, and each of them is instrumental in continually creating the school's special environment. Urioste in particular earnestly recounts her determination to get away from "pathology" and discipline and instead focus on students' strengths and view students as resources. She's even taken that philosophy to the Teacher's Lounge, where, as much to relieve stress as anything else (she seems to have banned stress from the school), she insists that staff relate funny stories involving Denison students instead of getting mired in the latest crisis or perceived failure. It's not a difficult task: The staff is immersed in the Denison philosophy. They're involved in the variety of activities offered by the school, they're involved in supportive relationships with students and with each other; and they're eager to make visitors—whether parents, other community members, or guests from outside the community—welcome.

Denison has results to support its philosophy, too: Students regularly score at or above grade level on the Iowa Test of Basic Skills. The school has repeatedly been cited as one of the 10 best in Denver. And parents volunteer thousands of hours toward working in the school; most of those hours are spent in classrooms.

ᴥ

A Norm of Caring
Aurora, Colorado
featuring the following assets: Caring School Climate, Parent Involvement in Schooling,
Youth as Resources, Safety, School Boundaries, Adult Role Models, Positive Peer Influence,
High Expectations, Achievement Motivation, School Engagement, Bonding to School,
Caring, Integrity, Responsibility, Interpersonal Competence, Cultural Competence,
Peaceful Conflict Resolution, Personal Power

Once upon a time, the story goes, a wild-animal trainer brought in several wolves to show the students at an elementary school. It was usually the case that the wolves, being jittery in the midst of lots of noise and activity, were kept tethered. But in this particular school, the trainer noticed that the wolves were remarkably calm. The atmosphere seemed not frazzled but peaceful; not erratic, but flowing. In music, it would have been the difference between the sharp, pointed bursts of *staccato* and the flowing, easy glides of *legato*. The trainer removed the restraints from the wolves, all the students approached the animals with wonder and joy, and everyone lived happily and unmauled—if not ever after, then at least for that afternoon.

The school is real; the story is true. It's Highline Community School, a 13-acre campus in the Cherry Creek School District, just outside Denver, Colorado. David Fischer is the principal of about 600 students from kindergarten to 5th grade from diverse socioeconomic and cultural backgrounds, and when you walk with him down the light, angular corridors of the school, you sense that he—as well as all the students and adults who greet him warmly as he passes—is glad to be there.

Fischer believes in building assets. He believes in walking his talk, and he believes that he needs to model behavior for school adults as well as students. When he first arrived at Highline, he says, teachers were isolated from one another and in some cases from the students, too. Expectations were low. He began by interviewing all the teachers to determine what they needed and what they wanted. He brought in a consultant and restructured the school into small groups. He began "looping," so that the 2nd- and 3rd-grade students and the 4th- and 5th-grade students now stay with the same teachers for two years. He made it a priority to know every student's name. He reached out to parents, and one of his most recalcitrant detractors gradually became one of his most ardent supporters. He went about establishing a climate of trust and high expectations. Only when he felt that teachers were comfortable with him, with each other, and with the school, did he begin seriously talking the asset-building language.

It seems to have worked. From 1996 to 1998, Highline students' scores on the Iowa Test of Basic Skills went up in reading, language, and math for every grade for every demographic. A "bully-proofing" program has been conceptually expanded from vio-lence reduction to encompass the idea that everyone is responsible for the health of the school. Students are now respected for their strengths and consulted for their input. And incidents of violence have decreased.

In fact, to a visitor accustomed to barely managed chaos in an elementary school, it is almost eerie to walk past open classroom doors and notice that in each classroom, students are attending to their teacher, engaged in work, or otherwise intently con-centrating on an activity. Vicki Temple and Paul Von Essen, respectively psychologist and social worker, are a big part of the change in norms around Highline. They helped institute the concept of what they call a "caring majority," in which it is *expected* that students care about one another.

When a student begins to bully other students in a classroom, for example, the other students don't let themselves be victimized. They challenge the bully, and soon children who insist on being aggressive find that their behavior doesn't work to bring them attention. The norm is that conflicts are settled peacefully, and teach-ers are there to help. The core of the environment at Highline is two-sided, each side complementing the other: on one side, clear boundaries, explicit expectations, and con-sistent consequences for transgressing those boundaries and failing to meet those expectations; on the other side, caring, support, and encouragement. Both sides build assets. And when both sides are accepted as the norm, students prosper. They suc-ceed academically, and they succeed in their relationships with one another. As Angela, a 2nd-grade student, replied when asked why she likes her school, "There's a lot of kids here who want to be your friend."

An example of such norm-changing—and asset building—comes from the activi-ty, facilitated by Temple and Von Essen, in which students recognize each other for having done caring and thoughtful deeds. On one occasion, a boy praised another boy in class for having reached out to a boy with Down's syndrome: When no one else would play with the boy, the classmate took it upon himself to throw him a football and start playing with him. Soon, other students joined in, and the norm of not play-ing with the boy changed to the norm of involving him in their games. Think of all the assets built in just that one boy's acknowledging his classmate.

Highline students also showed caring on the day after a teacher learned that his sister had died. The teacher was gone that day, and Temple and Von Essen led his 5th-grade class through a discussion about sympathy and empathy; besides writing cards to the teacher, the class determined that they would express their sympathy, ask what kind of support he would like, and then offer their support to their teacher.

Fischer tells a story that reflects the power of a simple gesture. In the midst of an event attended by about 100 students and family members, he stopped in front of one of his students to say, "Hi, Rachel," and ask how she was doing. Later in the week, Rachel thanked Fischer with a note that he still has tacked to his office wall.

You couldn't imagine how it felt to be recognized by the principal of the school in front of all those people, she wrote: "I almost burst."

⟡

The Conference
Gillette, Wyoming
featuring the following assets: Positive Family Communication, Parent Involvement
in Schooling, Youth as Resources, High Expectations, Achievement Motivation,
School Engagement, Responsibility, Planning and Decision Making, Personal Power

Danielle Anderson prepares to lead the parent-teacher conference later in the afternoon at Pronghorn Elementary School, in rural Gillette, Wyoming. She knows most of what she's going to say to the teacher, Marianne Baysinger, but she feels she still needs a little work on her conversation with the parent, Bronwen Anderson. The conversation with Bronwen Anderson has to be genuine, not only because she's a health education consultant with the Wyoming Department of Education as well as the Wyoming Community Coalition for Health Education, but also because Bronwen Anderson is Danielle's mother. Danielle is in the second grade.

This is not atypical at Pronghorn. Principal Steve Fenton says that many teachers, chief among them Baysinger and Carolyn Baker, ask students to facilitate the meetings. Students like Danielle rate themselves on how well they fulfilled the goals they set earlier in the year and which assets they feel they're improving. They tell the parents what they can do to help them improve academically. Near the end of the conference, they ask the parent and the teacher if they'd like to discuss anything with them out of the room. It's a prime example of students taking responsibility and using personal power to achieve. It's also a prime example of a school using students as a resource.

⟡

Animal House
Austin, Texas
featuring the following assets: Caring School Climate, Youth as Resources,
School Boundaries, Bonding to School, Caring, Responsibility, Self-Esteem

Cocoa is hungry. So are Cream, Little Bit, and Carrot. Luckily for them, Gullett Elementary School in Austin, Texas, has instituted a program in which they're fed and cared for. Also luckily, it's now a break between classes, and 5th-grade student Holly Meador is approaching the cage. She fills some food bowls and a few water containers, opens the window of the cage, and gently removes each of the ferrets to let them eat and drink.

The four ferrets are not the only animals in the "open" area of the school. They share the attention of the students with turtles, chinchillas, snakes, hedgehogs, and several birds. Janitors clean the aviary, but students are responsible for everything else. Classes rotate the responsibilities to make sure that each animal is cared for—and that each student has an opportunity to care for them.

Taking care of animals is not new to Gullett, and it's not the only program that gives students responsibility: For example, Gullett provides programs in intergenerational gardening, "peer buddies," and safety patrol. But principal Sherrie Raven believes that the animal program is the major reason why attitude problems and behavior problems have diminished in recent years. She perceives that caring for animals is a predecessor as well as a correlate of caring for people, and that kids feel good about themselves when they're involved in being responsible for another life. Even the climate is different, says Raven. "Kids are more relaxed. They walk slower in the halls; they know it's okay to stop and pet an animal."

Raven cites the example of a 4th-grade student who recently transferred into Gullett from a residential treatment center; the boy was diagnosed as both emotionally disturbed and as gifted/talented. "At the beginning of the year," says Raven, "we really didn't know if he would make it here." But then it was discovered that the boy's "most favorite thing in the world" was Gullett's guinea pig, Snowball. Soon, says Raven, the boy's entire behavior plan was built around Snowball: If the boy behaved well, then he could spend extra time with Snowball. If the boy excelled, then he could take Snowball home with him. The result? Raven says that the boy used to be referred to her for disciplinary reasons about once a week, but since initiating the "Snowball" plan over three months ago, he hasn't been referred to her once.

Raven believes that the animal-caring program exemplifies the motto of Gullett Elementary School: "A Living Experience."

✤

"Accidental" Asset Building
St. Louis Park, Minnesota
featuring the following assets: Caring School Climate, Parent Involvement in Schooling, Youth as Resources, Creative Activities, Youth Programs, School Engagement, Bonding to School, Responsibility, Personal Power, Self-Esteem

Les Bork is principal of St. Louis Park Junior High School, grades 7 and 8, in St. Louis Park, Minnesota. He's fond of saying that he "puts systems in place so things happen by accident." What Bork means is that when he establishes a school environment conducive to building assets, then assets will be built—not necessarily by any specific, directed program, but because, as a biologist might put it, the culture is ripe for growth. Here are some policies he's implemented:

- Students have the same teachers for both years.
- Teachers make home visits, about 15 homes for every teacher. Bork says that "We want to come to their house before they come to ours."
- Before students matriculate, they attend a week-long summer camp to explore the school and get information about study habits, campus life, and all the other details that might otherwise mystify and daunt a 7th-grade student.
- Teachers meet as a team for one hour every day to compare notes, plan, and discuss.
- Some students work at an on-site preschool.
- Students are required to take music both years.
- Athletic teams have a no-cut policy: Any student who wants to play on a team can.
- He frequently calls students in to the principal's office not to berate them for some misdeed but to praise them for some achievement. He then calls their parents. The phone call might go something like this: "Hello, Mrs. Dreaney. This is Principal Bork. . . . Yes, I have Cole standing right here next to me, and I'd like to speak to you about him. . . . Yes, he did do something, but it was something very good. His teacher tells me that not only has Cole been doing very well in English, but he's also been helping out the other students in the class. . . . Yes, well, we're very proud of him, too, and I just wanted to let you know that. . . . Thank *you*. Good-bye." Bork clearly relishes such conversations.

Bork believes that people can build assets continually, that school staff in fact are obliged to be "everyday heroes" for their students. He also believes that assessment tools such as Search Institute's *Profiles of Student Life: Attitudes and Behaviors* survey should drive programs. At St. Louis Park Junior High, it's obvious that he's established a climate along those lines.

✿

The Week-Long Student Conference
Aurora, Colorado
featuring the following assets: Other Adult Relationships, Caring School Climate, Youth as Resources, Service to Others, Adult Role Models, Positive Peer Influence, High Expectations, Youth Programs, Achievement Motivation, School Engagement,

Bonding to School, Caring, Responsibility, Planning and Decision Making, Interpersonal Competence, Cultural Competence, Peaceful Conflict Resolution, Personal Power, Self-Esteem, Sense of Purpose

Donna Curtis is counselor and Student Assistance Program coordinator at Overland High School in Cherry Creek School District, Colorado. She is currently sitting in a room listening to about 20 high school students discuss their upcoming week-long prevention conference, a conference based on assets that these same students selected to focus on during the year. The conversation is lively, directed, yet courteous and sensitive, as if these students—despite obvious external differences—really care about each other.

They do. Overland students receive an orientation about asset building when they're freshmen. They promote assets in class, in groups, and at conferences, and they lead by example. They enjoy the role of being a valuable resource, and they're determined to build their own assets—and the assets of their peers—regardless of what the adults in their school do. The actual conference is but a cap to the work these students do throughout the year; the assets they've built for themselves by doing it—Bonding to School, Planning and Decision Making, Interpersonal Competence, Cultural Competence, Peaceful Conflict Resolution, Personal Power, Self-Esteem, Sense of Purpose—are apparent when they speak. "I can feel their power," says Curtis. "I can feel their confidence grow."

Here is part of a letter Curtis and her students send out to potential speakers and sponsors:

> The Youth Advisory Board for Safe and Drug-Free Schools Task Force Committee has been working since early September . . . to plan activities for Substance Abuse Awareness Month. . . . Our theme is "Eye on Overland." Our committee meets every Wednesday, periods 4, 5, and 6 in the Counseling Office Conference Room. We have secured a grant from the Prevention Office and are in the process of seeking community and corporate contributions to fully fund our program. . . .
>
> Our Safe and Drug-Free Schools grant application includes promoting positive youth development by building assets. The committee carefully selected the assets on which they want to focus during the week of April 26–30. The committee has chosen to highlight 10 of the 40 assets: Positive Family Communication, Adult Role Models, Positive Peer Influence, High Expectations, Integrity, Responsibility, Resistance Skills, Personal Power, Self-Esteem, and Sense of Purpose (see attached).
>
> Youth Advisory Board Task Force members are all volunteers. These students are joined by two parent members, two sponsors . . . and other Overland staff volunteers. We need your commitment to help students build assets through participation in the program as a guest speaker and/or sponsorship via individual, business, or corporate funding as soon as possible. We look forward to working with you.

The rest of the letter requests the person's name, phone number, fax number, address, title and brief summary of the planned presentation, brief summary of the person's qualifications, size of audience the person prefers to speak to, and audiovisual equipment needed.

The result is a conference that speaks to and for young people. Here are some of the sessions that were scheduled:

- "Dating Violence and Rights in a Relationship"
- "Finding a Positive Adult Support System"
- "The Importance of Familial Communications"
- "Habitat for Humanity"
- "Simulated DUI Arrest"
- "Dealing with Discrimination"
- "Overcoming Tragedy and Adversity"
- "HIV and Teens: Prevention and Precaution"
- "Anything Is Possible"

Overland is a good example of *intentional* asset building. Curtis initiated the idea of the conference for two reasons: She thought that students would learn valuable life skills by planning and facilitating the conference themselves, and she believed that they should get the opportunity to learn from conferences just as adults do. She was right on both counts. First, students acquire a vast array of skills putting on the conference: They find speakers, fund the program, host the conference, arrange logistics, secure equipment, evaluate the conference, and write a final report. And second, the conference is a tool wielded by students to benefit other students. Most of the students and adults at Overland are aware of assets, they're guided by assets, and they're convinced that building assets benefits everyone in the school community, including themselves. As recent graduate Leonard Aragon-Rogers puts it, "You're helping to build your own assets by being involved. You're putting yourself in the position where you're not just helping other people—you're helping yourself."

The students speculate about teachers who don't seem to be building assets: How were *they* treated as adolescents? The consensus seems to be that teachers who build assets are essentially—excellent teachers. What the students say they want from school adults, though, is what we hear repeated across the breadth of the country: Relate to us. Focus on our strengths. See us as resources.

Create Your Own Stories: Asset-Building Environments

The Story	Some Things You Can Do
"Asset Building Everywhere"	◆ Ask new students to identify which assets they feel strong in and which present a challenge to them.
	◆ Give parents of new students an overview of the asset framework, and show them how they can build assets for their own children.
	◆ Analyze literature from an assets perspective.
	◆ Include students on the team to interview prospective school staff.
"The Architecture of Schools"	◆ Decorate the walls of your school with photographs of role models, projects that students have created, and anything else that will foster a connection between students and their school.
	◆ Invite local design and architecture firms to create a volunteer project of improving the appearance of your school, inside and out.
"The Spaceship"	◆ Provide a variety of activities to meet the needs of all your students.
"The Garden of Assets"	◆ Create a school garden that can be tended by students.
	◆ Create a school store that can be staffed by students and can sell supplies to students.
	◆ Reach out to involve parents as volunteers and as other resources.
"A Norm of Caring"	◆ Initiate "looping," so that students stay with the same teachers for at least two consecutive years.
	◆ Establish peaceful norms.
	◆ Recognize students—and encourage them to recognize each other—for doing caring and thoughtful deeds.
"The Conference"	◆ Have students facilitate parent-teacher-student conferences.
"Animal House"	◆ Provide opportunities for students to take care of animals in the school building.
"'Accidental' Asset Building"	◆ Institute a policy in which teachers make home visits.
	◆ Conduct an extended orientation for matriculating students.
	◆ Conduct teacher conferences every day.
	◆ Institute a no-cut policy for athletic teams.
	◆ Acknowledge students for their achievement, and communicate that to their parents.
"The Week-Long Student Conference"	◆ Give students the opportunity to plan and manage a conference that is based on the asset framework and that features topics of interest to students.

9

ℰ

Using Programs and Practices:

Stories from the Field

As we've mentioned before, many people jump immediately to the category of programs and practices when faced with a problem or a goal. But it's not as simple as that, for a few reasons: First, the goal or "problem" may not be sufficiently defined to be "fixable" or achievable by a program. For example, the possible causes of violence in school are many and varied: cliques and intolerance of different subcultures; perception of fighting as a way to solve problems; lack of self-control; poor management at home and at school; access to weapons; susceptibility to violent messages from media, to name but a few. A single program may not be equipped to address all these antecedents.

Second, a program may not be appropriate for all students. Consider a program designed to help students stay away from drugs. The program needs to appropriately address students with at least the following characteristics:

- Students of various ages and maturity levels;
- Students of both sexes and various sexual orientations;
- Students of different cultural backgrounds;
- Students of different socioeconomic backgrounds;
- Students in urban, suburban, and rural residences; and
- Students with various educational backgrounds in drugs and drug use.

More than that, though, the program needs to address students with different learning styles and abilities. Some students learn best by discussing issues, others by

143

reading, still others by doing projects. Any one program needs to reach as many students as possible, particularly the most vulnerable ones.

The third reason that problems may not be fixable by programs is a very basic one: Even if a program meets all the requirements we just discussed, it still needs to be implemented well. That means dedicated adherence to the way the program is designed. And *that* means training, monitoring, and evaluating. For that reason, the *teacher* is usually the most important component of the effectiveness of a program.

Given all that, are *any* programs and practices effective? Yes, of course; we're going to give you some examples of programs and practices that not only are effective but also help build assets, something that we believe is a higher standard. Some of the programs were designed and administered for very specific purposes; nonetheless, you may be able to adapt them to meet your own circumstances. A few of the programs are commercial products; again, you need to be sure that what you use meets the unique needs of your school community. Some programs have been shown to be very consistent with the developmental assets framework—e.g., *Communities That Care* and *America's Promise*, both of which seek to empower communities and promote positive development.[1]

And then there are the practices: Some practices—less formal than programs, more dependent on the dynamics of the classroom—have been shown to be very effective in achieving the results for which they were intended, when correctly implemented. Here are four examples:

- ◆ Social skills training, which teaches students how to get along with others, resist peer pressure, make decisions, use self-control, and communicate effectively;
- ◆ Cooperative team learning, which helps students achieve academic objectives while working with one another; and
- ◆ Service-learning, which gives students the experience of contributing to their communities while learning about various topics as well as themselves, and also sets up role models for students to emulate.

You can use any of these practices to build assets: You can teach students a conflict resolution skill (Peaceful Conflict Resolution). You can form cooperative learning teams in a classroom and assign students roles like facilitator, timekeeper, and reporter (Achievement Motivation, Responsibility). You can suggest that students try to persuade local businesses to adopt tough no-smoking rules (Youth as Resources, Caring, Personal Power), and you can also ask students who their heroes or "most unforgettable people" are and then discuss which qualities make those people special (Equality and Social Justice, Integrity, Honesty).

What follows are some of the programs and practices we've seen throughout the country that help students to build assets. Before you use *any* program or practice, however, think once more about intentionality: How is the program or practice helping your students to experience more assets?

✤

Assets and the Civics Lesson
Glenwood Springs, Colorado
featuring the following assets: Other Adult Relationships, Caring School Climate, Community Values Youth, Youth as Resources, Service to Others, Adult Role Models, Positive Peer Influence, High Expectations, Creative Activities, Youth Programs, Achievement Motivation, School Engagement, Bonding to School, Caring, Integrity, Responsibility, Planning and Decision Making, Interpersonal Competence, Cultural Competence, Peaceful Conflict Resolution, Personal Power, Self-Esteem, Sense of Purpose

"I'm more appreciated by the adults in my community," says Tracy Roseman, an 11th-grade student at Glenwood Springs High School in Colorado. She's talking about her participation in a "Fundamentals of American Democracy" class that's guided by the asset framework. The students meet to research, select, analyze, find solutions for, and implement a plan to solve a problem, resolve an issue, or build an asset in their community. They link up with community agencies, and they even have a modest budget. Just recently they hired a consultant to train their teachers on different learning styles.

Advisor Manette Anderson is understandably proud of her students and the work they've done. "Kids taking on these projects is a very effective way to not only build assets," says Anderson, "but build academic skills as well." Danielle Seymour knows about that. A member of Anderson's class, she formed a group of 22 high school mentors who work with teachers and students at both of the area's elementary schools. They help students struggling with literacy, and they also act as powerful role models. "All they have to do is say, 'That's not cool,'" says Anderson, "and the misbehaving stops." And Seymour has seen the effect on her classmates: "It gives them this great thing to be part of, and that's when you see them turn into this awesome tutor and mentor."

Anderson's students have accomplished other things, too. For over three years, they've worked with city planners, downtown business owners, and other community members to raise $50,000 and get permission to build a downtown pedestrian mall. For that enterprise, they won the Colorado Day Philanthropy Award for Youth Leadership and then the national Point of Light award.

Activities like these benefit at least three distinct groups. The first group is the people being helped by the high school students: the 3rd-grade students gain mentors, the teachers get a valuable in-service, and the community benefits in numerous ways, depending on the project undertaken by the students. The second group that benefits is of course the students themselves. Again, Manette Anderson: "Kids we haven't seen as the 'best' students have taken on leadership roles . . . Their talents are emerging." And the third group that benefits are those people in the community who are starting to change their stereotypical feelings about teenagers as do-nothings—except when they're making trouble.

The students' enthusiasm is boundless. Next on the agenda: writing and performing a two-act play about a world without assets and a world with assets. Students build their own assets while delivering the message to their audience.

⚜

Skills
University Place, Washington
featuring the following assets: Caring School Climate, Safety, School Engagement, Integrity, Responsibility, Planning and Decision Making, Interpersonal Competence, Resistance Skills, Peaceful Conflict Resolution, Personal Power, Positive View of Personal Future

Quincy Cook teaches 7th grade in a school just outside Tacoma, Washington. She's a great believer in teaching her students skills—academic skills, like how to take notes, how to work from an agenda, and how to take tests; and social skills, like how to use self-control, how to resist peer pressure, and how to resolve conflicts peacefully.

"It makes kids feel the power they have," says Cook, who tells the story of two students who were so impressed with learning the skills in a violence-prevention curriculum called *Get Real about Violence* that they wanted to share their experiences with younger students. One of the students had been "on the edge" of joining a gang. Learning to resist pressure from his friends made him realize that he was empowered *not* to join the gang.

Cook also uses cooperative learning teams in her classroom. Cook says that learning how to cooperate in groups not only helps students work together but also pushes them to figure out how the group will accomplish a task. "Even if there's a 'weak link,'" she says, "what are they going to do?"

Cook smiles when she thinks of the 7th-grade student who approached her recently by saying, "This is the perfect time to be teaching us these things." Why? "Because," he said, "we're starting to make all these choices that will affect us the rest of our lives."

⚜

Kids Leading Kids

Avalon, New Jersey

featuring the following assets: Caring School Climate, Community Values Youth,
Youth as Resources, Positive Peer Influence, High Expectations, Creative Activities,
Youth Programs, Caring, Responsibility, Interpersonal Competence, Cultural
Competence, Peaceful Conflict Resolution, Personal Power, Self-Esteem

Avalon Elementary School is a small school in rural New Jersey, with only 132 students in grades 1–8. Chief School Administrator Ron Bonner wanted to do something to help his students get along better with each other. He entered into a partnership with Cynthia Sosnowski of the Cape May County Health Community Coalition and Linda Conover of Cape Assist. Sosnowski showed Avalon teachers how they could use the asset framework to foster more respectful relationships among the students, and she, Conover, and Bonner designed a program focusing on older students teaching skills to younger students.

The program worked like this: All school staff participated in an outdoor experiential learning activity called a "Low Ropes" course. Students from grades 6, 7, and 8 then took the same course. Students from grades 5 learned the same kind of cooperative skills by visiting a county park and taking a similar course. All these students—from grades 5 through 8—then met for several months with leaders from Cape Assist to discuss what they learned: how to work together as teams, how to accomplish tasks, how to delegate responsibility, how to assume leadership. Peer leaders were chosen to oversee teams of five or six students to design a challenge—"The Avalon Challenge"—for the younger students, those in grades 1 to 4. On "Challenge Day," the younger students rotated through experiential cooperative-team activities facilitated by the older students. Finally, the older students debriefed, discussing what they learned from the entire experience.

Who benefited from this program? Everyone benefited. Older students learned firsthand that some of their classmates they might have previously ignored or even derided had much to contribute. Younger students got a healthy dose of cooperative team learning. Teachers and staff learned how to incorporate building assets into their routines. And the original goal—helping students get along better with each other—was met and sustained. The task now, says Bonner, who was impressed with students' insights about their experiences, is to keep the effort going, to help teachers incorporate cooperative activities into their routine, and to continue to build assets.

Community Night

Minneapolis, Minnesota

featuring the following assets: Other Adult Relationships, Caring Neighborhood, Caring School Climate, Community Values Youth, Adult Role Models, Creative Activities, Youth Programs, Responsibility, Interpersonal Competence, Cultural Competence, Self-Esteem

The larger community is a critical component in building assets in school communities. Principal Sue Thomas and Community Education Specialist Hedy Walls coordinate community activities at Northeast Middle School in Minneapolis. They believe that their students need to feel a part of several communities, and for that reason they bring in as much of the community around the school *into* the school in as many ways as possible. Twice a month is "Community Night," and families are bused in from a wide radius around the school. Perhaps the highlight of Community Night is a performance of the 70-member community band—people of all ages, colors, backgrounds, and experiences making music together.

It's more than just an apt metaphor for community. It's an example of how young people need to see, hear, and feel caring, positive, consistent messages repeatedly from a host of sources.

Walls also heads up the Helping Youth Promote Empowerment (HYPE) Council, local teenagers who regularly allocate state funds to nonprofit organizations with youth-driven and youth-run initiatives. Walls says that for years all funding had been allocated by an adult committee: "All of a sudden, we asked ourselves, where are the kids?" That insight led them, she says, to tell the adults, "'Thank you very much, but we don't need you anymore.' It was time to involve the youth."

⚹

SPARK

New Richmond, Wisconsin

featuring the following assets: Caring School Climate, Youth as Resources, Service to Others, Positive Peer Influence, High Expectations, Achievement Motivation, School Engagement, Caring, Responsibility, Planning and Decision Making, Sense of Purpose

Earlier in this book, we described New Richmond High School, in New Richmond, Wisconsin, saying that even without programs, it still would be characterized as an asset-rich environment. New Richmond does have programs and practices, though, that bear mentioning. One is SPARK, which stands for Supportive Peers As Resources for Knowledge. SPARK is a service club, according to its brochure, "committed to developing assets in youth by helping them reach their academic potential." The goal of SPARK is to give young people useful roles as peer tutors and improve school performance. Students can be referred by parents, teachers, and themselves, but they must have at least a 2.75 grade point average and at least a B in the class they're tutoring. They're also required to take six hours of training. Peer tutoring accomplishes many objectives, and often the tutor gets as much out of the activity as the tutee.

New Richmond does have other programs and practices. In fact, in preparation for a visiting film crew making a video about building assets in school communities, the Healthy Communities • Healthy Youth team compiled a list of asset-building activities within the school. The total was 103.

✦

Books and Hot Chocolate
Portland, Oregon
featuring the following assets: Family Support, Other Adult Relationships, Caring School Climate, Parent Involvement in Schooling, Adult Role Models, High Expectations, School Engagement, Reading for Pleasure, Self-Esteem

The spring 1999 issue of *Assets* magazine features a story about teacher Janet Muller's 3rd-grade class at Duniway Elementary School in Portland, Oregon. On the second Wednesday evening of every month, Muller, her 25 students, and the students' parents, all sit down at the Dragon's Breath Café to read and discuss books, drink hot chocolate and eat cookies. The idea, says Muller, was to create a positive environment for students who have difficulty reading: "They take these little kids out, isolate them from the other students, and put them in lower reading groups. I thought it would be great for them if just once, they could be like everyone else and be reading the same book."

There are obviously other advantages to this little program: The families grow closer, and the kids enjoy the interaction with their peers. Muller claims she knows what makes for success. "There is a clear definition between a successful student and an unsuccessful student," she says. "That's an adult who cares."

✦

Youth in Charge
Hampton, Virginia
featuring the following assets: Youth as Resources, Service to Others, Safety, School Boundaries, Positive Peer Influence, High Expectations, Youth Programs, Planning and Decision Making, Interpersonal Competence, Peaceful Conflict Resolution, Personal Power, Self-Esteem, Sense of Purpose

Hampton, Virginia, is an asset-building community. It wasn't always so. Hampton used to see its youth as problems: They were too violent, too dependent on drugs, too *something*. They were viewed as deficits, not as resources.

But things changed. In the 1990s alone, Hampton has created one of the most progressive and thorough citywide youth empowerment programs in the country. And the schools in Hampton are a reflection of the larger community. The newspaper *Youth Today* describes some of the schools' achievements in its December/January 1999 issue: "School superintendent William Cannaday uses youth committees to help craft school policies. When the schools wanted to change the absentee policy several years ago because 46 percent of all 7th- to 12th-grade students missed more than 10 days of school, the students came up with an idea to encourage attendance. Now students who earn A's and B's and who miss only certain numbers of days each year are exempt from finals. Currently, Cannaday says, only 26 percent of the students miss more than 10 days."

A student group at Phoebus High School is another example of changing attitudes. They formed the Phoebus High Action Team to determine issues to address during the school year. Last year, they worked on the Safety asset—specifically on the relationship between students and faculty. The result was a decrease in suspensions. They're also making connections with other schools. Teams of eight adults and students will come from each school to a summer asset-building workshop, during which they'll select assets to focus on for their respective schools.

Hampton's success is characterized by an attitude, an attitude that became a norm. The attitude is that young people have strengths and that they are resources. As one teenager said, "We're not broken. Don't try to fix us."

⚹

Natural Helpers
Newton, North Carolina

featuring the following assets: Other Adult Relationships, Caring School Climate, Community Values Youth, Youth as Resources, Service to Others, Safety, Adult Role Models, Positive Peer Influence, High Expectations, Youth Programs, Bonding to School, Caring, Honesty, Responsibility, Restraint, Planning and Decision Making, Interpersonal Competence, Cultural Competence, Resistance Skills, Peaceful Conflict Resolution, Personal Power, Self-Esteem, Sense of Purpose, Positive View of Personal Future

It was nine years ago when Melanie Elrod got a call from the North Carolina Department of Social Services. "What are you teaching your kids?" was the pointed question. "Um, what do you mean?" responded Elrod. Apparently, the department was suddenly receiving numerous referrals from the high school students in Elrod's school—mainly, referrals of child abuse. Because the students were asking all the right questions and providing all the right information, the department was wondering how they knew to make referrals. "They were amazed," says Elrod today, "that the kids were doing everything so properly."

What Elrod was teaching her kids was the *Natural Helpers* program, a peer-helping program that serves students in grades 6–12 who want to strengthen their communication and helping skills and who want to provide support to others and service to their schools and communities.

The program is based on a simple premise: Within every school, an informal "helping network" exists. When young people seek help, they usually do so from one source in particular—their friends. The program uses this existing helping network; it provides training to students and adults who are already perceived as "natural" helpers. It gives them skills to provide help more effectively to the young people who seek them out. The goals of the program are for students to help each other with little problems before they grow and to refer serious problems—such as child abuse, chemical dependency, and violence—to trained professionals.

The key to the effectiveness of *Natural Helpers* is its selection process. Everyone in the school—students and all school adults—simultaneously completes a survey that, among other things, asks students to name two adults and two students at the school they trust and with whom they feel comfortable talking about a personal problem. The names are tallied and then designated to the appropriate subgroups prevalent in the school, e.g., "band students," "athletes," various ethnic groups, and so on. The people selected to be prospective Natural Helpers then have two things in common: They're trusted by their friends, and they represent a subgroup in the school. Thus, theoretically, at least one helper is "naturally" accessible to everyone in the school community.

As student services coordinator at Newton-Conover City Schools, Elrod has coordinated the program for a decade; in fact, she says, it's the longest-running program in the district. She knows hundreds of students who have benefited from the program and who have helped others. "They even put it on their resumes," she says, "when they apply to be resident assistants at college. The skills they learn in the program help them to be more responsible."

The program helps them to be more sensitive, too. Elrod recalls a retreat training in which one of the participants was a boy with a police record. "It was probably the first time this boy was part of a school function," she says. And who among the other participants did the boy befriend? "The school valedictorian and the 'delinquent' hit it off," says Elrod. "Those two would never have talked if it weren't for the program. They would never have crossed the lines of their peer groups." The training marked a turning point for the boy with the police record. Today he's a responsible member of the community who has a family and a good job. "I've seen kids that had everything against them," says Elrod. She believes that becoming Natural Helpers has helped them feel good about helping others and given them a new sense of purpose. Elrod also says that, invariably, she is asked one question at the conclusion of the trainings: "Why don't you teach this to our parents?"

≈

The Adopted Bus Stop
St. Louis Park, Minnesota
featuring the following assets: Caring Neighborhood, Neighborhood Boundaries

Some asset-building programs have surprising origins. Karen Atkinson, coordinator of Children First in St. Louis Park, Minnesota, relates the story of several elderly women in the community who have "adopted a bus stop." They watch over the children waiting for their buses, they resolve conflicts, and they even bring children into their homes when it's raining. This "program" began with one or two women, and over the years it's grown so that there are bus-stop watchers all along the school routes.

Atkinson loves stories like this, because it reinforces her philosophy about how to operationalize assets. The St. Louis Park initiative was begun in 1993, and core-team member Atkinson believes in decentralization. "I empower asset builders," she says. When people in various sectors of the community ask her how they should build assets, she replies, "I don't know. What do *you* think?" That's how to get buy-in. That's how to get people emotionally and intellectually connected to the asset-building initiative. "The problems occur," says Atkinson, "only when we tell people what to do."

≈

The Listening Post
Carmel, Indiana
featuring the following assets: Other Adult Relationships, Caring School Climate

If you're in the lunchroom at Carmel High School, Carmel, Indiana, you'll see more than students. Every day you'll see several members of the community talking with students, listening to their issues, trying to tend to their needs. It's a program called Listening Post, and it's based on listening to students rather than telling them what to do. Here are some of the guidelines for the program:

- Student participation is voluntary.
- Listening Post volunteers work with students' personal matters and leave school matters to school staff.
- Listening Post volunteers provide feedback as needed to the school liaison.

- In cases of crisis or other serious matters—e.g., drug dependency, depression, or abuse—Listening Post volunteers inform the appropriate school personnel immediately.
- Confidentiality is honored in all matters not prescribed by the law.

The program can be summarized by the attitudes it sets out to engender in its volunteers:

1. Be yourself.
2. Be present.
3. Be a good listener.
4. Be consistent.
5. Be honest.
6. Be patient.
7. Be encouraging.
8. Be a role model.

> Above all, believe in young people. If we can help kids believe that we believe in them, they will start to believe in themselves.

Kevin Rowe, student assistance program coordinator at Carmel Clay Schools, sees great benefits from the program. First of all, he says, it shows students that people care about them. And second, he's been able to identify some potential suicides from reports of the Listening Post volunteers. That in itself, he says, has made the program worthwhile.

✦

Giraffes

Langley, Washington—and all over the world

featuring the following assets: Other Adult Relationships, Youth as Resources, Service to Others, Adult Role Models, High Expectations, Caring, Equality and Social Justice, Integrity, Honesty, Responsibility, Planning and Decision Making, Interpersonal Competence, Personal Power, Self-Esteem, Sense of Purpose, Positive View of Personal Future

Although asset building is not in itself a program, many programs and practices used around the country are consistent with the developmental assets framework: They give students opportunities to build assets, and they vest a lot of control in the students themselves. One such program is the Giraffe Project, out of Langley, Washington. The Giraffe Project is based on telling the stories of people who have "stuck their necks out for the common good," people who are courageous, people who are heroes—people who are "Giraffes." The philosophy of the Giraffe project is that by telling the stories of people like these, especially to students, others will emulate them.

Besides identifying and honoring such people, the Giraffe Project has developed and distributes a K–12 character education/service-learning program. This in turn has spawned a multitude of student projects from around the country—and from other countries, too—that have no doubt raised the levels of several assets, especially the Positive-Values assets of Caring, Equality and Social Justice, and Responsibility:

- Some of the service projects initiated by Mike Shannon's economics students at Foster High School in Tukwila, Washington, include doing a highway cleanup, organizing an after-school basketball tournament for younger kids, helping an elementary school teacher do a kids' tree planting on Arbor Day, teaching English as a second language, and making anti-gang presentations to 5th-grade students.
- In Tampa, Florida, at Twin Lakes Elementary School, 1st-grade students found that a classmate was diagnosed with leukemia. They determined to keep him involved in their service project, which was to collect books for a new children's hospital. Using two computers donated by a local phone company, the boy attended class electronically, and his classmates kept informed of his progress. He made it in person to the celebration at the end of the project. Thus, the students illustrated positive values in both their original service project and in their caring for their fellow student.
- At Doyle Elementary School in San Diego, 5th- and 6th-grade students painted trash cans for recycling, made posters urging people to recycle juice boxes, and placed the posters in the windows of stores in a nearby shopping mall.
- In Bostic, North Carolina, community volunteers were invited to speak about their work. Program Director Wanda Page says that the children were so impressed with the speaker from a local hospice that they "adopted" hospice patients and went on to adopt elders at a nursing home.
- In Winchester, New Hampshire, 7th-grade students at Thayer Junior/Senior High School designed and carried out a voter registration drive. They persuaded the city council to hold the drive, handed out flyers announcing it, canvassed the community, and by election day had registered over 200 new voters, many of them their own parents.

What more could you ask for than the response of a 4th-grade student in Ohio: "I really am having fun helping the world."

The Entrepreneurs Who Aren't Allowed to Fail

Denver, Colorado

featuring the following assets: Caring School Climate, Youth as Resources, Service to Others, School Boundaries, Adult Role Models, Positive Peer Influence, High Expectations, Creative Activities, Youth Programs, Achievement Motivation, School Engagement, Bonding to School, Responsibility, Planning and Decision Making, Interpersonal Competence, Cultural Competence, Personal Power, Self-Esteem, Sense of Purpose, Positive View of Personal Future

We started this book with a scene from an "asset-rich" school, the school where Giovanny DeLeon works on her vinyl letters—Mitchell Elementary School in Denver. The vinyl-letter program is called SPELL, for Students Producing Educational Letters in Learning. The letters are available by custom order and in "Word Wall" packages—groups of words designed to help build knowledge of a subject-specific vocabulary, such as music, sports, technology, career, or theater. The letters can be made in many different sizes, colors, and fonts. But the SPELL program is only a very small part of the Mitchell Elementary curriculum.

Mitchell Elementary School first opened its doors as a neighborhood school in August 1996; prior to that, it was a Montessori magnet program. Today, Mitchell is a model school for anyone who wants to serve neighborhood children. From the school's own archives, compiled by principal Lynn Spampinato: "It is a program built on a strong belief that all children, given high standards, support, and a relevant curriculum with active application of learning, can and will succeed. The goal, to prepare children to live freely, successfully, and independently in the highly technical world of the future, became the foundation of learning at the new Mitchell."

The Denver neighborhoods that surround Mitchell pose great challenges for Mitchell's students. For example, 96 percent of the students are eligible for free lunch programs. Crime, gang activity, and drug abuse are all prevalent. But Mitchell itself is a neighborhood—a caring, productive neighborhood, in its own way every bit as demanding as the neighborhoods outside its walls. Some features of this school community:

- Four K-5 teams move through four vertical curriculum strands: library and technology, arts, school-to-career, and wellness. The grades are "looped": Students stay in the same classrooms with the same teachers for kindergarten-grade 1, grades 2 and 3, and grades 4 and 5.
- Every classroom has a computer and a printer. Every class is connected to email and the Internet, including a home page linked to the public library.
- School is open year-round, with four breaks, none of which is longer than four weeks. The first quarter of school begins at the end of July.

This schedule results in 20 more school days per year—a total of 195—than a traditional schedule, and it was overwhelmingly approved by the local community. The schedule also includes six additional planning days for staff and one more paid holiday.

- Instruction relies on team teaching, multi-age grouping, and integrated technology.
- Some of the classes are same-sex only.
- Some of the learning processes used are the Lindamood-Bell Learning Process (phonemic sequencing focusing on decoding, visualizing and verbalizing to focus on comprehension, and symbol imagery focusing on encoding and high-frequency words) and Problem-Based Learning.
- Special education teachers are assigned to specific classrooms and team-teach with the regular classroom teachers.
- Core subjects are taught all day in Spanish, with ESL as a component for English language development. English transition rooms are in place at grades 3, 4, and 5.
- Parents who repeatedly attend school events have been eligible to win prizes like a trip to Disneyland; the prizes are donated by businesses.
- An adult education program offers daily classes from 2:45 PM to 6:30 PM, with free day care.
- Student-led conferences with teachers and parents help students take responsibility for their own learning and teach them organizational skills. Not only do they facilitate the conference, but they also complete a self-assessment ("things I do well" and "things to work on").
- Students at Mitchell can participate in a number of entrepreneurial and career-track programs. For example, besides the SPELL program, there is the teacher-supplies warehouse, in which students are given a budget and asked to store, take orders for, and deliver (usually by pulling a red wagon through the halls) supplies to classrooms; the store, which sells school materials—e.g., pencils, pads, book covers—to students, and which is staffed by students; and the Mitchell Mart, where students sell some of the flowers and vegetables they've grown in their own garden behind the school.

Virtually every great school has a great leader, and for Mitchell, Lynn Spampinato has been that leader. Spampinato built the "new" Mitchell from the ground up, hiring her entire staff and spearheading the design of the curriculum and the environment that envelops it. As you might expect, she has a lot to say about Mitchell, and she's justifiably proud of the academic progress her students have made in the past few years. But maybe Mitchell's success can best be summed up by something Spampinato says with force and conviction: "We simply will not let our students fail."

That, as much as anything, is a core statement about building assets. *"We simply will not let our students fail."* We will set high standards, we will use students' own strengths, and we will make sure they succeed.

Notes

1. White, J. (1999). Bridging frameworks: Linking assets to other youth development models. *Assets* Magazine, Spring 1999, pp. 10–11.

Create Your Own Stories: Asset-Building Programs and Practices

The Story	Some Things You Can Do
"Assets and the Civics Lesson"	◆ Encourage students to solve problems or build assets in their community.
	◆ Give students the opportunity to create activities relating to the asset framework.
"Skills"	◆ Teach students social skills so they can use self-control, resist peer pressure, resolve conflicts peacefully, make good decisions, and generally stay safe and healthy.
	◆ Incorporate cooperative learning teams in classrooms.
"Kids Leading Kids"	◆ Use cross-age teaching strategies.
"Community Night"	◆ Reach out to families by offering bus service to the school to participate in activities that interest them.
	◆ Establish a youth council who can allocate money for youth-centered projects.
"SPARK"	◆ Establish a youth club that can pair up peer tutors with students who need assistance.
"Books and Hot Chocolate"	◆ Start a reading club for students and their parents.
"Youth in Charge"	◆ Involve students in setting school policies and focusing on assets to build during the year.
"Natural Helpers"	◆ Institute a peer-helping program that involves all students in the school community.
	◆ Encourage students to refer serious problems to trained professionals.
	◆ Encourage students to break down barriers between different cultures.
"The Adopted Bus Stop"	◆ Encourage people in both the school community and in the greater community to create their own ways to build assets.
"The Listening Post"	◆ Ask for volunteers from the community to act as "good listeners" to students.
"Giraffes"	◆ Encourage students to perform service projects for their community.
	◆ Encourage students to identify and emulate heroes.
"The Entrepreneurs Who Aren't Allowed to Fail"	◆ Start "businesses" that can be managed by students and that will benefit the school.
	◆ Arrange the school year to maximize opportunities for education.
	◆ Incorporate team teaching with regular and special education teachers, multi-age grouping, and integrated technology.
	◆ Offer prizes that can be donated by businesses to motivate parents to participate in school events.

10

꙰

Sustaining the Change

Let's agree on one thing at the start: No school is ever going to reach the point where its leaders can honestly say, "We've brought every student up to 100 percent on each of the 40 developmental assets." Just as it takes continual heat to keep water boiling, it takes continual effort to keep students' asset levels where we'd like to see them. Because students, teachers, administrators, and support staff are constantly entering the school system, because they have new needs and new strengths, and because they interact with everyone else in the school community, any snapshot of a school is quickly outdated. When we agree on those points, then the conclusion is clear: The "work" of building assets is never done.

As you've read through these pages, you've no doubt noted that many of the people whom we cited as being asset builders *don't think of it as work*, and certainly not as extra work. When we discussed relationships with Helene Perry, the Minneapolis teacher who "lives the assets," she said that she treats her students the way she wanted to be treated when she was a student. When we discussed school environment with Marilyn Peplau, the counselor in New Richmond, Wisconsin, she implied that she was "merely" making her school into the kind of school she always thought a school should be. And when we discussed programs and practices with Cindy Carlson, the director of the Hampton Coalition for Youth, she said that the city started making positive changes to "make sure we were raising the kids to be a part of this workforce, rather than sucking up all of its resources."

Perry, Peplau, Carlson, and many others cited in this book began building assets for young people before they ever heard of assets. Once they did become acquainted with the asset framework, they felt empowered by the language, validated by the research, and relieved by the realization that they weren't alone. The framework was just that to them—a kind of skeletal structure that gave shape to their efforts and that they could "flesh out" with behaviors, attitudes, values, programs, activities, policies, procedures, and relationships, some new and some they'd already been experiencing or creating. It provided them with a focus, a direction—a way to use their relationships with young people to build assets.

The question remains, though, "How can you sustain your relationships, your school environments, your programs and practices?" We think you can do it in several ways:

- You continually evaluate what you're doing and make the appropriate adjustments.
- You continually inform, train, and guide people—including yourself—in the work of building assets.
- You continually work at changing the norms by incorporating the asset philosophy into everything you do.

Let's briefly examine each of these components.

Evaluation

No matter how large or small your efforts, whether you're talking about the intimacies and complexities of a relationship or the myriad permutations of a schoolwide program's effects on a group of students, you need to look at three basic questions:

- What are we doing?
- How are we doing?
- What is the connection between what we're doing and how we're doing?

Apart from those three important questions, one of the real benefits of evaluation is often overlooked. Evaluation is perceived by many people as a report card: You excelled, you passed, or you failed. But report cards do more than just present judgments; they can point the way to improvement. So it is with evaluations. The true worth of an evaluation is measured not only by how much it documents positive change but also by how much it *contributes* to positive change. Set up your evaluations so you can benefit from the information you gather.

Just as asset building is everyone's responsibility, so should everyone be involved in evaluating it. Ask all school staff, students, parents, and community partners what they see going on, what changes they think have occurred because of asset building, what they think should be done differently to build assets. Add those impressions to the more formal data you might collect, as well as records, anecdotes, and your own observations. Keep sharing the results with everyone. Asset building is not an exact science; you'll need to make course adjustments in your journey. And the best way to make adjustments is to base your changes on valid, reliable information.

Ultimately, you're also interested in the question, "What's in the way of our doing better?" The information you collect will be of little practical value if it doesn't lead to real changes and an ongoing commitment to doing even better.[1] For example, suppose you find out from your own surveys that a significant portion of students are feeling disenfranchised, unconnected to school. Further, you discover that a significant portion of *those* students are special education students. It's not enough to say, in effect, "We've identified some pieces of the picture to improve." What remains is to determine how to change the relationships, the environment, and the programs and practices to bring special education students into the fold, to make them feel as bonded to and as engaged in school as possible.

What Are We Doing

Determining the answer to "What are we doing?" depends on how carefully you've set up monitoring. Can you replicate what you've done? If you want to determine whether using cooperative teams, "looping" so that students stay in the same classroom with the same teacher for two or more years, and team-teaching produce more school engagement, then you need to know exactly how the cooperative teams, the looping, and the team-teaching were established and facilitated. In essence, you need to find out whether asset building is really happening in your school, and how faithfully the actions individuals are taking actually adhere to the assumptions and principles of asset building (such as a focus on all youth, not just "well-behaved" or "at-risk" youth).

What are individual teachers, administrators, and other staff doing to build assets in your school? What are students doing? Does everyone hold a common understanding of what asset building means and what it implies for personal actions? What steps are being taken in curriculum and instruction, school organization, cocurricular programs, community partnerships, and support services to bring the asset philosophy to life? Asking staff, students, and parents about these questions; observing classes, lunchrooms, hallways, and other campus areas; and analyzing staff meeting minutes, grant applications, and other records all can give you an idea of what you're doing.

In this chapter, we've included two additional ways (Handouts 10.1 and 10.2) of assessing what you're doing. Using the first tool, "Where Are We Now? Asset-Building Culture Shift Assessment for Schools," with any group of school adults, you

Where Are We Now? Asset-Building Culture Shift Assessment for Schools

Think about your school today. Circle where you think your school is on the following dimensions. The closer you are to 5, the more your school is making the culture shifts in thinking and action that are characteristic of a deep commitment to asset building.

1. We focus on naming youth problems that should be fixed.

1. We focus on enhancing young people's positive development.

    1   2   3   4   5

2. We focus most of our energy and resources either on troubled youth or on high-achieving youth.

2. We distribute our energy and resources to benefit all students.

    1   2   3   4   5

3. We emphasize age- and grade-specific opportunities.

3. We promote frequent cross-age contacts, among students and between students and adults.

    1   2   3   4   5

4. We each take care of our "own" students, not other teachers' or staff's students.

4. All staff understand and act on their responsibility to take care of all students.

    1   2   3   4   5

5. We emphasize formal programs and curricula in our work with students.

5. We emphasize the informal supportive relationships we have with students.

    1   2   3   4   5

6. Staff in different departments or positions have different visions for young people's healthy development.

6. All staff are committed to a common vision of young people's healthy development.

    1   2   3   4   5

7. Students in this school are exposed to conflicting and inconsistent messages about what is important and valued.

7. Students in this school are exposed to consistent messages about what is important and valued.

    1   2   3   4   5

8. We try to be efficient in this school and not offer too many programs that duplicate each other.

8. Students are provided with multiple opportunities to build the same developmental assets.

    1   2   3   4   5

> **Where Are We Now? Asset-Building**
> **Culture Shift Assessment for Schools (cont.)**

9. Students do not feel valued at this school.			9. Students are treated as valuable resources at this school.	
1	2	3	4	5

10. At this school, we tend to shift our focus from issue to issue, depending on what is fashionable.			10. At this school, we have a long-term commitment to building students' developmental assets.	
1	2	3	4	5

11. At this school, most staff and students aren't involved in major decisions about the quality of our school life.			11. At this school, most staff and students are involved in major decisions about the quality of our school life.	
1	2	3	4	5

12. At this school, we focus on how school personnel and programs can promote students' learning and growth.			12. At this school, we engage parents and other individuals and organizations from the community in promoting students' learning and growth.	
1	2	3	4	5

can quickly learn whether they see fundamental "culture shifts" occurring that indicate the school is moving collectively toward real commitment to the asset-building philosophy. Using the second tool, "Are We an Asset-Building School Community?," you can get a more comprehensive perspective of the degree to which school staff think asset building is currently reflected in your relationships, environment, and programs and practices. This tool allows you to match priorities (things that are important in your school culture) with practice (what you're doing and how well you're doing). You can look at the gap to discover areas that are highly important but where your school doesn't seem to be doing as well as it needs to.

It's important to point out, though, that these are not "research" instruments; they haven't been validated, and no statistical studies have shown them to be "reliable." These can, however, be very useful learning tools or aids for discussion and planning. The staff in your school community will then be able to interpret the information you get from these learning tools and what the results suggest about how to change and improve what you're doing.

How Are We Doing?

Determining the answer to "How are we doing?" is far more complex. It starts with making sure you've identified your hoped-for outcomes clearly, and that those outcomes can realistically be affected by asset-building efforts in the time span you're examining. For example, if you make a commitment to doing asset building in the second quarter, and you hope for students' mean Grade Point Average to be higher in the third quarter because of what you're doing, you've set up an unrealistic goal. On the other hand, if you hope to see a greater proportion of students thinking they have a caring school climate, and you look at your progress over the course of a whole school year, that's an outcome that may be possible to achieve and document.

For several reasons, administering the Search Institute *Profiles of Student Life: Attitudes and Behaviors* survey at regular intervals—say, every year or two—is insufficient to determine whether what you did brought about any changes, nor is it a way of adequately measuring an individual student's progress. Although a longitudinal study is currently under way in Colorado, the survey in normal use is scored anonymously, so individual students can't be tracked. In addition, reports of some of the assets, such as Self-Esteem, tend to be very stable in most adolescents, and levels don't show much meaningful change under most circumstances. Responses to some survey items are likely to change as a predictable result of normal adolescent development. For example, more 12th-grade students will have sexual intercourse than 6th- or 8th-grade students, regardless of whether you do asset building, simply because of their increasing age and maturation. Surveying students every few years can give you a series of portraits of your school's student body, though, and can provide some indications of where efforts are working and where they need to be intensified.

What may make the most sense is to use that survey and other tools selectively, based on *what* you're doing, to give clues about *how* you're doing. For example, if you're focusing on the assets that we outlined in Chapter 3 as the ones most directly affecting academic success, then you may want to target your evaluation efforts toward understanding how those particular areas may have been affected. Your district research and evaluation specialist, local college researchers, and Search Institute can all provide helpful guidance. In addition, you can use grades, standardized test scores, attendance and behavior referral records, teacher observations, parent observations, self-assessments, and a host of both quantitative and qualitative tools—some of which you can develop yourself—to give you increasingly clearer pictures of your students' progress. Ultimately, you want to know whether more students are realizing their full potential as a result of your adopting an asset-building philosophy.

Another way to tell how you're doing is to assess various activities from an asset-building perspective. Educators in the field have created a number of useful tools to help with this task, and we've included a sampling to get you started. (Additional evaluation tools that are in development at Search Institute are available at the

Search Institute Web site: www.search-institute.org.) The first is a simple form (Handout 10.3) that gives you an opportunity to consider how well an activity builds assets in each of the asset categories and how to improve that activity.

In New Richmond, Wisconsin, the guidance team, consisting of Kelly Curtis, Wayne Whitwam, and Marilyn Peplau, developed a variety of informal evaluations based on the asset framework, slight adaptations of which are included in this chapter. One of them (Handout 10.4) is called the "Independent Study Performance Worksheet"; with it, student performance is assessed for six of the eight asset categories. A similar worksheet (Handout 10.5) is provided for student aides to rate their experience.

What Is the Connection?

Determining the answer to "What is the connection between what we're doing and how we're doing?" is the most difficult task, primarily because so much else is going on in the lives of your students that it's difficult to separate out the influence of an asset-building effort. You may be building assets intentionally in your school, but are students experiencing the same in the rest of the community or in their homes? In addition, if you look at averages of different things as your outcomes (average Grade Point Average, average behavior referrals, etc.), you can't be confident asset building had anything to do with the results, either positive or negative, unless a critical mass of students actually are experiencing a lot of informal and formal asset building.

The more you can document that asset-building actions are systematic, intentional, ongoing, repeated, and pervasive, the better the case you can make for linking your asset-building effort to your chosen outcomes, for connecting the "what" with the "how." In the same way, the more you can demonstrate that both informal and formal asset building are going on at those levels, the more you can be confident that your school culture is being affected in all three key areas we've identified: relationships, environment, and programs and practices. If you've implemented a lot of changes in programs and practices but people's relationships aren't really changing, then once again, you've given yourself a chance to only partially affect students, and so it would be unrealistic to expect asset building to have made truly deep impacts in those young people's lives.

An example: Suppose you adopted a mentoring program in which 6th-grade students from a nearby middle school came in once a week for three months to read to your 1st-grade students. You tested the 1st-grade students before the program began, you tested them just after it ended, and you tested them two months after it ended. Let's say that you were really ambitious, and you tested a control group, too, as well as the 6th-grade students. Finagle the statistics as you will, it doesn't appear that the 1st-grade students who were mentored increased their reading ability any more than the 1st-grade students who weren't mentored.

Are We an Asset-Building School Community?

Read each statement and decide how important you think each statement is for your school (3=very important, 2=moderately important, 1= a little important).

Then, decide how well you think you do what the statement describes, in your school or your classroom (3=we do it very well, 2=we do it moderately well, and 1=we don't do it well at all).

Then look at the items that you labeled as being very important. How well are you doing on all of those?

Items that are very important and that you're doing well on are successes. Celebrate them! And make sure you have an explicit plan to keep on being successful with those.

Items that are very important, but that you're not doing really well on might be appropriate to focus on in your asset-building agenda.

And remember—you're describing your school, not just your "own" students or classes. If you don't know how to describe your school on an item, ask the relevant people for their input.

	How Important Is This? 3=very important 2=moderately important 1=a little important	How Well Do We Do This? 3=we do it very well 2=we do it moderately well 1=we don't do it well at all

Relationships

1. The great majority of adults on the school staff are interested in their students as persons. ____ ____

2. There is a feeling of collegiality among administrators, faculty, and other staff. ____ ____

3. Parents are genuine partners in children's learning and schooling. ____ ____

4. We effectively promote caring relationships among students, teachers, and other school staff. ____ ____

5. Each student is known by name and talked with several times a week by at least several adults on staff. ____ ____

6. The main decision-making style is for teachers, administrators, other school staff, and students to share in decision making. ____ ____

7. We foster close teacher-student relationships by doing things like breaking the school into small "houses" or teams, and using advisor-advisee or teacher-based guidance programs. ____ ____

8. Counselors explicitly talk about future plans, short- and long-term, with every student several times a year. ____ ____

	How Important Is This?	How Well Do We Do This?

Environment

9. Students feel valued and cared for. ____ ____

10. Students feel they belong in and are connected to the school. ____ ____

11. All students get encouragement and care. ____ ____

12. All staff get encouragement and care. ____ ____

13. Adults and students consistently express high expectations for student performance and behavior. ____ ____

14. Adults consistently express high expectations for each other's performance and behavior. ____ ____

15. The great majority of students consistently put forth great effort in their schoolwork. ____ ____

16. We effectively maintain student motivation and engagement. ____ ____

17. We effectively strengthen the social expectations among teachers and students that promote achievement. ____ ____

18. It is common to see and hear laughter, interest, smiles, and other indications of pleasure and joy in the majority of students. ____ ____

19. All staff, not only teachers, feel student success is their personal responsibility. ____ ____

20. Building staff, parents, district personnel, and community members share a commitment to building assets among all students. ____ ____

21. We ensure staff and student safety (freedom from harassment as well as violence) through consistent rule enforcement and positive role modeling. ____ ____

22. In this school, students routinely contribute to the determination of rules and consequences. ____ ____

23. We provide challenging curriculum to all students as an expression of our high expectations for them. ____ ____

	How Important Is This?	How Well Do We Do This?

Programs and Practices

24. Commitment to asset building is a criterion used to select new school staff, including teachers and administrators.

25. The annual review of teachers includes assessment of their commitment to and engagement in asset building.

26. There are plentiful and systematic opportunities for students to learn key social and decision-making skills.

27. All students are asked to contribute to the betterment of the school community.

28. Average and underachieving students have as many chances to be leaders and contributors as do above-average students.

29. Students are treated as valuable resources and active players in building our school community.

30. There is very little "tracking" of students into courses grouped by ability levels.

31. Most instruction is offered through interdisciplinary teacher teams.

32. We don't have a rigid departmental organization.

33. The great majority of students have to synthesize and interpret more than they have to memorize.

34. Most students can connect what they're learning to the world beyond school, through things like service-learning and internships with community resources.

35. Cocurricular programs are usually run cooperatively with youth-serving organizations, congregations, and other community groups, not just by the school.

	How Important Is This?	How Well Do We Do This?
36. This school is a significant partner in a community-wide coalition or initiative on behalf of children and youth.	____	____
37. We often use cooperative learning strategies to provide constructive group interaction.	____	____
38. We typically keep students in the same teams for several years to help nurture deeper relationships.	____	____
39. We train numerous children and youth—and not only the highest-achieving students—to be peer tutors and mediators.	____	____
40. All students are actively recruited for participation in school- or community-sponsored after-school programs.	____	____
41. We collaborate with a wide range of community resources to expand the types and operating hours of school- and community-sponsored youth programs.	____	____
42. All students participate in health and sexuality education that focuses on fostering personal and social health and wellness.	____	____
43. Our parent communications emphasize suggestions for supporting learning at home (e.g., talking about what goes on at school, expressing the value of education) even more than parents' attendance at school functions.	____	____
44. We often collect data on students' needs through strategies like surveys and focus groups.	____	____
45. We know and often celebrate what is currently being done to build assets.	____	____
46. We annually assess our current organization, structures, and strategies in light of asset building.	____	____

Assessing Youth Activities through an Asset-Building Lens

In order to continually increase the asset-building strength of youth activities, take time to debrief or reflect on youth activities using the eight categories of developmental assets. Complete this worksheet after an event, then refer to it the next time you plan a similar activity.

Description of Activity: _____

Date: _____

ASSET CATEGORY	HOW THE ACTIVITY BUILT THESE ASSETS	OTHER WAYS IT COULD BUILD THESE ASSETS
Support: How did the activity reinforce caring relationships and a warm climate in which all youth felt welcomed and accepted?		
Empowerment: How did the activity empower youth to serve and lead? How well did it offer physical and emotional safety?		
Boundaries and Expectations: How did the activity support appropriate boundaries for behavior? How did it challenge youth to be and do their best?		
Constructive Use of Time: How did the activity use young people's time for enrichment and growth?		
Commitment to Learning: How did the activity reinforce curiosity, learning, and discovery?		
Positive Values: How did the activity reinforce and articulate positive values?		
Social Competencies: How did the activity build young people's life and relationship skills?		
Positive Identity: How did the activity nurture in youth a sense of purpose, value, and possibility?		

Adapted from E.C. Roehlkepartain, Building Assets in Congregations *(Minneapolis, MN: Search Institute, 1998).*

Independent Study Performance Worksheet

Name _____

Supervisor _____

Student # _____

Date _____

Semester _____

ELEMENT	UNSATISFACTORY (D)	BASIC (C)	PROFICIENT (B)	DISTINGUISHED (A)
PLANNING AND PREPARATION				
ASSET CATEGORY: Constructive Use of Time				
Task completion	Student is inefficient and undependable in task completion	Student usually completes work according to timelines.	Student completes work efficiently and accurately according to timelines provided.	Exceptionally dependable and conscientious in all tasks assigned; finds tasks to do without being assigned.
Task transitions	Much time is lost transitioning from one task to another.	Task transitions are sometimes inefficient resulting in loss of productive time	Transitions occur smoothly with little loss of productive time.	Excellent in transitioning from task to task without loss of focus.
Accuracy	Does not make effort to insure that all tasks are completed accurately.	Most tasks completed accurately.	Very competent at completing tasks according to given specifications.	Makes an exceptional effort to complete tasks accurately and professionally.
ENVIRONMENT				
ASSET CATEGORY: Social Competencies				
Interaction with others	Student does not demonstrate respect toward others; little attempt to establish harmonious relationships.	Interactions with others are usually respectful but may have difficulty working with some individuals.	Interactions with others are friendly, warm, and respectful; attempts to work through differences and is sensitive to the feelings of others.	Student genuinely respects and understands others and deservingly earns the respect of others.

ELEMENT	UNSATISFACTORY (D)	BASIC (C)	PROFICIENT (B)	DISTINGUISHED (A)
Flexibility/ adaptability	Finds it difficult to be receptive to new ideas or tasks.	Generally open to new ideas and will change his/her approach if asked.	Typically receptive to new ideas and tasks; deals with new situations well.	Superb flexibility to handle new situations and adapt approach to meet a need.
Attitude Toward Supervision	Views constructive feedback negatively and makes little effort to learn from the process.	Accepts feedback and requests advice when in doubt.	Seeks feedback from which to learn and improve skills.	View supervision as an excellent opportunity for growth and models positive outlook for others.
ASSET CATEGORY: Positive Values (Responsibility)				
Management of materials and supplies	Materials are handled inefficiently resulting in waste of resources	Routines for handling materials and supplies are followed moderately well.	Routines for handling materials and supplies are followed without any difficulty.	Offers positive input to improve efficiency in routines for handling materials and supplies.
Confidentiality	Frequent lapses in respecting confidentiality issues have occurred.	Usually respects confidentiality issues.	Understands and follows standards for confidentiality; corrects others who may violate confidentiality.	Demonstrates a high degree of confidentiality for students, parents, and staff.
Work area environment	Work area is generally disorganized and untidy.	Work area is clean.	Keeps work area organized and presentable.	Work area is exceptionally well-organized and aesthetically pleasing.

SERVICE DELIVERY

ELEMENT	UNSATISFACTORY (D)	BASIC (C)	PROFICIENT (B)	DISTINGUISHED (A)
ASSET CATEGORIES: Commitment to Learning/Social Competencies				
Punctuality	Frequently late/does not make deadlines.	Arrives at start of work day and leaves at end of day.	Arrives early to be ready at his/her designated time.	Arrives early to be ready at his/her post and has prepared for next day's activities before departure.

Independent Study Performance Worksheet (cont.)

ELEMENT	UNSATISFACTORY (D)	BASIC (C)	PROFICIENT (B)	DISTINGUISHED (A)
Oral and written language	Student's spoken and/or written language is inappropriate and may contain many grammar or syntax errors.	Spoken and written language skills are adequate. Vocabulary and grammar are correct, but may be limited or inappropriate at times.	Spoken and written language is clear and correct. Vocabulary is appropriate to student's age and interests.	Spoken and written language is correct and expressive with well-chosen vocabulary for student's age and interests.
Knowledge of age group	Student displays minimal understanding of developmental characteristics of age group.	Displays generally accurate understanding of this age group.	Displays good understanding of the characteristics of this age group of students.	Displays understanding of the developmental characteristics of this age group as well as exceptions to general patterns.
Correcting student work	Frequent errors and/or sloppiness is noted in correcting student work.	Generally accurate in correcting student work.	Dependable and accurate in correcting student work.	Takes initiative and is consistently conscientious in handling student work.
ASSET CATEGORY: Boundaries and Expectations				
Expectations	Student does not appear to have established standards of conduct for self or others.	Standards of conduct appear to have been established for most situations, and student seems to understand them.	Standards of conduct are clearly followed by the student.	Student exceeds expectations.
PROFESSIONAL RESPONSIBILITIES				
ASSET CATEGORY: Positive Identity				
Attitude	Student's lack of enthusiasm is a detriment to the educational process.	Student usually demonstrates a positive outlook.	Student shows considerable enthusiasm and a positive attitude.	Student manifests an uncommonly positive attitude which gives others an uplift.

Independent Study Performance Worksheet (cont.)

ELEMENT	UNSATISFACTORY (D)	BASIC (C)	PROFICIENT (B)	DISTINGUISHED (A)
Personal appearance	Presents an inappropriate appearance; does not look presentable.	Is frequently careless or inappropriate in appearance.	Dependably presents an appropriate, well-groomed appearance.	Always presents an excellent example of appropriate professional appearance.
Goal setting	Has made no attempt to set/work toward individual goals for growth.	Has demonstrated some difficulties focusing on goals for growth.	Positive effort to set and plan implementation steps in meeting goals for growth.	Uses goal setting and implementation as an excellent opportunity for growth.
Acceptance of new responsibilities	Unwilling to accept new or different responsibilities.	Has some difficulty accepting new responsibilities but attempts to follow through to best of ability.	Typically receptive to new responsibilities and willingly implements to best of ability.	Eagerly seeks opportunities to broaden field of responsibilities and skills.

Quarter 1 2 3 4

Grade _____

Final Grade _____

FOR STUDENT AND SUPERVISOR'S USE

Student and Supervisor have reviewed and understand performance criteria.

_____   Date _____
Supervisor's signature

_____   Date _____
Student's signature

174

Independent Study Aide Self-Evaluation

Name: _____ Supervisor: _____

We want to know that we're helping you to build assets! Please rate yourself on the following expectations. You'll discuss this self-evaluation with your supervisor.

Expectation

(1=mostly not true → 4=mostly true)

Support

1. I feel that my supervisor provides me with encouragement and support.   1   2   3   4

Empowerment

2. The tasks I'm given make me feel useful and provide service to others.   1   2   3   4

Boundaries and Expectations

3. I know what I'm supposed to do and am encouraged to do the best I can.   1   2   3   4

Constructive Use of Time

4. I am an efficient worker.   1   2   3   4
5. When I complete a task, I ask what else needs to be done.   1   2   3   4

Commitment to Learning

6. I care about what I do.   1   2   3   4
7. I enjoy what I do.   1   2   3   4

Positive Values

8. I sign in to the attendance sheet.   1   2   3   4
9. I take initiative in projects.   1   2   3   4
10. I complete tasks as assigned.   1   2   3   4
11. I am a reliable, independent worker, and my supervisor can depend on me.   1   2   3   4

Social Competencies

12. I'm able to plan what I do and follow through with that plan.   1   2   3   4
13. I'm able to express my needs and balance them with the needs of my supervisor.   1   2   3   4

Positive Identity

14. I feel good about what I've accomplished as an aide.   1   2   3   4

What does this tell you? Does it tell you that the mentoring program failed? Not at all. Does it tell you that the mentoring program succeeded? No, of course not. The tests don't tell you anything worthwhile—not until you get answers to a lot more questions, questions like the following:

- How were the mentors selected? Did they volunteer, or were they assigned? Were they themselves good readers? Did they relate well to 1st-grade students?
- What did the mentors read? Did the reading material interest the 1st-grade students? Did it interest the mentors?
- Was each mentor always paired with the same 1st-grade student?
- How was the program explained to the 1st-grade students?
- What role did the teacher have in the program?
- What did the 6th-grade mentors miss as a result of having to travel to the elementary school? What did they gain?
- What were the non-mentored students doing during mentoring times that may have affected *their* reading skills?
- What did the 1st-grade students miss while they were being read to?
- What did the 1st-grade students say about the program?
- What did the 6th-grade students say about the program?

The judgment rendered by the evaluation isn't meaningful until these questions and more are answered. What *is* meaningful is how the new information will help improve the program.

Remember that evaluating an asset-building effort involves more than just the development of your students; it involves the development of your school, and it spills over to the larger community. School development results from three kinds of change and the interactions among them:

- Planned change, i.e., what you're doing with asset building;
- Changes that occur naturally in the school's life cycle, e.g., the hiring of a new principal; and
- Unforeseeable, unplanned events, both positive and negative, e.g., a rise in school spirit as a result of a successful girls' basketball season, an infusion of numerous adult volunteers thanks to a new business-sponsored mentoring program, sharp rises in inflation and consequent budget cutbacks, tragedies like drinking/driving accidents and school shootings.

The hard truth is that school development occurs less frequently because of deliberate efforts than because of unplanned and even unforeseeable events.[2] Your asset-building work is only part of what shapes students and schools, and so in your evaluation you should not expect it to be otherwise. The asset framework might also help you make thoughtful, creative responses to those unforeseeable events.

What's in the Way of Doing Better?

Finally, most of us have been involved in situations in which everything in sight is evaluated and nothing comes of it. Surveys are administered, data are collected, priorities are established, and tasks are assigned—but *nothing really happens*. Even though evaluations are necessary in order to maintain funding from particular sources, to meet state standards and learning requirements, and even to justify the very existence of certain programs, evaluation is not an end in itself: It serves your goals and the people who benefit from those goals being met. Commit not just to "continually evaluate what you're doing," as we stated earlier; commit to the second part of that statement, to "make the appropriate adjustments." That happens by looking at the information you've gathered and applying it honestly and consistently to your relationships, your environment, and your programs and practices. The hallmark of an effective evaluation is the change it produces.

Training

Working out of Augsburg College, in Minneapolis, Joseph Erickson teaches a course in asset building for K–12 teachers in which he trains teachers to take leadership roles in their communities' asset-building efforts. Erickson believes that for teachers to be involved in building assets for young people, they first need to examine their own philosophies as individuals: What is important to them? Why do they do what they do? Erickson's second focus is for teachers to examine the philosophies of their schools: What are their schools' missions? What is important to *them*? Why do *they* do what they do? Finally, Erickson explores with teachers how to operationalize the asset philosophy—how to build assets based on teachers' personal credos and their schools' missions. Erickson believes that by helping teachers to understand the philosophy behind building assets, they'll be more able to build assets in a way that's consistent with their particular circumstances.

⚜

John Morefield, the former Seattle principal who greeted his students as they emerged from the bus every morning, has views similar to Erickson's. He also believes that change must begin with the individual, and that some old attitudes must be acknowledged and challenged, attitudes that especially affect young people who are poor or who have certain ethnic, religious, and cultural backgrounds—attitudes that cast some cultures as not only different but also deficient, that posit the immutability of intelligence, and that narrowly define intelligence in the first place. Morefield believes that only by changing these attitudes and by *intentionally* building assets for and with young people—identifying and working with strengths as opposed to "fixing" weaknesses—can real change be effected.

Morefield, like many others who believed in building assets before there was research and a vocabulary to describe it, felt relieved upon discovering the asset framework. These days, he's no longer "the principal that makes house calls" because of his practice of meeting all new kindergartners in their homes before they entered his school for the first time. These days, he shares his views with like-minded educators across the country. "I don't feel alone with this anymore," he says.

ᘓᘠ

Educators like Erickson and Morefield, who are training people not merely to build assets but to embrace the asset framework, have to address the issues on several levels: the personal, the school, and the district. These levels roughly correspond to the "implementation" components we presented earlier: individual relationships, school-wide environment, and in some cases district-wide programs and practices. Not one of these components is sufficient by itself to build assets effectively. And that's why information, training, and guidance are needed simultaneously on all these levels:

- ◆ In order to be successful in building assets, school adults need not only to establish caring relationships but also to take the opportunity to give students information and skills so they can, for example, resist negative peer pressure or learn how to be responsible.
- ◆ In order to be successful in building assets, schools need to provide an environment in which students enjoy going to school, in which all students receive the structure, encouragement, challenge, and support they need.
- ◆ In order to be successful in building assets, school adults need not only to implement asset-building programs but also to see and use students as resources.

ᘓᘠ

Others in the field are also concerned with having educators and other school staff understand and use the asset philosophy in their work. At New Richmond High School, New Richmond, Wisconsin, they even use the assets to guide them in hiring. (See Handout 10.6 for an example of standards for hiring guidance counselors.)

The challenge is clear: For building assets to persist, school adults and students

Guidance Counselor Hiring Standards

Distinguished	Basic	Unsatisfactory
General Asset Building		
1. Provides numerous examples of incorporating asset building in classroom, group, and individual guidance. Uses newspaper articles and other community resources to promote the assets.	1. Has created some asset-building activities, using the language.	1. Has not incorporated asset-building techniques. Limited knowledge of assets.
2. Can give examples of how s/he has helped build each of the 40 developmental assets.	2. Can give examples of how students build assets using the language.	2. Seldom uses asset-building techniques.
Support		
3. Demonstrates a hallway-friendly, approachable manner, willing to seek out opportunities to engage with youth. Has created an innovative support system for youth.	3. Demonstrates a congenial, friendly manner.	3. Does not seek out student contact.
4. Offers multiple opportunities to promote parent involvement in schooling, e.g., by facilitating orientations, regular individual parent contact, and meetings to promote assets.	4. Maintains parent contact. Uses parents as a resource.	4. Maintains parent contact on a limited basis.
Empowerment		
5. Can give examples of establishing programs that use youth as resources. Seeks opportunities to use youth talents in existing programs.	5. Has established and participated in youth-focused programs.	5. Has seldom participated in youth-focused programs.
Boundaries and Expectations		
6. Can give examples of demonstrating initiative. Has high expectations of self, students, and counseling program. Shows evidence of understanding consequences of behavior. Acts as a role model to peers and others in setting appropriate boundaries and facing and resolving conflicts.	6. Demonstrates a motivated manner and seeks to improve self.	6. Shows limited evidence of professional growth.

Constructive Use of Time

7. Prioritizes youth as the center of the counseling position. Manages large projects and programs effectively. Makes attempts to connect youth with activities and programs in the school and community.

7. Is able to prioritize counseling duties effectively.

7. Accomplishes minimum counselor requirements.

Commitment to Learning

8. Can give examples of varied teaching methods used to match different learning styles, e.g., kinetic, auditory, and visual. Students are active participants. Evaluates and seeks to improve curriculum.

8. Varies teaching method to meet student needs.

8. Tends to use the same teaching style.

9. Can give examples of improvements made to counseling program. Has presented professionally, sharing knowledge and innovative ideas with other counselors.

9. Looks for ways to improve counseling. Gives examples of ideas that have been improved.

9. Has made limited improvements to the curriculum or program.

10. Seeks opportunities and has creatively integrated guidance into existing curriculum, using asset language.

10. Gives examples of integrating developmental guidance.

10. Uses developmental guidance model in isolation.

11. Promotes school engagement by planning, organizing, and facilitating parent and youth transition programming.

11. Has initiated and participated in transition programming.

11. Has seldom participated in transition programming.

12. Gives examples of learning and using new technologies. Uses school system, Microsoft Office, Internet capabilities, and email to enhance job performance.

12. Uses scheduling, word-processing, and E-mail. Has used software and the Internet for career and education exploration.

12. Has seldom used new technology and software.

Positive Values

13. Gives examples of "above-and-beyond" efforts to help youth.	13. Demonstrates a caring manner, placing a high value on helping others.	13. Appears to care about youth.

Social Competencies

14. As a cooperative team player, participated actively in K–12 guidance department goals and curriculum development. Demonstrates thoughtful planning and decision making, individually and through annual professional goals. Seeks to teach social skills—e.g., resistance skills and peaceful conflict resolution—to youth.	14. Sets specific annual goals and evaluates. Emphasizes to youth the importance of social skills, e.g., resistance skills and peaceful conflict resolution.	14. States general goals.
15. Can give examples of teaching interpersonal competence by initiating, promoting, and facilitating support groups. Uses and promotes cultural competence. Uses the developmental assets as a tool to encourage positive choices.	15. Has facilitated a variety of support groups, but without using the asset language.	15. Has seldom facilitated support groups.
16. Uses an eclectic approach to individual counseling. Strives to improve counseling skills. Integrates the Wisconsin Developmental Guidance Model into practice and demonstrates proficiency with post-secondary planning.	16. Is familiar with and uses various counseling strategies. Knows the Wisconsin Developmental Guidance Model.	16. Is comfortable working with students.

Positive Identity

17. Appears to counsel with a sense of purpose. Believes s/he can help make a difference. Can give examples of job being a rewarding experience.	17. Believes s/he can make a difference.	17. Work provides a monetary means to fulfill other areas in life.
18. Helps youth to feel and use their own personal power so that they can resolve their own problems and come to their own decisions.	18. Works with youth on a shared-control basis.	18. Makes decisions for youth.

must believe that caring, respectful, genuine relationships are important and attainable; must contribute to a friendly yet challenging environment; and must adopt programs and practices that give everyone multiple opportunities to succeed. The challenge can be met, though, if for no other reason than that's what people seem to *want*. Chris Templin, a coordinator and trainer in the asset framework out of Colorado Springs, says she begins many of her training workshops by asking participants, "What would you want for *your* kid?" And David Fischer, the principal of Highline Elementary School, says that he's never met any parents who didn't want the best for their children. By incorporating the asset framework into your staff development plans, parent education workshops, and other training opportunities, you can equip all the members of the school community to provide the best for students.

Norms

One of the more pleasant duties of Delta-Menominee District Health Department health educator Brett Peterson is to coordinate awards. Each month, this rural Michigan county hands out an award to one youth (8–12 years old), one teenager, and one teacher who best exemplifies building assets. Students may be nominated by anyone—other students, teachers, school staff. Teachers are nominated by students, who write a story describing why the teacher is worthy of the award. There are actually three awards given to each person: the first is recognition and instant status as a role model; the second is a $25 gift certificate to a local business chosen by the person receiving the award; and the third is a plaque citing the person for "making a difference" and for "recognition of positive accomplishments in your community." Peterson says that the people receiving the award are typically thrilled; what he doesn't say but clearly believes is that making these awards keeps the idea of assets in people's minds, and reaffirms that it's a good thing to care about others.

Something else is going on here, and it's why we want to introduce the topic of "norms" in this manner: Peterson's awards help to establish the norm that building assets is a valuable thing to do—so valuable, in fact, that it's rewarded. Celebrating achievements is another way to establish that norm. It also focuses on good things being achieved, gives everyone a lift, and points everyone to the future.

The awards program is a good example of the actions that are needed to change norms: The new norm (in this case, making a difference in the community through building assets) needs to be identified and recognized. Social influences need to be in place, so that everyone seems to be doing it, especially influential people. People need ongoing reminders about and orientation to the new norm. And systems, programs, and policies need to come into being that reinforce and "standardize" the norm.

This pattern of rewarding positive behaviors and celebrating achievements is similar to the pattern we discussed earlier, when the Highline Elementary School student in Cherry Creek, Colorado, established the norm that it was good to reach out to and play with a boy who had Down's syndrome. We saw it again in Glenwood Springs, Colorado, when the community norm changed from viewing teenagers as problems to viewing them as resources. And we saw it in possibly the most pronounced way in Denver with Lynn Spampinato's little entrepreneurs: The norm changed from those students viewing themselves as unsuccessful in everything to viewing themselves as not only succeeding academically but also running legitimate business enterprises. When you change the norms, you fix the model in people's consciousness and they begin to live it. And when you do that, you've begun to make an impact that goes deeper than an individual or a handful of people changing their behavior for a short time—you've begun to change systems, and for the long term.

The last examples we'll offer in the book illustrate a different kind of "norm changing," a more concrete kind. The change isn't in people's minds, though that invariably follows. The change is in policies, on the school level and on the district level. Think of your school—or district—as an individual who gradually comes to accept the asset framework as necessary, and the actions based on it as *normal, socially expected behaviors.* As individuals, we accept such changes in norms by shifting our attitudes as a result of some information, experience, or emotional insight. But schools and districts accept such changes in norms in much less subtle ways: Strong leaders have a vision, and they persuade others to incorporate that vision into policy.

⚜

In Salt Lake City, Utah, Shelley Stevens, coordinator of drug and alcohol prevention programs for Granite School District, keeps schools on top of implementing ideas to build assets. Each of her 15 staff people is responsible for knowing several assets, inside and out—what they mean and how they can be operationalized. Schools in the district incorporate asset building into their School Improvement Plans, and often they'll call Stevens's office for an in-service. Stevens assigns the appropriate specialist, and that person discusses with school staff how best to implement a strategy for building the assets chosen by the school to focus on. Stevens says that school staff are very impressed when they learn how building assets is associated with reducing risk factors: "That's how we get the teachers with us," she says. Stevens is currently working on an evaluation of asset building that will use attendance and disciplinary referrals as indicators of progress.

⚜

As PTO president at Belleview Elementary School in Cherry Creek School District, Colorado, Robin Thorsen made asset building the topic of a standing PTO committee; she secured the support of the principal, teachers, and other staff members; and she incorporated asset building into the School Improvement Plan, resulting, she says, in "accountability." One of the ways the school currently builds assets is by having students make 2- to 3-minute presentations on individual assets that are televised live on Monday mornings to the entire school. The activity is called "PAM," for "Power Asset Moments" (Belleview's principal is also named "Pam"). Thorsen, though, seems happiest when she's talking about another effect of her involvement with assets: She's now much more communicative with her own sons, ages 7 and 11.

※

The District Improvement Agenda is a document that guides the work of Minneapolis Public Schools. Last approved on June 30, 1998, the agenda itself states that it is "intended to be a 'living' document. It includes responsibilities for all stakeholders to improve student achievement." The first of three goals in the agenda is to "accelerate achievement of all students," and the last of four objectives under that goal states that "Each student will acquire assets they need to achieve academic success and develop in healthy ways." Conspicuously included in the document are assets/task management skills that delineate each goal, for the district, for schools, for teachers and other school adults, for students, for families, and for the community. Here are several examples for middle-school students:

- Create an atmosphere of mutual respect in which students' opinions and contributions are valued. (district)
- Involve families in planning for learning. (schools)
- Set clear rules and consequences. (teachers and other school adults)
- Expect to achieve at high levels. (students)
- Establish a family routine that includes regular supervised time and a place for studying. (families)
- Help provide after- and out-of-school activities. (community)

Thus does Minneapolis Public Schools, under the leadership of superintendent Carol Johnson, weave asset building into the fabric of school life. From top to bottom, asset building figures prominently into the sectors we mentioned previously in this book: curriculum and instruction, school organization, cocurricular programs, community partnerships, and support services. *Systematically*, asset building infuses, nourishes, informs the public schools throughout the city. *Individually*, the effort is guided by something that Carol Johnson says when she speaks to groups about building assets: "Raise your children so that other people love them."

Let's return to a metaphor we used earlier: Incorporating the asset framework into school and district policies is like finding the right plot for a plant. Once it's secure, it can grow and flourish. Once the asset framework is "planted" inside a policy, it can "grow" to meet the needs of school adults and students alike.

The Next Steps

If you've read this book carefully, you've probably picked up at least four strong messages:

- Building developmental assets in school communities can help young people succeed and thrive in many ways.
- Building developmental assets in school communities can be accomplished by a systematic, sustained effort by the entire school community.
- Building developmental assets in school communities involves forming relationships that are mutually respectful, caring, and genuine; creating a structured, challenging, caring environment that encourages asset building; and using programs and practices that provide specific opportunities for asset building to all students.
- Keeping the asset-building effort going relies on reliably and meaningfully evaluating your efforts as well as your outcomes; training; networking; and establishing healthy norms that are conducive to asset building.

But what now? Where do you go from here? Of course, that depends on your role in your school community and what your school community has already done in terms of incorporating the asset framework. But here are a few ideas:

If you haven't set up a core team in your school, think about who those people would be and approach them. Start awareness raising by giving them some of the handouts from this book or tell them some of the stories from Chapters 7–9. Show them the video *"You Have to Live It": Building Developmental Assets in School Communities,* a Search Institute film that introduces the assets through interviews with educators. Discuss with them the concept of asset building in general and asset building in your school in particular.

If you haven't surveyed your students, consider calling Search Institute at 800-888-7828 and ask about administering the *Profiles of Student Life: Attitudes and Behaviors* survey.

If you want to broaden and deepen the reach of asset building in your school, meet with a group as representative of your school as possible—e.g., teachers, administrators, students, support staff—for visioning, planning, networking, and discussing strategies.

Finally, forget for a moment that you are a worker in a school community and just think about yourself as an everyday person. Think about how you relate to young people in your everyday life outside work. Do you know them? Do you know *about* them? Do they know about you? What can you do—on an individual, one-to-one basis—to build developmental assets for and with those young people?

Think about what specific steps you can take—now, this minute—to do on a personal level what we've been talking about on a school level. Think about being intentional yet informal. For instance, when you stop at the coffee shop or the grocery store, don't just say "thanks" to the young person who waits on you. Try complementing an unusual hairstyle, interesting jewelry, or her or his competence, or ask whether working there is fun. Use the response to open the door to getting acquainted. Ask the worker's name, and next time you're there, greet the young person by name. It's small steps like these that help you incorporate the developmental assets into your life. And the sooner you "live" the asset framework, the sooner you can be a model for others, and the sooner an increasing number of young people can reap the benefits of your efforts.

⚜

We started this section by stating that the "work" of building assets is never over. But we've consistently heard from people that they *want* to build assets, that in fact they *do* build assets, and that they believe that young people thrive from building assets. What remains is tactics and commitment. After all the awareness presentations have been made, after all the survey results are tabulated and communicated, after all the strategies are implemented, and after all the evaluations are examined, there's a bottom line. The bottom line is you. And in this case, we do mean "you," the person who's reading this book. Building assets is about you—how you relate to the people in your life, how you influence others to relate to the people in their lives.

This is one case in which individuals do make a big difference. When you treat a teenager as a resource instead of a problem, it matters to the teenager. When you call a seven-year-old by her name, it matters to the seven-year-old. If you do these things often and publicly, then others will see it and maybe do the same thing. It doesn't take much energy; in fact, it saves energy, even creates energy. And it doesn't matter who you are or what your position is; you can do it. Just imagine if everyone considered everyone else's strengths before their liabilities! Just imagine if all our schools, our businesses, our families were rich with assets!

The work of building assets may never be over, but the work of living as a caring, responsible human being is never over, either. When you build assets—for yourself, for and with young people, for other adults—you're living as a caring, responsible human being.

It's as simple as that.

Notes

1. For more on overcoming barriers to action, see Benson, P.L. (1997). *All kids are our kids: What communities must do to raise caring and responsible children and adolescents.* San Francisco: Jossey-Bass.
2. Louis, K.S., Toole, J., & Hargreaves, A. (1999). Rethinking school improvement. In J. Murphy & K.S. Louis, (Eds.), *Handbook of research on educational administration, 2nd edition* (pp. 251–276). San Francisco: Jossey-Bass.

Resources for Further Exploration

From Search Institute

"You Have to Live It": Building Developmental Assets in School Communities. (1999). Use this new video, filmed in schools in four states, to introduce the asset framework to groups in your school community, including teachers and paraprofessionals, counselors, support staff, parents, and more. Inspiring stories and creative, practical ideas make it easy for viewers to start building assets right away.

Learning and Living: How Asset Building for Youth Can Unify a School's Mission (1998). This 16-page booklet looks at the role of school staff as asset builders, shows how the asset model brings focus to school agendas, and provides readers with background, rationale, and ideas in a quick-to-read format.

Assets: The Magazine of Ideas for Healthy Communities & Healthy Youth. This quarterly publication provides regular, timely information about asset building from all parts of a community, including schools, along with stories, strategies, and ideas for new things to try. Especially useful for teachers and staff, the staff lounge, parents.

Building Assets Together: 135 Group Activities for Helping Youth Succeed (1998). This book gives creative, easy-to-use activities to introduce youth to developmental assets. It includes 94 interactive group activities and 41 photocopiable worksheets for 6th- to 12th-grade youth. Great for classroom and small-group use.

Ideas for Parents Newsletter Master Set (1997). With this ready-to-use newsletter set, you can offer parents in your community practical tips on how to build each of the 40 assets for and with their own children. The set includes a users guide with an overview of each newsletter and helpful suggestions for customizing, promoting, and distributing the series.

Pass It On! Ready-to-Use Handouts for Asset Builders (1999). For anyone in a school wanting to spearhead increased awareness of the assets among colleagues, parents, bus drivers, child-care workers, members of the school board, neighborhood residents, and others, this book of 92 handout masters lets you spread the word with ease. Includes a section of handouts in Spanish.

Developmental Assets: A Synthesis of the Scientific Research on Adolescent Development (1999); A Fragile Foundation: The State of Developmental Assets among American Youth (1999); and *Starting Out Right: Developmental Assets for Children (1997).* These three books are important tools for those interested in the research behind the developmental assets. The book *Developmental Assets* examines more than 800 scientific articles and reports on adolescent development that tie to each of the 40 assets. *A Fragile Foundation* is a report that features data from communities that used the *Search Institute Profiles of Student Life: Attitudes and Behaviors* survey during the 1996–97 school year. And *Starting Out Right* extends the asset framework, originally developed for youth ages 12–18, to children from infancy on.

What Teens Need to Succeed: Proven, Practical Ways to Shape Your Own Future (1998). Written for young people, this handbook provides more than 120 true stories about teen and adults who are building assets for themselves, along with eye-opening checklists and quizzes, fun lists of things to do and try, and other tools and tips for helping young people be independent, self-sufficient, competent, and caring.

These resources, as well as posters, workbooks, trainings, and survey services, are available from Search Institute. For more information and a free catalog:

Search Institute
615 First Avenue NE, Suite 125
Minneapolis, MN 55413
612-376-8955
800-888-7828

www.search-institute.org

From the Field

The following list of resources is provided for the reader as a jumping-off point for further inquiry and as a mere sample of the many resources available for envisioning and promoting healthy youth development.

PROFESSIONAL DEVELOPMENT

Other People's Children: Cultural Conflict in the Classroom
Lisa D. Delpit, The New Press, 1996

Describes how cultural heritage/home influences language and how misunderstandings in the classroom can arise from cultural differences that are unexplored.

The Courage to Teach: Exploring the Inner Landscape of a Teacher's Life
Parker J. Palmer, Jossey-Bass Inc., San Francisco, 1997

and the companion guide

The Courage to Teach: A Guide for Reflection and Renewal
Rachel C. Livesy with Parker J. Palmer, Jossey-Bass Inc., San Francisco, 1999

The book and companion guide are explorations of how teaching is a passion that needs to connect all the threads of life in order to be done well. Palmer advocates a nondenominational spiritual approach to professional development by making meaning and connections in everyday life.

You Can't Say You Can't Play
Vivian Gussin Paley. Harvard University Press, Cambridge, MA, 1992

Paley is a Kindergarten teacher who captures the dialogues within herself, among her students, and between her and her students on topics such as race, exclusion, play, friendship, fear, risk, and other aspects of being a student and teacher that weave into the school day. She is an intimate storyteller who documents her growth along with the students' and speaks honestly about her own fears, failures and learning.

WHOLE SCHOOL/SYSTEM CHANGE

Rallying the Whole Village: The Comer Process for Reforming Education
Editors: James P. Comer, Norris M. Haynes, Edward T. Joyner, Michael Ben-Avie.; Teachers College Press, New York, New York, 1996

Comer outlines the design of the holistic school. The school structure includes school partnerships, community involvement, emphasis on the support of caring adults, and evaluation.

Way to the River Source: A Community's Journey to Supporting Diversity in Schools through Family and Community Involvement
Judith Katz and John G. Mentos, COMPAS, St. Paul, MN, 1997

This novelized report presents the stories of people involved in a six-year program seeking to divest schools of racial prejudice. The program involves parents, communities, and schools.

LISTENING TO YOUNG PEOPLE

Take Time to Play Checkers and Other Wise Words from Kids
Misti Snow, Penguin Books, New York, New York, 1992

A collection of *Mindworks* columns compiled by the editor from the topical newspaper writings of young people. The Introduction describes how the column started, its evolution, and the impact it has had on the Minneapolis community.

STUDENT ACHIEVEMENT AND PERFORMANCE

Multiple Intelligences: The Theory in Practice
Howard Gardner, HarperCollins Publishers, Inc., New York, New York, 1993

This book provides descriptions of the practical applications of Gardner's theory of the several human competencies that should be recognized and taught in schools.

Educating Everybody's Children: Diverse Teaching Strategies for Diverse Learners
Editor, Robert W. Cole. Association for Supervision and Curriculum Development. Alexandria, VA

This book is an accessible and practical guide to improving academic achievement as indicated by research and practice. There are clear connections between chapter topics and the asset framework.

BEST PRACTICES IN PREVENTION AND INTERVENTION

Safe Passage: Making It Through Adolescence in a Risky Society
Joy G. Dryfoos, Oxford University Press, New York, New York, 1998

Dryfoos summarizes the elements and examples of effective programs and approaches for promoting healthy youth development. She provides practical descriptions for parents, schools, and communities.

Fostering Friendship: Pair Therapy for Treatment and Prevention
Editors, Robert L. Selman, Caroline Watts, Lynn Hickey Schultz; Aldine De Gruyter, New York, New York, 1997

Describes the implementation of pair therapy using case descriptions and reflections by practitioners and researchers. Pair therapy is a prevention/intervention service designed to promote social and emotional development.

STUDENT INVOLVEMENT

Empowering Students to Transform Schools
Gary Goldman and Jay B. Newman, Corwin Press, Inc., Thousand Oaks, CA, 1998

Goldman and Newman present their theories and practical tools for improving schools through the authentic involvement of students in the visioning, planning, leading, and evaluation of the school community.

Asset Builders Cited in This Book

In Schools

Manette Anderson
Glenwood Springs High School
1340 Pitkin
Glenwood Springs, Colorado 81601
970-945-5762

Kayleen Bonczek
Principal, Franklin Middle School
1501 Aldrich Avenue North
Minneapolis, Minnesota 55411
612-668-2600

Ron Bonner
Chief School Administrator, Avalon
    Elementary School
32nd Street and Ocean Drive
Avalon, New Jersey 08202
609-967-7544

Les Bork
Principal, St. Louis Park Junior High School
2025 Texas Avenue South
St. Louis Park, Minnesota 55426
612-928-6300

Sheryl Burgstahler
Director, DO-IT
University of Washington, Box 354842
Seattle, Washington 98195
206-685-3648

Kenneth Burnley
Superintendent, Colorado Springs Public
    School District 11
1115 North El Paso
Colorado Springs, Colorado 80903
719-520-2000

Quincy Cook
Narrows View Intermediate
7813 44th Street West
University Place, Washington 98466
253-566-5630

Donna Curtis
SAP Coordinator, Overland High School
12400 East Jewell Avenue
Aurora, Colorado 80012
303-696-3714

Judi Edwards
Program Coordinator, Linn-Benton-Lincoln
    ESD
905 4th Avenue SE
Albany, Oregon 97321
541-967-8822

Melanie Elrod
Student Services Coordinator, Newton-
    Conover City Schools
605 North Ashe Avenue
Newton, North Carolina 28658
828-464-3191

Joseph Erickson
Department of Education, Augsburg College
2211 Riverside Avenue, C.B. #312
Minneapolis, Minnesota 55454
612-330-1647

Steve Fenton
Principal, Pronghorn Elementary School
3005 Oakcrest Drive
Gillette, Wyoming 82718
307-682-1676

David Fischer
Principal, Highline Community School
11000 East Exposition Avenue
Aurora, Colorado 80012
303-364-7657

Teresa Garcia
University Hill Elementary School
956 16th Street
Boulder, Colorado 80302
303-442-6735

Sally Goddard
Aquila Primary Center
8500 West 31st Street
St. Louis Park, Minnesota 55426
612-928-6500

Rick Heiden
Assistant Principal, Bismarck High School
800 North 8th Street
Bismarck, North Dakota 58501
701-221-3518

Brenda Holben
Prevention Advisor, Cherry Creek Schools
4700 South Yosemite Street
Englewood, Colorado 80111
303-486-4247

Michael Kerosky
Coordinator, Safe and Drug-Free Schools
Anchorage School District, P.O. Box 196614
Anchorage, Alaska 99519
907-269-2471

Terry Knisler
Superintendent of Schools
P.O. Box 591
Philomath, Oregon 97370
541-929-3169

Pam Livingston
Principal, Belleview Elementary School
4851 South Dayton Street
Englewood, Colorado 80111
303-771-2840

Joe Madril
Monroe Elementary School
15 South Chelton Road
Colorado Springs, Colorado 80910
719-520-2310

Janet Muller
Duniway Elementary School
7700 S.E. Reed College Place
Portland, Oregon 97202

Hilde Newman
Social Worker, Dry Creek Elementary School
7686 East Hinsdale Avenue
Englewood, Colorado 80112
303-770-2144

Barb Nielsen
Principal, Adams Elementary School
6110 28th Avenue NW
Seattle, Washington 98107
206-706-3870

Marilyn Peplau
New Richmond High School
1232 200th Avenue
New Richmond, Wisconsin 54017
715-246-2790

Helene Perry
Clara Barton Open School
4237 Colfax Avenue South
Minneapolis, Minnesota 55409
612-668-3580

John Preston
Consultant for Comprehensive School Health
Area Education Agency 7
3712 Cedar Heights Drive
Cedar Falls, Iowa 50613
319-273-8215

Sherrie Raven
Principal, Gullett Elementary School
6310 Treadwell Boulevard
Austin, Texas 78757
512-414-2082

Suzanne Siler
Coordinator, Safe and Drug-Free Schools
Hickman Mills School District
Baptiste Educational Center
5401 East 103rd Street
Kansas City, Missouri 64137
816-612-8063

Lisa Sloan
Susan Lindgren Intermediate School
4801 West 41st Street
St. Louis Park, Minnesota 55416
612-928-6700

Lynn Spampinato
Principal, Mitchell Elementary School
1350 East 33rd Street
Denver, Colorado 80205
303-296-8412

Shelley Stevens
Drug and Alcohol Prevention Programs
Granite School District
340 East 3545 South
Salt Lake City, Utah 84115
801-268-8560

Bob Tift
Principal, Benilde-St. Margaret's School
2501 Highway 100 South
St. Louis Park, Minnesota 55416
612-927-4176

Martha Urioste
Principal, Denison Montessori School
1821 South Yates Street
Denver, Colorado 80219
303-934-7805

Hedy Walls
Community Education Specialist, Northeast
  Middle School
2955 Hayes Street NE
Minneapolis, Minnesota 55418
612-627-3042

Connie Wirz
Kenai Middle School
201 Tinker Lane
Kenai, Alaska 99611
907-283-4896

In Communities

Barb Alfrey
Manager of Volunteer Programs, The Pillsbury
  Company
Mail Station 37X5, 200 South 6th Street
Minneapolis, Minnesota 55402
612-330-4581

Nancy Ashley
Owner, Heliotrope
1249 N.E. 92nd Street
Seattle, Washington 98115
206-526-5671

Karen Atkinson
Coordinator, Children First
karen-atkinson@qm.stlpark.k12.mn.us

LeAnn Bauer
Coordinator, Youth First
101 East 4th Street
Hastings, Minnesota 55033
651-480-2366

Cindy Carlson
Director, Hampton Coalition for Youth
22 Lincoln Street
Hampton, Virginia 23669
757-727-1381

Don Draayer
5906 Holiday Way
Minnetonka, Minnesota 55435
612-934-9680

Phil Heath
Prevention Education Coordinator
Northwest Iowa Alcoholism and Drug
  Treatment Unit
25 East State Street, P.O. Box 307
Algona, Iowa 50511
515-295-5158

Rick Jackson
Vice-President for Program Development,
  Greater Seattle YMCA
909 4th Avenue
Seattle, Washington 98104
206-382-5334

Tom Koplitz
Executive Director, Community Partnership
  with Youth and Families
38694 Tanger Drive
North Branch, Minnesota 55056
612-674-4085

Bev Lackey
President, Albuquerque Assets
New Mexico Advocates for Children and
  Families
801 Encino Place NE, F21
Albuquerque, New Mexico 87102
505-344-8860

Colleen Mahoney
Director, Center for Health Promotion
ACHVE Department, 316 White Hall
Kent State University
Kent, Ohio 44242
330-672-7977

Ann Medlock
President, The Giraffe Project
197 2nd Street, P.O. Box 759
Langley, Washington 98260
360-221-7989

Judith O'Leary
Executive Director, Communities in Action
141 Franklin
Stamford, Connecticut 06901
203-978-1881

Barbara Pearce
Executive Director, The Georgetown Project
P.O. Box 957
Georgetown, Texas 78627
512-930-1154

Brett Peterson
Health Educator, Delta-Menominee District
   Health Department
2920 College Avenue
Escanaba, Michigan 49829
906-786-4111

Kevin Rowe
Student Assistance Program Coordinator,
   Carmel Clay Schools
5201 East 131st Street
Carmel, Indiana 46033
317-844-9961

Mark Scharenbroich
Scharenbroich & Associates
5702 Seven Oaks Court
Minnetonka, Minnesota 55345
612-939-9080

Cynthia Sosnowski
Director, Cape May County Healthy
   Community Coalition
Blueprints 2000 Project
310 95th Street
Stone Harbor, New Jersey 08247
609-368-2935

Desiree Voorhies
Health Education Specialist, Genesee Valley
   BOCES
40 Munson Street
LeRoy, New York 14482
716-768-9540

About the Authors

Neal Starkman has been a curriculum developer since the 1970's. He has developed numerous materials in the field of health education, including comprehensive curricula in drug education, AIDS prevention, violence prevention, and peer helping. In addition, he has written or produced books, videotapes, audiotapes, plays, songs, posters, and learning games on a variety of topics. He has also designed training workshops and marketing materials.

Starkman holds a Ph.D. in Social Psychology from the University of Connecticut (1975); his company, Flashpoint Development, specializes in developing innovative health education. He has written two novels and published fiction, nonfiction, and academic papers in national magazines and journals.

Peter C. Scales is a developmental psychologist who is widely recognized as one of the nation's foremost authorities on adolescent development, family life and sexuality education, middle schools, and healthy communities. He received his B.A. in psychology, and M.S. and Ph.D. in child and family studies from Syracuse University. He is Senior Fellow with Search Institute in Minneapolis, where he conducts research on the role that youth developmental assets play in risk reduction and promoting adolescent health. Among his positions, Dr. Scales has served as director of national initiatives for the Center for Early Adolescence at the University of North Carolina—Chapel Hill, chair of the Alaska Governor's Commission on Children and Youth and executive director of the Anchorage Center for Families, national director of education for Planned Parenthood Federation of America, senior social scientist for Mathtech Social Science Group, and Research Director at Syracuse University's Institute for Family Research and Education.

Scales has authored more than 200 professional and popular articles, books, and other publications, and has given more than 250 keynote speeches to groups ranging from the National Governor's Association to the National Council on Family Relations and the American School Health Association. His awards include the 1988 US Administration for Children, Youth, and Families Commissioner Award for outstanding child abuse prevention, and the American Camping Association's 1998

Hedley S. Dimock award for outstanding contributions to youth development. Among his books are *Developmental Assets: A Synthesis of The Scientific Research on Adolescent Development* (Search Institute, 1999), *A Fragile Foundation: The State of Developmental Assets among American Youth* (Search Institute, 1999), and *Growing Pains: The Making of America's Middle School Teachers* (National Middle School Association, 1994).

Clay Roberts is the founder and president of Roberts & Associates, a company dedicated to the development of healthy, contributing young people. A developer, trainer, and speaker, he has developed five national model school-based programs. These programs include *Here's Looking at You 2000,* a K-12 drug education program, and *Natural Helpers,* a peer helper program.

Roberts has been a consultant and keynote presenter throughout the United States and abroad and has served as an educational consultant to Search Institute. He earned his M.A. from the University of Oregon in health education, and is active in initiating an asset-building movement in his own community.